SpeechSH**A**RK.™:

A Public Speaking Guide

SECOND EDITION

Penny Joyner Waddell, Ed.D.

Travice Baldwin Obas, M.Ed.

Kendall Hunt
publishing company

Cover designed by Cassandra West

www.kendallhunt.com
Send all inquiries to:
4050 Westmark Drive
Dubuque, IA   52004-1840

Printed in the United States of America

SpeechShark Logo, Book Cover Design, Shark Bites and SpeechShark Terms Design

created by

Cassandra West, Graphic Artist

E-mail: Cwest@SpeechShark.com

"YOU DO NOT HAVE TO BE GREAT TO START, BUT YOU HAVE TO START TO BE GREAT!"

Zig Ziglar

LET'S GET STARTED!

Table of Contents

Presenting a speech may be frightening, like standing on a dock and being afraid to jump into deep water. However, once you learn the basics of public speaking, you can become an expert.

Unit #4: Visual Aids

Unit #5: Presenting the Speech

Foreword

Penny Waddell's newest book, *SpeechShark*, guides novice and experienced speakers to create a professional presentation in a quick and organized way. This book and the *SpeechShark App* are practical tools to prepare you for success! Whether you are planning a speech for a special occasion, group presentation, or an informative talk, Penny's advice will help you feel more confident by giving a well-structured presentation and knocking it out of the park or, perhaps I should say, knocking it out of the water!

    Nick "Sunshine" Tokman, a former four-year cast member of the hit show **Deadliest Catch** is now a professional speaker, empowering others to conquer negative influences and connect with their voice to create their own definition of success.

Website: www.nicktokman.com   **Facebook:** NickSunshineTokman
Instagram: NickTokman   **Twitter:** NickTokman

Writing a speech is different from writing a story, proposal, or article. It takes preparation, discipline, and, when the big day comes, confidence. As a long-time communications consultant and speech app developer, I believe being a powerful, persuasive, articulate speaker is the single most pivotal skill that gets us ahead in life. This *SpeechShark* guidebook provides everything you need to develop successful speech-writing skills. As a foundational guide, Penny Joyner Waddell, author, speech coach, speech program director, and instructor, provides an easy-to-follow method for both novice and experienced speakers. The bundled SpeechShark app is the best on the market, provides templates and prompts for creating speeches from a variety of genres, and is a great way to prepare. Simply brilliant.

Audrey Mann Cronin
Co-founder/President, Say It Media, Inc. (creators of LikeSo app),
Founder/President Mann Cronin PR, Inc.

Drawing inspiration from her effective public speaking app, Dr. Penny Joyner Waddell's newest book, *SpeechShark: A Public Speaking Guide*, goes right to the heart of the issues that most determine communication success or failure. Readers will come to understand that public speaking intimidation is not a permanent state and can be overcome with preparation and practice. There's no doubt *SpeechShark* can help public speakers turn their biggest fear into their greatest strength.

Joel Schwartzberg
Public Speaking Coach and Author of
"Get to the Point! Sharpen Your Message and Make Your Words Matter"

Meet the SpeechSharks!

Dr. Penny Joyner Waddell
PWaddell@SpeechShark.com

Travice Baldwin Obas
TObas@SpeechShark.com

With years of experience as public speaking coaches and instructors for novice and experienced speakers, Dr. Penny Joyner Waddell and Travice Baldwin Obas teamed up to write a guidebook designed just for you. This practical step-by-step approach is user-friendly and offers just the right amount of instruction along with easy to use guides to help you begin thinking like a professional speechwriter. Tips and tools for making speech presentations will have you speaking like a pro in record time. Start by learning about the foundations of public speaking, the types of speeches, and methods of delivery. From there, move on to planning the outline, creating visual aids, rehearsing, and then delivering the speech. This simple, easy to use formula takes the guesswork away from planning a great speech and you can count on a standing ovation every time!

Both authors are available as speakers separately or as a team for conferences, conventions, and professional development opportunities. Topics include: Overcoming the Fear of Public Speaking, PREP for Impromptu Speaking, Planning a Speech, Understanding Non-Verbal Communication, Creating and Using Effective Visual Aids, Managing a Tech Team, Adding Movement and Energy to Presentations, and more!

"Start by learning about the foundations of public speaking, the types of speeches, and methods of delivery."

Contributing developers: Marcus Smith, Maurice McFarlane, Cassandra West, and Charles Hardnett.

Marcus Smith is a developer for both Android and iOS versions of SpeechShark. He started his education at Gwinnett Technical College in the Game Development program; then graduated from Kennesaw State University as a Software Engineer. He has worked on several group projects experienced with mobile platforms and web APIs, as well as principles of software design, also as QA analyst identifying software defects and recommending improvements. Don't let his serious expressions fool you! In his free time, he is often working on small fun mobile projects, practicing for casual video game tournaments, and re-watching favorite TV shows like *Game of Thrones.*

Maurice McFarlane, when not perfecting his serious face, spends time doing copious amounts of push-ups in inappropriate places, sipping Earl Grey tea, and coding iOS applications as part of the SpeechShark development team. An accomplished applications developer and karaoke singer, includes adventures working with Tier 1-2 retailers (many of which you have probably shopped with) on Point-of-Sale system customizations, building custom APIs for payment devices, and implementing P2Pe/ EMV solutions. Adventures consist of bar hopping, purchasing Udemy tech courses in an effort to, as he puts it, ". . . become one with the machine," binging on One-Punch-Man, hanging with his homies, and preparing for the inevitable coming of the Sharknado.

Cassandra West is the graphic designer for SpeechShark. Her expertise includes brand identity, corporate presentations and campaigns, web collaboration, UI design, package design, book cover/layout design, and more.

Cassie has worked with many of the top companies in the Atlanta area and a few outside the state of Georgia. This talented designer is a wonderful combination of beauty and brains with a side of pizazz! Her smile is infectious and her artistic flair, along with a positive outlook on life, makes her a shark you will always want to have around!

Charles Hardnett is the project manager and senior developer for SpeechShark. His career includes a vast array of experiences as a computer science professor and researcher, software developer, educational administrator, and software architect. He has worked on projects involving the development of compilers for high-performance computing, access and switching for telecommunications, web applications for a variety of domains, and mobile applications for entertainment, productivity, and education. A fun fact about Charles is that he is a certified wedding and party DJ.

Preface

Several years ago, I had the inspiration to develop a speech writing app that would help students and business leaders plan and write speeches. Through my many years as a speech instructor and speech coach, I learned that when people say they have a fear of public speaking, it is more a fear of not knowing what to say. Speakers who have a clear message and a plan for the clear points they will cover, take time to rehearse, and incorporate trained tech support to make the presentation shine, realize they have cured their own fear of public speaking or speech anxiety. The SpeechShark app was developed to be a tool for speakers to help organize thoughts and put content into a package that would be well received by any audience.

Speakers are not sharks, like vicious man-eaters; instead, they are a focused species with a key role to share a message with an audience. Instead of an ocean, SpeechSharks navigate stages and platforms. Instead of sharp, pointed teeth, they use their intelligence and problem-solving skills to strategize and create a calculated plan for success. To a speaker, the audience is not a large, deep abysmal pit. The audience is an opportunity for the speaker to go deeper!

With the help of a talented App Design Team, SpeechShark was born! Charles Hardnett, project manager, worked closely with Maurice McFarlane (IOS Specialist) and Marcus Smith (Android Specialist). Cassandra West (Graphic Artist) designed the SpeechShark icon, logo, and colors used within the app, along with the cover for this book. My job was to provide the idea storyboards, the plan that a speech should follow, and troubleshoot content issues that would rise to the surface.

You've heard the saying, "It takes a village to raise a child," and I can tell you that it takes a dedicated team to build an app. This is not as easy as it looks and I am sure this team became quite frustrated with me on many occasions as I was asking them to help develop the app while all of them were working other full-time jobs! True to the SpeechShark theme, they threw themselves one hundred percent into the turbulent waters and assumed the sharky attitudes that made this dream a reality. Over the past few years, I have lovingly referred to my friends as "The Sharks." Before this project, I might have considered sharks as cold, blood-thirsty predators in the ocean. Now, I have a true respect for a species that remains in constant motion, never vulnerable with armor plated skin and with a reputation of power and skill not held by many!

Did you know that a group of sharks is called a shiver? Have you ever walked on to a stage to make a presentation and felt a shiver of excitement or anxiety? Now, perhaps you understand why we have taken on the title of SpeechShark for the app and also for the book. This companion guidebook was requested by Kendall Hunt Publishing Company. They realized that an app as effective as SpeechShark would also benefit the public if an accompanying guidebook were available. Brittanie Tucker with Kendall Hunt suggested that I ask someone to co-write the project with me and the very first person who came to mind was Travice Baldwin Obas. I was so pleased when she accepted the challenge and joined our SpeechShark team! Travice and I first met eight years ago as we served together on the Georgia Communication Association Board. Quickly, I learned that this public speaking professional was committed to excellence in all things.

For anyone old enough to remember the television show *Happy Days*, the main character Fonzarelli, also known as Fonzie or The Fonz, was waterskiing in the ocean and decided to jump over a shark to prove just how cool he really was. This is where I first heard the term, "jumping the shark." To do this means that you are doing something so amazing that everything after that event pales in comparison. I'm reminding you of this story because I hope that it will let you know that overcoming the fear of public speaking is just like Fonzie jumping the shark. Sometimes, you just have to take a deep breath, believe in your own abilities, and go for it! Or, to quote The Fonz, "Heyyyy!"

Having a good plan and a strategy for crafting an effective speech allows you to say, "Bite me!" to speech anxiety. Stay out of the water? Not you, because you will put on your shark skin suit, better known as thick skin, and walk confidently to the stage because you are no longer the guppy in the shark tank! You are a SpeechShark and this public speaking guidebook was designed just for you!

How Do I Use the SpeechShark App?

Did you purchase the SpeechShark app? Excellent! If not, visit our website at www.SpeechShark.com to see a demonstration. The app is available for Android users in **GooglePlay** and for iOS users in the **Apple Store**. Using the app means you are on your way to creating effective and exciting speech presentations for your audience! Click on your SpeechShark app and let's get started!

Here are steps to follow:

1. Open the SpeechShark app.
2. Select "Hxome" to see options to create speeches, manage speeches, or select preferences.
3. If you want to create a NEW speech, select "Create Speeches."
4. A page will open that asks about the purpose of your speech. Read through each type of speech and choose the type that works best for your purpose. If you need more information about each type of speech, simply "LONG PRESS" the speech type to receive a brief tutorial regarding the speech. A "SHORT PRESS" of the speech type will take you directly to the next step in creating a speech.
5. Answer each prompting question using a complete sentence. Use correct grammar and spelling as this information will automatically begin building a speech outline.
6. Take your time and work through each step—one at a time—answering each prompting question and when finished touch the "Continue" bar.
7. SpeechShark takes all of the guesswork out of crafting an effective speech, but it is up to you to answer the prompts, keep the purpose of your speech as your goal, and consider who will be listening to your speech. What does your audience need to know? What does your audience WANT to know? What can you do and say to connect with the audience and engage them?
8. As you have answered all of the questions, you will notice that SpeechShark will then deliver a full written outline that you can print, share, or e-mail. Additionally, you will see that SpeechShark will automatically generate three note cards that can be used for notes on your phone or tablet/iPad. This will make you a Card Shark because instead of standing in front of your audience with awkward note cards, your notes are easily accessed using your electronic device and are available with a simple swipe.
9. Once the speech has been written, you can always retrieve it by going back to the "Home" file on the SpeechShark app and selecting "Manage Speeches." Every speech you craft will be stored there in a file with the "TITLE" that you give to the speech.
10. You, too, can be a **SpeechShark!**

Acknowledgments

Deep appreciation is extended to the following: Co-author, Travice Baldwin Obas; the dedicated members of the SpeechShark app design team: Charles Hardnett, Maurice McFarlane, Marcus Smith, and Cassandra West; personal editor and the greatest mom in the world: Ruth Rowell Joyner; the publishers and editors of Kendall Hunt, Brittanie Tucker and Kim Schmidt; and most importantly family support from my husband, Bill, our children, Katie, Steven, Maggie, and Halie, and our sweet grandbabies, Will, Bailey, and Hunter.

Unit #1:

Foundations of Public Speaking

Public Speaking

Speaker and Audience Responsibilities

Key Terms to Know

Chapter 1—Public Speaking

- Active Listening
- Appreciative Listening
- Communication
- Critical Listening
- Decoding
- Empathetic Listening
- Encoding
- Feedback
- Informative Listening
- Noise
- Public Speaking

Chapter 2—Speaker and Audience Responsibilities

- Active Listener
- Attention Step
- Connectors
- Conversational Tone
- Empathetic Listener
- Empathy
- Establish Credibility
- Establish Relevance
- Imagery
- Shark-o-licious Treat
- Startling Statement
- Thesis
- Transitions

Chapter One
Public Speaking

In this chapter:

Have you ever felt like a guppy in a shark tank?

Do you need help finding your voice?

What is the difference between communication and public speaking?

Why are listening skills important?

How do I use the SpeechShark app?

HAVE YOU EVER FELT LIKE A GUPPY IN A SHARK TANK?

One day, I approached a client who was scheduled to present his first informative speech and he looked terrified! He was sweating, had almost no color in his cheeks, and his hands were shaking. I sat with him in the corner of the room for a few minutes and tried to help calm his fears. Following my instincts, I told the client that I was confident he would do a great job! For weeks, I watched this same man present impromptu speeches and he clearly had no trouble communicating his ideas to others. Yet, here he was looking quite frazzled. After a few minutes of "pep talk," I asked him to take a deep breath and then tell me exactly how he felt. He looked directly at me and said with a shiver, "Have you ever felt like a guppy in a shark tank?"

Truthfully, we can all say that we have felt like a guppy in a shark tank when faced with presenting a speech! We feel like ALL eyes are on us and that we are the tender morsel of the day. We believe the audience members are staring at every part of our bodies, evaluating every piece of clothing, shoes, even judging the fact that we brought note cards to the lectern. They are listening to every word and hearing every unplanned pause, every stutter or stumble, and are critically judging us and finding fault with the information we are trying to share. Yes, we know what it feels like to be the guppy in a shark tank!

You don't have to feel like a guppy any longer—YOU are the Shark! Using the information in this book, along with the SpeechShark app, you can maneuver your way through murky waters and move confidently and fearlessly toward your goal! So, grab your device, click over to your speech notes, and walk to the stage area prepared to knock your audience out of the water! Make your points clearly because you wrote the speech with the end purpose and your audience in mind! No longer are you a guppy, you are a SpeechShark!

DO YOU NEED HELP FINDING YOUR VOICE?

Have you ever been asked what you think about an issue? Were you able to answer immediately? Did you feel confident with your answer? Did you feel like your answer was delivered effectively? Since before the time of Aristotle, it was evident that speaking and sharing opinions and facts are important to our society.

We all have opinions and the right to voice those opinions. Becoming a competent speaker is a goal that most of us have, but many of us are not entirely sure how to find our own voice, to exercise the freedom of speech, and to use our voices to bring about societal change.

Quite often, you will be asked to participate in group presentations or to make solo presentations. The higher you proceed in a college education and the more you advance in your company or organization, the more often you are going to be challenged with the prospect of public speaking. Since this is going to be an ongoing reality in your life, why not take time now to find your voice and learn to speak professionally and eloquently?

WHAT IS THE DIFFERENCE BETWEEN COMMUNICATION AND PUBLIC SPEAKING?

When going into the ocean or into a business meeting, many things can go wrong. *Sharks* can be the changing business climates, creative investment strategies, communication opportunities, or problem-solving strategies. You might ask yourself, "Why do we keep swimming in spite of calculated risks that we can't always navigate?"

My plan to avoid a shark attack is to not resemble the seal! Understand your strengths and weaknesses. Become informed. Learn the difference between communicating and speaking in public! Just as sharks maximize water safety, SpeechSharks maximize stage safety. Become an educated communicator, focus on your goals, and swim confidently toward your prize!

Communication is defined as a process in which ideas or information are transmitted, shared, or exchanged. In other words, you can communicate through various methods that are verbal and non-verbal: writing, speaking, art, music, movement, food, clothing, e-mails, videos, gifts, and the list goes on.

Public Speaking is a communication process in which speakers and listeners participate together. Public Speaking operates with the intention that speaking will be done in a public setting and with an audience. This type of speaking integrates theory and practice. While theory is important, speaking situations demand that content should be adapted to the speaking situation and to the audience for which the speech is intended. The speaker will share content, which can be received by the listener. In turn, the listener communicates to the speaker through verbal or non-verbal cues to indicate understanding or the lack thereof. In other words, communication is a *transactional* process.

With public speaking, there is participation between the sender (speaker) and the receiver (audience). This diagram shows how the communication process might look.

First, the speaker decides to send a message. Before sending the message, the speaker encodes the message and content to send. **Encoding** is a process by which a person derives meaning and understanding. It may involve finding a common understanding to develop a deeper understanding of the point or topic. Many speakers find that conducting research or speaking to someone with experience about the topic will help them develop a deeper understanding of the topic.

Once the speaker has a good understanding of the content, **the speaker delivers the message** to the audience. Each rhetorical situation is different; therefore, the speaker needs to consider many factors when deciding how to deliver the message. Finding common ground between the speaker and the audience, emphasizing the sharing of an idea with the audience, and determining an effective approach will help the speaker achieve the intended goal.

The audience receives the message, but the message may be distorted according to distractions in the surrounding area or by preconceived ideas and opinions of each audience member. As the audience receives the message, they decode what they have heard and understood before sending verbal and/or non-verbal feedback to the speaker. **Decoding** is a process by which we translate or interpret the content into meaning. The decoding process can be altered depending upon "noise" in the environment. **Noise** can be defined as distractions in the speaking environment, but also can include preconceived notions, opinions, and ideas. Sometimes **feedback** is verbal, but many times feedback is non-verbal. Feedback helps the speaker know if the content delivered has been effectively decoded and received. In order to have feedback, the receiver (audience) will need to listen.

WHY ARE LISTENING SKILLS IMPORTANT?

Consider how sharks find their prey. They do this using sensory receptors found along the sides of their bodies. These receptors perform much like our ears. They can feel vibrations or movement in the water around them with these receptors and respond to the message received.

SpeechSharks (that is you) also use sensory receptors to navigate communication waters to detect and gather information from that which we hear. **We listen!** Some of us are better listeners than others. You will also find that at times, you may be a better listener than you are at other times. What we hear often is determined by the amount of distractions that interfere with content being delivered. Instead of hearing a full sentence spoken to us, we might only hear bits and pieces of that sentence and decode the message into something that is not what the speaker intended. It happens all of the time. Business deals, marriages, and friendships are often broken because of this breakdown in communication. Become a better listener and you will be a more effective employee, a better marriage partner, and a more reliable friend.

Listening is quite different from hearing. Without any effort, you can hear something; however, it takes a conscious effort to listen. Hearing is a physical process that occurs as sound waves vibrate against eardrums and then that sound moves to the brain where it is decoded into a message or response.

Perhaps this table will make this clearer for you:

Listening	Hearing
Activity	Process
Learned Skill: can be taught and learned	Response to stimuli: involuntary
Active: requires the listener to be engaged, encode/decode, and respond	Passive: requires no action on the part of the listener
Choice: requires focus and attention	Continuous: if no hearing loss, hearing is ongoing
Message or content is consciously received and message gets a response	Sound is received, but will not always elicit a response

Effective speakers are great listeners! They must listen to find out what is needed by their potential audience and then go the extra mile to research main points within the content to provide the audience with credible information.

What keeps us from being good listeners?

In the section above we discussed "noise" that can be distractors during communication. Let's spend time now discussing these distractors in more detail. They include things we hear, see, do, know, and perceive/feel. These distractors are all prevalent whether we are in a public speaking situation or a private conversation. I'm sure you will be able to relate to all of these.

Things we hear: Have you ever tried to talk to someone in a crowded restaurant and the environmental noise surrounding you was so loud that you couldn't carry on a cohesive conversation? This could be anything from background music, other people's conversations, dishes rattling, glasses clinking, to chairs scraping on the floor. Extraneous noise can make it difficult to enjoy the person with whom you are sharing dinner. Do unusual accents cause you to reflect on how the speaker is pronouncing or saying a certain word resulting in misunderstanding content that was being shared? Perhaps you are visiting with friends during a play date with your children, and you are trying to listen while your friend tells you about an issue she is having with her phone company, but you are also trying to tune in to the chatter going on with the children. Chances are you didn't hear your friend's entire story and you also did not gather the full meaning of the tug-of-war going on with the children. You may be hearing lots of sounds, but are you really listening?

Things we see: Often, we have trouble focusing on a message if things we see are interfering with the message. It could be a glare off the windshield of a car parked outside, the speaker's choice of clothing, decorations on the stage, or other people in the audience. I am sure this distraction is something with which all of you can identify.

Things we do: What are your own listening habits? Do you have a tendency to tune out conversations while you check your text messages, Facebook, Instagram, or Twitter? Are you completing a sentence on your computer while a colleague is trying to tell you about a problem they are having in their department? Does the heavy cologne worn by the speaker distract you from listening to the content? Do you anticipate how you will respond before your speaker finishes the sentence? What poor listening habits do you have that might keep you from actively listening?

Things we know or don't know: Have you ever been confused by meanings of words and spent the next few minutes trying to decide the meaning of the word or correct pronunciation of the word instead of listening to the message? Do you wonder, "How is that spelled?" or look up the meaning on your phone? Do you find yourself pondering over incorrectly cited research or questioning facts offered by the speaker? Too many facts presented during a speech can also cause us to miss the speaker's main point because we are too focused on details. These things can prevent us from active listening.

Things we feel or perceive: Illness, pain, hunger, anger, extreme happiness, or exhaustion can keep us from hearing all that is being said. Negative attitudes, prejudices, beliefs, or feelings toward a topic can cause us to lose our desire to actively listen as a topic is presented. We are more critical of speakers who have views which differ from our own. Consequently, we will receive less of the intended message that we would have heard had we listened with an open mind. Likewise, we might listen closer to those who speak about a topic with which we agree. To become better listeners, resist positive or negative distractions, focus on verbal and non-verbal messages, try to see the speaker's point of view, take notes, and concentrate on active listening.

What are the types of listening skills?

Active Listening: Listen to understand. Determine if non-verbal cues being sent by the speaker mirror the speaker's message. Position your body so that your shoulders are facing the speaker, body posed forward, and use positive head nods and smiles to send a non-verbal cue that you are actively listening to the speaker.

Critical Listening: Resist outside noises and distractions to use critical listening skills. This involves looking past a speaker's distracting behavior and the environmental distractions that are around you. Avoid concentrating on yourself and your own feelings or perceptions. Instead, concentrate on the speaker and message being delivered.

Empathetic Listening: Try to see the speaker's point of view, even if you do not share the speaker's views. We often find ourselves in diverse audiences and it is imperative that we actively try to understand the speaker's message and offer positive non-verbal cues in support for the speaker.

Informative Listening: Taking notes during a speech will help you to use informative listening skills. Make notes of the main points, research, or data presented, and examples that are especially interesting to you. Even if your colleague is speaking to you about an issue, take notes about the issue and show active listening skills with strong body posture.

Appreciative Listening: This is my favorite type of listening skill. As we show enjoyment of a speaker and their content, we exhibit appreciative listening. Send non-verbal cues that you are listening and enjoying the speech. This is important and also helps the speaker to be less anxious due to the positive non-verbal cues sent during the speech.

WHAT TYPE LISTENER ARE YOU?

Instructions: Evaluate the following by answering the question truthfully as you are at this time. Later, take the same evaluation to see if you can notice improvements. When finished, tally your score using the key found at the end of the evaluation.

Questions:	Never 1	Rarely 2	Sometimes 3	Often 4	Always 5
1. I pay attention to the speaker.					
2. I can ignore distractions during the speech.					
3. I can listen to a speaker's ideas without letting my ideas/opinions get in the way.					
4. I can ignore distracting personal habits of the speaker (Throat clearing, movements, note cards).					
5. I take notes to organize the speaker's main points.					
6. During the speech, I am thinking of questions to ask about ideas I do not understand.					
7. I can understand the meaning of unknown words from the balance of the speaker's message.					
8. I can separate fact from opinion, without it being verbally cited.					
9. I can tell the difference between important and unimportant details.					
10. I listen to hear the speaker support points with research or personal stories.					
11. I agree and respect that others have differing points of view.					
12. I evaluate the speaker and the content of the speech.					
13. I identify specific words or phrases that impress me as I listen.					
14. I get caught up in the story or poem the speaker shares.					
15. I put what I hear into my own words so that I can recount it to others.					
16. I listen to what the speaker is saying and try to feel what the speaker feels.					

Questions:	Never 1	Rarely 2	Sometimes 3	Often 4	Always 5
17. I find hidden meanings revealed by subtle verbal and non-verbal cues.					
18. I use good listening skills and resist the urge to multi-task by listening to a speech and checking my cell phone.					
19. In a small group setting, if the speaker is struggling to explain something, I want to step in and assist.					
20. When people speak to me, I give head nods and verbal confirmations like, "OK" or "Yes."					
Calculate Score by Adding Points **MY SCORE IS:** _____					

Due to many different types of situations and speaker variables, responses to this questionnaire may not always reveal the same results. However, this assessment should give an idea of your average listening skills. **Circle the evaluation that corresponds with your score.**

15–30 — POOR — Continue work to improve your listening skills

31–74 — AVERAGE — But, you need to set your goals higher

75–100 — GOOD — Never stop working to be a better listener

WHERE CAN YOU PRACTICE YOUR PUBLIC SPEAKING SKILLS?

Many people enjoy belonging to professional development organizations that encourage public speaking presentations and provide opportunities to improve leadership skills. Take public speaking courses through your local college's continuing education program. Find organizations in your area that provide a public forum to practice your skills. Options to consider are Toastmasters International, National Speaker's Association, National Communication Association, Church or Religious Organizations, College Clubs, Meet-ups, Civic Organizations, Community Functions, Sports Events, Political Organizations, Book Clubs, Craft Clubs, and Business Networking Events. Speak at every opportunity to improve your communication skills, and you will become a more effective listener, communicator, and leader!

The key to being a good speaker is to speak so that others can understand you and your message! Every time you speak, give your audience something wonderful to remember. Make it a pleasant experience and they will ask you to speak again. Speak again and you will get more experience. The more experience you have the better speaker you will be.

The key is . . .

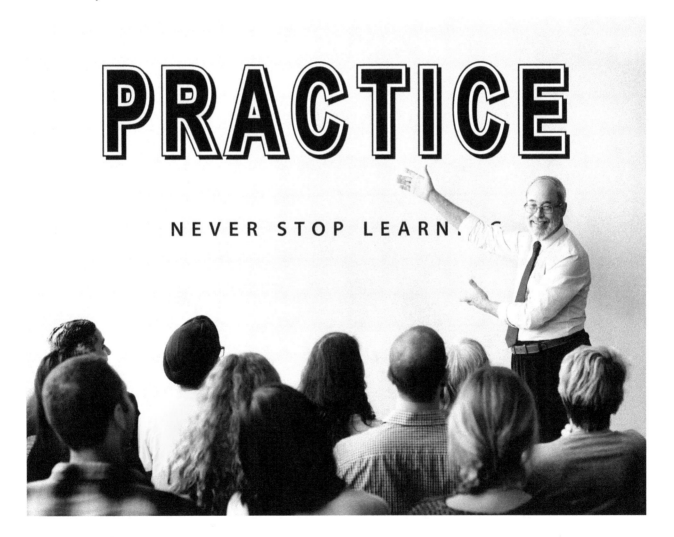

Public Speaking

After reading this chapter, you will be able to answer the following questions:

1. What is the definition of communication? _____

_____

_____

2. What is the definition of Public Speaking? _____

_____

_____

3. What are the six steps found in the communication process? _____

_____

_____

4. What happens through the encoding process? _____

_____

_____

5. Why should the speaker find common ground with the audience? _____

_____

_____

6. What happens during the decoding process? _____

_____

_____

7. What is noise? _____

_____

_____

8. Describe feedback. _____

_____

_____

9. Is listening an activity or a process? _____

_____

_____

10. Is hearing an activity or a process? _____

_____

_____

11. Is listening a learned skill or an involuntary response? _____

_____

_____

12. What distractors can keep us from receiving communication signals sent our way? _____

_____

_____

13. List the five types of listening skills: _____

_____

_____

14. What is active listening? _____

_____

_____

15. What is critical listening? _____

_____

_____

16. What is empathetic listening? _____

_____

_____

17. What is informative listening? _____

_____

_____

18. What is appreciative listening? _____

_____

_____

19. What type listener are you (Poor, Average, Good)? _____

_____

_____

20. When is your next speech? Are you prepared? _____

_____

_____

Shark Bites

IMPROVING LISTENING SKILLS

Let's work on our bad habits and explore cures!

Bad Habit: Often it is hard for me to concentrate on things people are saying because I tend to focus on their speech patterns, posture, clothes, or appearance.

Example: Last week while attending a church service, the pastor was explaining a Bible verse that was particularly hard to comprehend. I was so distracted by the number of filler words the pastor was using that I completely quit listening to the content and began counting the filler words.

Cure: _____

_____

_____

Here is another one:

Bad Habit: Sometimes I may pretend to be listening, but my mind is on other things. I will often look directly at the speaker, smile and nod like I am listening to them, when actually I am thinking about something else.

Example: Last week, my co-worker friend was telling me all about her weekend away with another set of friends. I am sure the plans must have been fun for her, but my mind was on a work deadline that I had to meet by that afternoon. I was smiling, head nodding, and acting like I was truly listening to her, but in reality, I was thinking about how I was going to meet the deadline. When I came back around to hearing her conversation, she was asking me if I wanted to join them next weekend. I had no idea what she was wanting me to join!

Cure: _____

_____

_____

Chapter Two

Speaker and Audience Responsibilities

In this chapter:

What are the speaker's responsibilities?

What are the audience's responsibilities?

SPEAKER RESPONSIBILITIES

Speakers have a responsibility to the audience. It is your job to know who will be in your audience and to plan your speech for them! Just because it is your opportunity to deliver the speech does not mean that you can stand on your soap box and use the time with a captured audience to share just exactly what you think about anything and everything. No, you will need to provide content that the audience needs and it is your responsibility to present it in a way that is effective, clear, and to the point. Prove you are a competent speaker by the content that you provide and the manner in which you provide the content.

Speak to your audience using a conversational tone. Your speech should not sound canned or rehearsed. It should sound as if you are sitting with one person in your audience at your kitchen table and discussing the topic over a nice cup of hot tea! Audiences do not want to be talked at. They want a conversation between you and them. This is the type of interaction you want on a small scale between you and another person. This is also the type of interaction an audience desires with a speaker. Talking "with" someone, sharing information, feelings, convictions are so much more enjoyable than having someone talk "at" you! It is a more intimate transaction. Just remember, the same type of interpersonal communication skills that work on a one-on-one or in a small group setting will also work beautifully between a speaker and an audience.

Show the audience that you care about them with the content you provide. Mention their names or the town where you are speaking. Say something positive about their local sports team, mayor, or director of the business where you are speaking. This will help your audience to feel like you wanted to be there with them enough to know what is important to them. It will help you to get the audience in your corner and will also make your speech so much more effective! Consider yourself as a host or hostess at a gathering. Your job is to make your audience comfortable and to supply their every need. Serve them a "Shark-o-licious" speech!

SERVING UP A "SHARK-O-LICIOUS" TREAT?

My daughter brought home a bag of gummy treats yesterday that were shaped like sharks! Isn't that fun? Sharks are everywhere! These fun shark treats made me think about great speeches and how they have a lot in common with a great meal. Since you might be presenting a speech soon, I wanted to share this with you so that you can serve a "Shark-o-licious" treat to YOUR audience.

Every memorable meal begins with an appetizer and then moves to a second dish before leading to the main course which usually includes a protein dish, starch, and vegetable before concluding with a delicious dessert.

Memorable speeches should follow the same type of menu as I will explain in the following table:

Memorable Meal	Memorable Speech	Similarities
Appetizer	Attention Step	Just as you arrive at a meal hungry and ready to eat, your audience will arrive anxious to hear your speech. This is where you set the stage, get the audience's attention, and provide your audience with a "taste" of what is to come.
Soup	Establish Relevance for the Topic Establish Credibility to Speak About the Topic Preview of Main Points (Thesis)	The soup prepares your palate for the main course of a meal, but it is this step in the speech that prepares your audience for the topic. First, explain why it is important that the audience hear about the upcoming topic. Then, tell your audience why YOU are credible to speak to them about the topic. The next thing that you will do during this phase is to clearly state the three main points that you will cover. This prepares your audience and allows them to anticipate the "main course"!
Bread	Transitions	Bread during a meal is often used to cleanse the palate and is enjoyed between courses. For the speech, transitions, also called connectors, are essential as they transition the content from one thing to the next. A great speaker will use clear transitions to move from the Introduction Step to the Body of the speech, to each Main Point, and then finally into the Conclusion.
Main Course: Protein Starch Vegetable	Body	The main course is the purpose of the meal and the body is the purpose of your speech! The body of the speech contains three main points that support the topic. Often the main points include research, stories, and examples that further define the topic.
Dessert	Conclusion	All great meals culminate with a sweet treat! The dessert that concludes the memorable meal is my favorite part of the meal because it leaves a sweet taste in my mouth! A great speech conclusion should leave your audience wanting more! Signal that you are concluding the speech, re-state the three main points, and then provide closing statements or an Appeal that will make your audience wish the speech could last just a little longer! Now, isn't that sweet?

It is time to start cooking, or should I say, writing the speech! How are you going to make sure your next speech is "Shark-o-licious"? Plan, Prepare, and Persevere! Keep these tips in mind and your next speech is sure to be a crowd pleaser with your audience having an appetite that will have them demanding an encore!

Plan

Even the simplest things need to be considered as you prepare for your presentation. And, yes, there are still more questions:

- What can you say or do to get your audience's attention from the very beginning?
- How can you get your audience to relate immediately to your topic?
- Why are YOU credible to talk to an audience about this topic?
- How can you conclude the speech so that your audience continues thinking about your speech topic even after your speech is over?

Answering these questions will help you prepare an Introduction Step that introduces the topic to your audience and will have them in the palm of your hand before you actually begin speaking about the topic. A strong Introduction Step (appetizer and soup) is important for an effective presentation, but this step cannot be written until AFTER you have planned the body (main course) of your speech (topic and three main points). This will also help you to prepare a Conclusion Step (desserts) that ends your speech with a BANG!

Prepare

The speaker has a responsibility to begin the speech with an Attention Step or Opener that will get their attention within the first few seconds of your presentation. Consider how you would feel if you were one of the audience members sitting and waiting to hear a great speech from YOU. Start strong with an engaging Attention Step. Here are some suggestions and why they work:

1. **Questions:** This works because a well-designed question is just begging to be answered. Be careful that your question leads directly to the topic you will be covering and remember that presentation is everything. A great question with a weak delivery will not make for a memorable Attention Step.

2. **Empathy:** This allows you to connect with your audience on a personal level. This starts the feeling of an intimate relationship between you and the audience in the first few seconds of your speech. Ask, "Have you ever thought about why. . .", "I'll never forget the moment when", or "Just like YOU, I was brought up to believe. . .".

3. **Announcement of a NEW Policy or Procedure:** While this might not always be met with full cooperation, it does get the attention of your audience and they will be very interested to see how this change will affect their own area or their lives.

4. **Secrets:** Everyone loves a secret! Start your speech by saying, "I want to let you in on a little secret—this is a secret that not even my husband knows. . ." Doing this provides you with the opportunity to promise something to your audience that they simply cannot refuse. They want to know the secret!

5. **Startling Statement:** Beginning your speech with a shocking statement that makes your audience feel like they may be making a huge mistake about something will certainly give them reason to sit up straight and listen to what you have to say!

6. **Warnings:** If you start your speech by saying, "There are three warning signs to look for when. . .", then your audience will want to hear you identify the three warning signs.

7. **Quotes:** This is always a good strategy, but can get a bit boring if every speaker that day begins with a quote. If you are going to use a quote, make sure that it is a quote that will make the audience want to sit up and take notice! Also, make sure you have the name of the person correct who is cited with the quote.

8. **Imagery:** You can start by saying, "Imagine, if you will. . ." People love imagery and they will enjoy an Attention Step that begins with imagery!

9. **Stories:** Everyone loves a good story. Start by saying, "Do you mind if I share a story with you? Last week when I was a XYZ, I heard about. . ." Now, they want to hear about it, too!

10. **Choices:** If I were to ask you to choose between this donut and an apple, which would you choose? Wait for the answer? Of course, you are hoping they will choose the apple, but you notice that more than half of your audience raised their hands saying they would choose the donut! Give them a choice! Then, allow that choice to help shape the direction of your speech topic.

Don't introduce yourself in the opening words of your speech. Save your introduction for the portion of your introduction step where you will establish your own credibility as a speaker for the topic. Here is an example:

Introduction to the Speech:

Attention Step:

Establish Need/Relevance for the Topic:

Establish Credibility: For the past twenty years, I have been a public speaking coach helping young people to prepare for interviews and competitions. Hello, my name is Dr. Penny Joyner Waddell and I am happy to be here with you today to discuss the importance of dressing for success when giving a speech presentation.

Thesis:

Persevere

Using the speech writing formula that we have presented in this book, we want you to begin thinking like a speech writer. You are on the right path—you are a SpeechShark swimming easily toward your target! Take a deep breath. It's almost time to meet your audience!

AUDIENCE RESPONSIBILITIES

Audiences have a responsibility, too! As the speaker enters the stage, please show appreciation for the speaker by giving your undivided attention and clapping until the speaker has taken his/her place on stage and is ready to begin the presentation! Your next task is to LISTEN to the speaker. Put away cell phones and electronic devices that would cause distractions and position your body to face the speaker. Using your nonverbal cues, show the speaker that she has your full attention and that you are anxious to hear her message. Smile at the speaker, nod your head in agreement, and show support with your face and body posture.

Prepare yourself to hear the speech. Listen carefully to identify the message delivered. Get plenty of rest and a good meal prior to the presentation. Just as the speaker has to prepare for you, it is your job to prepare yourself. Not enough sleep? You could be tempted to take a short nap during the presentation. YES, your speaker will know you are napping and that sends a negative non-verbal cue that you are bored and what the speaker is saying is of no consequence to you. If you are hungry, your stomach may growl or you could spend her speech thinking about what you might eat just as soon as the speech is over. Here are some tips to help you be a great audience member:

1. **Be an active listener** by showing appreciation for the speaker. Sending positive non-verbal cues such as smiling, head nods, leaning forward toward the speaker, and establishing eye contact, will show the speaker that you are glad to hear the speech. Just using the active listener posture will help you focus more on the speaker and become a better audience member.

2. **Resist distractions** and use your critical listening skills to focus in on the speaker and the message.

3. **Practice empathetic listening** and try to see the speaker's point of view, even if it differs from your own.

4. **Focus on verbal and non-verbal cues** being sent by the speaker. Are the speaker's verbal and non-verbal cues matching with the content of the speech?

5. **Take notes and create a presentation outline** during the speech. Informative listening is used during this time of the speech. Write down questions you may have so that you can ask them after the speech is over. Never interrupt the speaker to ask a question. Always save the questions to ask during a question and answer session or to pose privately to the speaker after she leaves the stage area.

Speaker and Audience Responsibilities

After reading this chapter, you will be able to answer the following questions:

1. What is the speaker's responsibility to the audience? _____

   _____

   _____

2. What type of tone should be used when speaking to an audience? _____

   _____

   _____

3. When should the speaker introduce themselves? _____

   _____

   _____

4. What audience responsibilities should be expected? _____

   _____

   _____

5. What is the difference between an active listener and an empathetic listener? _____

   _____

   _____

Shark Bites

Consider how you might plan your next Shark-o-licious Speech using this table:

Memorable Meal	Memorable Speech	What are YOUR plans?
Appetizer	Attention Step	
Soup	Establish Relevance for the Topic Establish Credibility to Speak About the Topic Preview of Main Points (Thesis)	
Bread	Transitions	

Main Course:
  Protein
  Starch
  Vegetable
	Body
	
	Three Main Points
		1.
		
		2.
		
		3.

Dessert	Conclusion End with a BANG!	

SpeechSHARK.™

Unit #2:

Types of Speeches
and
Methods of Delivery

Key Terms to Know

Chapter 3—Types of Speeches

- Attitudes
- Behaviors
- Beliefs
- Central Idea Speech
- Ceremonial Speeches
- Demonstration Speech
- Entertaining Speech
- Group Presentation
- Informative Speech
- Key Idea Speech
- Moderator
- Motivational Speech
- Persuasion Speech
- Question and Answer Session
- Questions of Fact
- Questions of Policy
- Questions of Value
- Sales Presentation
- Social Occasion Speeches
- Special Occasion Speeches
- Values
- Work-Related Speeches

Chapter 4—Methods of Delivery

- Conversational Quality
- Memorized Speech
- Manuscript Speech
- Impromptu Speech
- Extemporaneous Speech

Chapter Three
Types of Speeches

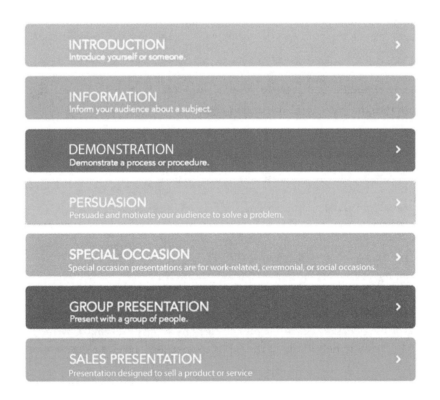

INTRODUCTION
Introduce yourself or someone.

INFORMATION
Inform your audience about a subject.

DEMONSTRATION
Demonstrate a process or procedure.

PERSUASION
Persuade and motivate your audience to solve a problem.

SPECIAL OCCASION
Special occasion presentations are for work-related, ceremonial, or social occasions.

GROUP PRESENTATION
Present with a group of people.

SALES PRESENTATION
Presentation designed to sell a product or service

In this chapter:

What are the different types of speeches?

How do I use brainstorming worksheets to plan my speech?

What plan should my speech outline follow?

TYPES OF SPEECHES

There are three basic purposes or types of speeches: informative, entertaining, and motivational. Some speeches will address just one purpose or type, but there are many speeches that will include all three.

Informative speeches are designed for the speaker to provide interesting and useful information and to add knowledge to the listener's existing understanding of the topic. For this type of speech, the speaker takes on the role of an instructor and will teach, instruct, explain, report, and/or describe.

Entertaining speeches are enjoyable speeches. Some organizations list this type of speech as a humorous speech. Although not all speeches are categorized as entertaining speeches, it is possible for all speeches to contain entertaining aspects. Audiences enjoy speeches that are light-hearted, incorporate humor, and provide entertaining factors within the speech. Storytelling is considered one strategy for delivering an entertaining speech. Special Occasion Speeches usually include entertaining aspects. Due to the nature of this type of speech, speakers are able to build relationships, bond with the audience, and enhance networking possibilities.

Motivational speeches are designed to inspire the audience to act on information. Most often, Persuasion and Special Occasion Speeches will incorporate motivational strategies. Speakers who have the purpose of motivating the audience will need to consider incorporating information, research, and stories which will influence the audience's values, beliefs, attitudes, or behaviors. More information about this is covered in the Persuasion Speech section of this book.

Before you decide which type of speech to present, determine the purpose of the speech and ask yourself:

- What must I say to the audience to provide content they want to hear?
- Is your purpose to introduce yourself or someone else?
- Do you need to inform your audience about a specific topic?
- Will you need to demonstrate a process, product, or procedure?
- Do you want to persuade your audience to solve a problem?
- Is this a special occasion and will require a roast, toast, or presentation about the occasion? Is it a ceremony, work related, or a social event?
- Are you making a group presentation or trying to sell a project?
- Are you taking part in a fun PechaKucha event?
- Are you competing in a debate, oral interpretations, improvisation, or story telling competition?

Unsure about how to write a speech? The SpeechShark app was created just for you! Select the type speech you need, answer the questions in full sentence format, and SpeechShark will do the rest of the work. For those who want to know more details about the types of speeches, here is a description and important facts about each type.

Introduction Speech

In your personal and business life, you will have plenty of opportunities to introduce yourself or others. Whether your introduction is planned or unplanned, understanding the tips below will help you complete the introduction with ease. Introduction Speeches are informative in nature because the purpose of the speech is to provide your audience with information about you or the person you are introducing.

Usually, Introduction Speeches are not very lengthy and last between two and three minutes. This isn't much time, so you will need to consider specific points to include, but without too much detail.

When introducing yourself, choose a theme and plan the introduction around the theme. If the setting is casual or informal, then you could introduce yourself with a theme about your hobbies, work, or family. Personal introductions on an informal scale will often include a handshake along with eye contact and a smile.

If the setting is business or formal, then you should introduce yourself by including information about your work, innovative ideas, experience in the field, and future goals. In both cases, consider the setting and provide information you think the audience would like to know. Avoid giving so much information that your introduction becomes tiresome! It should be light and positive.

One safe rule of thumb for an introduction speech is to follow a chronological or time-ordered sequence to introduce yourself or someone else. Begin your speech by briefly covering the **past**, then move to the **present**, and finally, share your hopes for the **future**.

If you are using the SpeechShark app to create this speech, then you can begin now to craft the speech. If you are not using the app, you may want to use the Introduction Speech Brainstorming Worksheet to get your thoughts together and prepare to write your presentation outline. Remember that all speech writers follow the **Standard Outline** procedure for creating a speech outline. We will only show you this type of outline in this book so that you will begin thinking like a professional speech writer!

Consider your audience and the speech making situation so that you know what type of information to include. **Answer the following questions:**

• What is your ultimate purpose for the introduction? _____

_____

_____

_____

• Are you speaking to a room full of people or to one person? _____

_____

_____

_____

• Is the introduction in a formal or informal setting? _____

_____

_____

_____

• What information do you need to share? _____

_____

_____

_____

• How much time do you have for the speech? _____

_____

_____

_____

• What can you do to make the introduction relevant to the audience?_____

_____

_____

_____

SPEECH BRAINSTORMING WORKSHEET

Speech Category: Introduction Speech

Speech Title: Give your speech a clever title. _____

Specific Purpose: Write a full sentence to show what you plan to accomplish by introducing yourself or introducing someone else.

_____

_____

Introduction:

Attention Step: Consider how you will get your audience's attention. Write all you plan to say using full sentences.

_____

_____

Establish Need/Relevance: Explain why this introduction should interest the listener. Write all you plan to say using full sentences.

_____

_____

Establish Credibility: Explain why YOU are credible to introduce yourself or another person. Write all you plan to say using full sentences.

_____

_____

Thesis (Preview) Statement: Write a complete sentence and clearly state the three points you will cover:

_____

Point #1: Past _____

Point #2: Present _____

Point #3: Future _____

Body:

Transition Sentence: Write a full sentence to transition from the Introduction Step to the first main point.

_____

_____

    I. First Main Point—Past: (Share information about your past—stay with a theme.)
       A. First Sub-Point
          1. First Sub-Sub-Point (Not all points will require sub-sub-points.)
          2. Second Sub-Sub-Point
       B. Second Sub-Point
          1. First Sub-Sub-Point
          2. Second Sub-Sub-Point

Transition Sentence: Write a full sentence to transition from the past to the present.

_____

_____

    II. Second Main Point—Present: (Share information about your present—stay with the theme.)
       A. First Sub-Point
          1. First Sub-Sub-Point (Not all points will require sub-sub-points.)
          2. Second Sub-Sub-Point
       B. Second Sub-Point
          1. First Sub-Sub-Point
          2. Second Sub-Sub-Point

Transition Sentence: Write a full sentence to transition from the present to the future.

_____

_____

III. Third Main Point—Future: (Share information about your goals for the future—stay with the theme.)
    A. First Sub-Point
        1. First Sub-Sub-Point (Not all points will require sub-sub-points.)
        2. Second Sub-Sub-Point
    B. Second Sub-Point
        1. First Sub-Sub-Point
        2. Second Sub-Sub-Point

Transition Sentence: Write a full sentence to transition from the third main point to the conclusion.

_____

_____

Conclusion:

Summary: Write in full sentence format a summary of your three main points.

_____

Point #1: _____

Point #2: _____

Point #3: _____

Appeal to Action: Leave your audience thinking about your introduction. End with a **BANG!**

(NOTE: Be sure to add a Works Cited Page as a page separate from the Outline. Include all sources used.)

Works Cited

(Note: If you use Visual Aids, please include a Visual Aid Explanation Page as a page separate from the Works Cited Page and separate from the Outline.)

Visual Aid Explanation Page

INTRODUCTION SPEECH OUTLINE TEMPLATE

Last Name 1

First Name/Last Name
Introduction Speech
Day Month Year

Speech Category: Introduction Speech
Title:
Purpose:

Introduction:
Attention Step:
Establish Need/Relevance:
Establish Speaker Credibility:

Thesis: Today, I want to share three points about (Topic): (1) _____,

(2) _____, and (3) _____.

Body:

Transition/Link: First, I will start at the beginning by sharing a little about (Point #1).
    I. First Main Point
        A. Sub-point
        B. Sub-point

Transition/Link: I've shared (Point #1) with you, now I'd like to tell you about (Point #2).
    II. Second Main Point
        A. Sub-point
        B. Sub-point

Transition/Link: You've heard about (Point #1 and Point #2), now I'll cover (Point #3).
    III. Third Main Point
        A. Sub-point
        B. Sub-point

Transition/Link: My purpose today was to (insert purpose and add a statement about the topic).
Conclusion:

Summary: Today, I shared with you three points: (1) Point #1 _____, (2) Point #2 _____

_____, and (3) Point #3 _____.
Appeal to Action: As I conclude this speech, (End with a BANG).

(NOTE: Be sure to add a Works Cited Page as a page separate from the Outline. Include all sources used.)

Works Cited

(Note: If you use Visual Aids, please include a Visual Aid Explanation Page as a page separate from the Works Cited Page and separate from the Outline.)

Visual Aid Explanation Page

EXAMPLE: INTRODUCTION SPEECH OUTLINE

Penny J. Waddell
Introduction Speech
30 June 2017

Speech Category: Introduction Speech
Title: A Penny Saved Is a Penny Earned
Purpose: The purpose of this speech is to introduce myself to the readers of this book.

Introduction:
Attention Step: Benjamin Franklin, one of the most famous Americans in our history, once said, "A penny saved is a penny earned" (*Benjamin Franklin Quote*s 1).
Establish Need/Relevance: My father would say this quote every time he introduced me to someone because he loved my name. Since we will be spending time together this fall, it is important that you get to know a little about me. Through the years, my name, Penny, has become a way to start conversations with complete strangers and so I wanted to share this quote with you and a few tidbits of information to let you know how a person's name can help that person build a life.
Establish Speaker Credibility: Hello, my name is Penny and I am credible to introduce myself to you because I know myself better than anyone else in this room, unless of course, it is my father!
Thesis: Today, I want to share three points about my life as a speech coach: (1) Past Speaking Experiences, (2) Present Speaking Experiences, and (3) Future Speaking Experiences.

Body:

Transition/Link: First, I will start at the beginning by sharing a little about my past speaking experiences.
    I. Past Speaking Experiences
        A. Learning Public Speaking Tips
        B. Not a Penny to My Name
        C. College Experiences Worth Every Penny

Transition/Link: I've shared past speaking experiences with you, now I'd like to tell you what is going on presently.
    II. Present Speaking Experiences
        A. Not a Bad Penny, But a Good Penny
        B. Turning a Penny Postcard into a SpeechShark Postcard
        C. Developed a SpeechShark app for Speech Writing and Author of the *SpeechShark* textbook

Transition/Link: You've heard about my past and present speaking experiences, but the best is yet to come!
    III. Future Speaking Experiences
        A. Throwing a Penny Over My Shoulder into a Wishing Well
        B. A Good Penny is Worth a Pound of Cure
        C. A Penny for your Thoughts

Transition/Link: My purpose today was to introduce myself to you and to help you know a little more about me. Do you think you might be able to remember my name, if we met again somewhere along the way?
Conclusion:

Summary: Today, I shared with you three sweet points—you might call them Penny Candy: (1) Past Speaking Experiences, (2) Present Speaking Experiences, and (3) Future Speaking Experiences of a new friend named Penny.

Appeal to Action: As I close this speech, the next time you see me at a meeting or in a crowd, I hope you will remember that I am not a "bad penny." I am a "good penny" and a speech coach that can help you "Save" face when asked to speak in public and "Earn" the respect of those in your audience. Remember, "A Penny Saved Is a Penny Earned" (*Benjamin Franklin Quotes* 1).

(NOTE: Place the Works Cited Page on a page separate from the outline).

Works Cited

Benjamin Franklin Quotes. Your Dictionary. Lovetoknow.com 2017. Accessed 12 March 2017.

Informative Speech

What is an **Informative Speech**? It is an opportunity to share something of value with your audience. You may choose to provide information about a hobby, career, politics, religion, or something that is happening in your school, college, or community. The purpose of an informative speech is to share knowledge with your audience. Often, the audience may already have a good understanding of the topic, but you will then be able to expand their knowledge by providing credible research, data, and personal stories to support your main points.

Conducting research will allow the opportunity to provide a strong attention step and conclusion for the informative speech. You may choose to begin the speech with a great quote or startling statistics that will get your audience's attention and will also lead to the informative speech topic you will present. Research can also provide options for the conclusion to keep your audience thinking about the information you shared. Supplementing your informative speech with credible research and personal experiences will make the topic come alive for your audience and will help your audience to remain more attentive.

Once you know who will be in your audience, consider choosing a topic that will be interesting to those in your audience. Also, consider a topic that interests you. Remember, enthusiasm is contagious! If you are enthusiastic about your topic, then your audience will enjoy your speech so much more.

Don't be afraid to share a topic that may be personal in nature. Audiences truly enjoy hearing personal stories and your experience with the topic will help support the points in the speech. Let us see your personality and passion for the topic.

An **Informative Speech** is often called a **Key Idea Speech** or a **Central Idea Speech**. You will hear these titles interchangeably because you begin with one general topic idea, but find it necessary to narrow your topic down to one key or central idea. From that point, you will have a better chance of informing your audience about the topic you have chosen.

The best informative speeches have titles that lead to the information the speaker wishes to share. Most of these titles will begin with *"How to. . .", "Why You Should. . .", Did You Know. . .", "Tips for. . .", "The Pros and Cons of . . .", "Examples of. . .", and "The Problems With. . .".*

Here are some examples of informative speech titles:

Informative Speech Topics	
How to Make Brownies	How to Choose a Church That Is Right for Your Family
How to Start a College Club on Your Campus	Where to Go on Your Next Vacation
Why You Should NOT Text and Drive	The Problem with an HOA (Home Owners Association)
Why Homeowners Should Have an HO3 Insurance Policy	Examples of GMOs (Genetically Modified Organisms)
How to Hang Glide	Time Management Skills
Tips for a Winning Interview	How to Name Your Child
The Pros and Cons of Being a Stay-At-Home Mom	The Problem with Sugar

Visual aids are often used during informative speeches to help the audience visualize content being shared by the speaker. If you are not familiar with creating effective visual aids for a speech, please refer to Unit #4 of this textbook to learn more.

An important visual aid tip to remember for an informative speech is to keep it simple and show one slide per main idea. Too many slides and too much information will be distracting, but a visual aid that is effectively designed will help the audience to visualize the speaker's points. No murky waters here for Speech Sharks who know how to combine quality research, personal experience, and visual aids to paint a clear picture of the speech topic!

Whether you are informing your audience about people, places, careers, hobbies, objects, procedures, or events, you can be sure that the more time you spend crafting a speech FOR your audience, the more successful you will be communicating that information TO your audience. Use the Informative Speech Brainstorming Worksheet to help craft your next Informative Speech.

INFORMATIVE SPEECH BRAINSTORMING WORKSHEET

Speech Category: Informative Speech
Speech Title: Give your speech a clever title. _____
Specific Purpose: Write a full sentence to show the purpose of your speech.

_____

_____

Introduction:
Attention Step: Consider how you will get your audience's attention. Write all you plan to say using full sentences.

_____

_____

Establish Need/Relevance: Explain why this informative speech topic should interest the listener. Write all you plan to say using full sentences.

_____

_____

Establish Credibility: Explain why YOU are credible to speak about this topic. Write all you plan to say using full sentences.

_____

_____

Thesis (Preview) Statement: Write a full sentence clearly stating the three points you will cover:

_____

Point #1: _____

Point #2: _____

Point #3: _____

Body:

Transition Sentence: Write a full sentence to transition from the Introduction Step to the first main point.

_____

_____

    I. First Main Point:
      A. First Sub-Point
        1. First Sub-Sub-Point (Not all points will require sub-sub-points.)
        2. Second Sub-Sub-Point
      B. Second Sub-Point
        1. First Sub-Sub-Point
        2. Second Sub-Sub-Point

Transition Sentence: Write a full sentence to transition from the first main point to the second.

_____

_____

    II. Second Main Point:
      A. First Sub-Point
        1. First Sub-Sub-Point (Not all points will require sub-sub-points.)
        2. Second Sub-Sub-Point
      B. Second Sub-Point
        1. First Sub-Sub-Point
        2. Second Sub-Sub-Point

Transition Sentence: Write a full sentence to transition from the second point to the third point.

_____

_____

    III. Third Main Point
      A. First Sub-Point
        1. First Sub-Sub-Point (Not all points will require sub-sub-points.)
        2. Second Sub-Sub-Point
      B. Second Sub-Point
        1. First Sub-Sub-Point
        2. Second Sub-Sub-Point

Transition Sentence: Write a full sentence to transition from the third main point to the conclusion.

_____

_____

Conclusion:

Summary: Write in full sentence format a summary of your three main points.

_____

Point #1: _____

Point #2: _____

Point #3: _____

Appeal to Action: Leave your audience thinking about your speech. End with a **BANG!**

(NOTE: Be sure to add a Works Cited Page as a page separate from the Outline. Include all sources used.)

Works Cited

(Note: If you use Visual Aids, please include a Visual Aid Explanation Page as a page separate from the Works Cited Page and separate from the Outline.)

Visual Aid Explanation Page

INFORMATIVE SPEECH OUTLINE TEMPLATE

Last Name 1

First Name/Last Name
Informative Speech
Day Month Year

Speech Category: Informative Speech
Title:
Purpose:

Introduction:
Attention Step:
Establish Need/Relevance:
Establish Speaker Credibility:

Thesis: Today, I want to share three points about (Topic): (1) _____,

(2) _____, and (3) _____.

Body:

Transition/Link: First, I will start at the beginning by sharing a little about (Point #1).
   I. First Main Point
      A. Sub-point
      B. Sub-point

Transition/Link: I've shared (Point #1) with you, now I'd like to tell you about (Point #2).
   II. Second Main Point
      A. Sub-point
      B. Sub-point

Transition/Link: You've heard about (Point #1 and Point #2), now I'll cover (Point #3).
   III. Third Main Point
      A. Sub-point
      B. Sub-point

Transition/Link: My purpose today was to (insert purpose and add a statement about the topic).
Conclusion:

Summary: Today, I shared with you three points: (1) Point #1 _____, (2) Point #2 _____

_____, and (3) Point #3 _____.
Appeal to Action: As I conclude this speech, (End with a BANG).

(NOTE: Be sure to add a Works Cited Page as a page separate from the Outline. Include all sources used.)

Works Cited

(Note: If you use Visual Aids, please include a Visual Aid Explanation Page as a page separate from the Works Cited Page and separate from the Outline.)

Visual Aid Explanation Page

EXAMPLE: INFORMATIVE SPEECH OUTLINE

Waddell 1

Penny J. Waddell
Toastmasters International Meeting
30 June 2017

Speech Category: Informative Speech
Title: How to Dress for An Interview
Purpose: The purpose of this speech is to inform my audience how to dress for an interview.

Introduction:
Attention Step: (Show pictures on a PowerPoint slide of different people dressed in different ways. One person is dressed in jeans, flip-flops, and a T-shirt; another is dressed in a short minidress with tattoos showing on her arms and legs; another is dressed business casual.) Take a look at the pictures of these three candidates who are about to interview for a job position at a Fortune 500 Company. Which candidate do you think will get the job?
Establish Need/Relevance: The truth is that any one of these candidates MAY get the job. The secret is knowing with which company the candidate is interviewing. If interviewing for a position at GOOGLE, the jeans and T-shirt may be appropriate. If interviewing for a position with The Coca Cola Company in Atlanta, the candidate dressed business casual may get the job. Before interviewing for a job position, be sure to know what type of dress is expected.
Establish Speaker Credibility: I am credible to speak to you today about dressing for an interview because I have recently interviewed for a job position and got the job! For the position, I needed to dress in an upscale suit, very little jewelry, and I needed to project extreme professionalism.
Thesis: Today, I will cover three points to inform you how to dress for an interview. (1) Research the company, (2) Understand the culture of the company, and (3) Put your best foot forward.

Body:
Transition/Link: Let's begin with the first point, research the company.
    I. Research the Company
        A. What type of business does this company do?
        B. For this position, what type of work responsibilities are expected?

Transition/Link: I've shared the importance of researching the company with you, now I'd like to tell you how to understand the culture of the company.
    II. Understand the Culture of the Company
        A. Make a trip to the company prior to the Interview (Quast).
        B. Watch to see how other employees dress.

Transition/Link: You've heard how to research the company and how to understand its culture, now I want to show you how to put your best foot forward.
    III. Put Your Best Food Forward (Smith).
        A. Choose clothing, shoes, and accessories that mirror how other employees in this company dress.
        B. Always err on the conservative side, but don't forget to show your personality.

Transition/Link: Now you should understand a little more about how to dress for an interview.
Conclusion:

Summary: Today, I shared with you three points: (1) Research the company, (2) Understand the culture of the company, and (3) Put your best foot forward.

Appeal to Action: As you interview for what might very well be the most important interview of your life, be sure to remember that "You never get a second chance to make a first impression" (Quast). With this quote, I want to challenge you to dress for success and make sure this interview is the one that will help you get your dream job!

(Note: The Works Cited page is a separate page from the Outline).

Works Cited

Smith, Chris. "Dress to Impress: what to wear for a job interview." *The Guardian.* Guardian Careers. (2017).

Accessed 12 March 2017.

Quast, Lisa. "8 Tips to Dress for Interview Success." *Forbes.* (2014). Accessed 12 March 2017.

(Note: The Visual Aids Explanation page is a separate page from the Outline and the Works Cited page).

Visual Aids Explanation Page

PowerPoint Presentation:

Slide #1: Title of Speech—How to Dress for an Interview

Pictures of Three People Dressed Differently

Slide #2: (Point #1): Research the Company

Bullet Points:

- Type of Business
- Type of Work Responsibilities

Slide #3: (Point #2): Understand the Culture of the Company

Picture of Business with Employees Entering the Door

Slide #4: (Point #3): Put Your Best Foot Forward

Picture of Professionally Dressed Employee

Slide #5: "You Never Get a Second Chance to Make a First Impression" (Quast)

Picture of a Group of Professionally Dressed Employees

Demonstration Speech

Sometimes the audience needs to see a **Demonstration Speech** in order to fully comprehend the process or procedure needed to complete a task. Demonstration speeches are informative type speeches, but will include a demonstration to complete the purpose. Usually this speech is a bit longer than the Central Idea (Informative) Speech and involves audience participation. This type speech also includes an entertaining aspect. Perhaps that is why this type of speech is so popular! Audiences are able to retain and comprehend information better when they actively take part in the demonstration and can visualize how the process or procedure works. It is because of this fact that Demonstration Speeches often appeal to diverse audiences and to people with varying learning styles. To summarize, the audience will hear the information, see the demonstration, and participate in the demonstration to retain the information much longer.

As with any speech topic, the speaker will need to choose a topic tailor-made for the intended audience. This is a great speech to incorporate your creativity and bring an element of entertainment to the speaking arena. Make it informational and useful so that you can add value to your audience's knowledge of the topic. Topics may include crafts, sports, hobbies, food preparations, horticulture, home or automotive repairs, but can also include how to budget, create a will, or participate in stock trading. If you have more time, your topic could involve the process of flipping a house, starting a business, or designing a website. Again, the topic you choose needs to be a topic that will be interesting and useful for the audience that will hear your speech. Demonstration Speech titles almost always begin with, "How to. . .". The title lends itself to the purpose of the speech.

Here are examples of good Demonstration Speech titles:

Demonstration Speech Topics	
How to Arrange Flowers	How to Organize Your Closet
How to Bake a Cake	How to Pack for a Trip
How to Clean a House	How to Paint a Room
How to Tie a Bow Tie	How to Play Dominoes
How to Change a Diaper	How to Wrap a Gift
How to Use Twitter	How to Write a Resume
How to Make Egg Rolls	How to Fold a Flag
How to Make a Picture Frame	How to perform CPR

The best plan to follow for a Demonstration Speech is to: (1) describe the history of the process or procedure you will demonstrate, (2) list and describe the materials needed for the demonstration, and (3) demonstrate the process or procedure. This plan may seem simple, but it truly is the clearest way to present demonstration information in such a way that will make sense to the audience.

Handouts and visual aids are important for a successful Demonstration Speech. The visual aids can help with the actual demonstration and handouts are given to audience members following the demonstration as a reminder of the process or procedures followed.

Understanding the setting of where the speech will be given may help you choose the topic and visual aids. Where will you be giving the demonstration speech? Will it be inside or outside? Will it be in a traditional classroom setting or in a public hall?

Rehearsals for a Demonstration Speech are different from rehearsals needed for other types of speeches. The Demonstration Speech will incorporate more visual aids than an Informative Speech. You might have a PowerPoint or Prezi Slide Presentation to illustrate steps in the process or procedure, but a table display is almost always used for a Demonstration Speech. The speaker stands behind the table and uses the props on the table display to demonstrate the process or procedure while speaking. It is for this reason that rehearsals should always include the actions that will be taken during the speech. Rehearse using the PowerPoint or Prezi Slide Presentation, but also using the props on the table display. Rehearse completing the steps needed to demonstrate the process or procedure. You'll notice that your speech time will actually last longer when you are giving the speech using the props to demonstrate than when you rehearse the speech without the props. This speech will involve using a Tech Team to help set up and break down the demonstration stage. Rehearse with your Tech Team so they know exactly what you want them to do and when you want them to do it.

DEMONSTRATION SPEECH BRAINSTORMING WORKSHEET

Speech Category: Demonstration Speech
Speech Title: Give your speech a clever title. _____
Specific Purpose: Write a full sentence to show the purpose of your speech.

_____

_____

Introduction:

Attention Step: Consider how you will get your audience's attention. Write all you plan to say using full sentences.

_____

_____

Establish Need/Relevance: Explain why this demonstration speech topic should interest the listener. Write all you plan to say using full sentences.

_____

_____

Establish Credibility: Explain why YOU are credible to demonstrate this topic. Write all you plan to say using full sentences.

_____

_____

Thesis (Preview) Statement: Write a complete sentence and clearly state the three points you will cover:

_____

Point #1: The history of _____

Point #2: Materials needed for the demonstration: _____

Point #3: Demonstration of _____

Body:

Transition Sentence: Write a full sentence to transition from the Introduction Step to the first main point.

_____

_____

    I. **First Main Point:**
        A. First Sub-Point
           1. First Sub-Sub-Point (Not all points will require sub-sub-points.)
           2. Second Sub-Sub-Point
        B. Second Sub-Point
           1. First Sub-Sub-Point
           2. Second Sub-Sub-Point

Transition Sentence: Write a full sentence to transition from the first main point to the second.

_____

_____

    II. **Materials needed**
        A. First Sub-Point
           1. First Sub-Sub-Point (Not all points will require sub-sub-points.)
           2. Second Sub-Sub-Point
        B. Second Sub-Point
           1. First Sub-Sub-Point
           2. Second Sub-Sub-Point

Transition Sentence: Write a full sentence to transition from the second point to the third point.

_____

_____

    III. **Demonstration**
        A. First Sub-Point
           1. First Sub-Sub-Point (Not all points will require sub-sub-points.)
           2. Second Sub-Sub-Point
        B. Second Sub-Point
           1. First Sub-Sub-Point
           2. Second Sub-Sub-Point

Transition Sentence: Write a full sentence to transition from the third main point to the conclusion.

_____

_____

Conclusion:

Summary: Write a full sentence summary of your three main points.

_____

Point #1: The History of (Product or Process) _____

Point #2: Materials needed: _____

Point #3: The Demonstration _____

Appeal to Action: Leave your audience thinking about your demonstration. End with a **BANG!**

(NOTE: Be sure to add a Works Cited Page as a page separate from the Outline. Include all sources used.)

Works Cited

(Note: If you use Visual Aids, please include a Visual Aid Explanation Page as a page separate from the Works Cited Page and separate from the Outline.)

Visual Aid Explanation Page

DEMONSTRATION SPEECH OUTLINE TEMPLATE

Last Name 1

First Name/Last Name
Demonstration Speech
Day Month Year

Speech Category: Demonstration Speech
Title:
Purpose:

Introduction:
Attention Step:
Establish Need/Relevance:
Establish Speaker Credibility:

Thesis: Today, I want to share three points about (Topic): (1) _____,

(2) _____, and (3) _____.

Body:

Transition/Link: First, I will start at the beginning by sharing a little about (Point #1).
   I. First Main Point
      A. Sub-point
      B. Sub-point

Transition/Link: I've shared (Point #1) with you, now I'd like to tell you about (Point #2).
   II. Second Main Point
      A. Sub-point
      B. Sub-point

Transition/Link: You've heard about (Point #1 and Point #2), now I'll cover (Point #3).
   III. Third Main Point
      A. Sub-point
      B. Sub-point

Transition/Link: My purpose today was to (insert purpose and add a statement about the topic).
Conclusion:

Summary: Today, I shared with you three points: (1) Point #1 _____, (2) Point #2 _____

_____, and (3) Point #3 _____.
Appeal to Action: As I conclude this speech, (End with a BANG).

(NOTE: Be sure to add a Works Cited Page as a page separate from the Outline. Include all sources used.)

Works Cited

(Note: If you use Visual Aids, please include a Visual Aid Explanation Page as a page separate from the Works Cited Page and separate from the Outline.)

Visual Aid Explanation Page

EXAMPLE: DEMONSTRATION SPEECH OUTLINE

Penny J. Waddell
SkillsUSA Culinary Arts Demonstration
25 April 2017

Speech Category: Demonstration Speech
Title: Manners Matter
Purpose: The purpose of this speech is to demonstrate how to set a table for dinner.

Introduction:
Attention Step: Two weeks ago, I went to a formal dinner that included several courses. The young lady seated to my left was quite nervous, so I asked her how she was doing. She told me that she was terrified because she had no idea which fork to use for each course. As she said this, she looked down at the place setting in front of her that had four forks, two knives, and two spoons. Have you ever been in this type of situation? Do you know which fork to use?
Establish Need/Relevance: Emily Post, whose name has become synonymous with etiquette and manners, said in her article, "The Table Setting Guide" that "Setting a proper table is not as difficult as it seems."
Establish Speaker Credibility: At a young age, I learned how to set a Basic Table Setting and a Formal Table Setting. As I grew older and had daughters of my own, I taught them to do the same. As they were growing older, I taught a course called, "Oops Your Manners are Showing." In that course, I was able to teach young people about table setting etiquette; therefore, I feel credible to share this information with you.
Thesis: Today, I will share three points about setting a proper table. (1) First, I will tell you about the history of setting a table. (2) Second, I will list the materials needed to set a table, and (3) Third, I will demonstrate the proper setting of a table.

Body:

Transition/Link: Before you learn how to set a proper table, let's first look at the history of setting a table.
    I. **The history of setting a table**
        A. How it Began
        B. Origins of Cutlery

Transition/Link: I've shared the history of table setting with you, now I'd like to tell you the materials needed to set a basic table.
    II. **Materials needed to set a Basic table ("Table Setting Guide")**
        A. Dinner Plate, Bread Plate
        B. Drinking Vessels, Cutlery and Napkin

Transition/Link: You've heard about the history of setting a table and learned the materials that you will need. Now, please allow me to demonstrate how to set a basic table.
    III. **Demonstrate the setting of a table**
        A. Step #1—Placement of Plates
        B. Step #2—Placement of Drinking Vessels, Cutlery and Napkin

Transition/Link: My purpose today was to show you how easy it is to set a basic table.
Conclusion:

Summary: Today, I shared with you three points: (1) First, the history of setting a table. (2) Second, materials needed to set a table. (3) Third, the proper setting of a table.

Appeal to Action: Do you remember the young lady that I told you about in the beginning of this speech? She did a great job that night at the formal dinner party. She just watched others around her and then picked up the fork she saw them pick up. We learn by watching. Be careful because your manners are showing!

(Note: The Works Cited page is a separate page from the Outline.)

Works Cited

"Table Setting Guide." *The Emily Post Institute.* 2017. Accessed 2 April 2017.

(Note: The Visual Aid Explanation page should be placed on a separate page from the Outline and Works Cited page.)

Visual Aid Explanation Page

PowerPoint Presentation:

Slide #1: Title of Speech

Picture of a Table Setting

Slide #2: History of a Table Setting

Picture of a Table Setting

Slide #3: List of Materials Needed

Picture of Materials

Slide #4: Demonstration of a Table Setting

Picture of a Table Setting

Slide #5: Conclusion Slide—Picture

Table Display:

Table with a tablecloth and dishes arranged in a Basic Table Setting ("Table Setting Guide")

Persuasion Speech

We use persuasion strategies all day long as we inspire or motivate others to do something. It begins in the morning when you are persuading your child to get dressed for school, it continues as you go to work and try persuading your co-workers to embrace a new policy or procedure at the office. Then at night when you go home, you are still using your persuasion strategies to motivate your family to get outside for a little exercise after supper. Just face it, we will use this type of skill more often than any other. Not only are you attempting to persuade others to think of something in a different way, but they will also be attempting to persuade you to think another way.

Did you sit with friends or family members after the last presidential election and try to persuade them to think like you? Were they trying to change your mind about the way you think about politics? These types of interactions happen quite often. Sometimes we actually stop to consider another way of thinking. What strategy motivates you to think of things in a different way? What strategy motivates you to action?

The key word here is—motivate! That is because as we attempt to persuade someone to consider the view we present, we are actually motivating or influencing their values, beliefs, attitudes, or behaviors. Let's look at an explanation for each one of these areas.

Area to Influence (Motivate):	Explanation
Values	Do you think something is right or wrong? Do you consider something is good or bad?
Beliefs	Do you perceive the topic to be true or false?
Attitudes	Do you look at the topic in a favorable or unfavorable light? What is your attitude toward the topic?
Behaviors	Behaviors are a combination of your personal values, beliefs, and attitudes. We behave a certain way when we are reacting to these different areas.

The best strategy for being persuasive without sounding preachy or gimmicky is to follow **Monroe's Motivated Sequence**. Perhaps you would like to know a little more about Monroe's Motivated Sequence, especially if you have never heard of this term before. According to Frymier and Shulman, authors of the article, "What's in It for Me?" published by the *Communication Education Journal*, one way to truly motivate someone to do something or to think differently about something is to show the benefits or "What's in it for me?" This allows the speaker the opportunity to make the content relevant to the listener and to increase their motivation toward a solution.

The person who developed the Motivated Sequence Theory was Alan H. Monroe, a professor at Purdue University and well known for his theory of persuasion. **Monroe's theory involves five steps:** begin with a strong attention step, describe a problem showing a need for change, introduce a realistic solution which includes having the listener help solve the problem, help the listener visualize the results of solving the problem, and finish by challenging the listener to solve the problem.

First, the speaker should describe the problem using examples that will get the attention of the audience and will cause the audience to agree that there is, indeed, a problem.

Second, credible research and/or experiential research should be used to support the problems listed. Explain the problem in detail and show how this problem affects listeners. It is important that the audience relate to problems described in order for them to be motivated to take part in the next step.

Third, the speaker should propose realistic solutions to solve the problem. The solutions should be something that every person in the audience can do to help solve the problem. If the solution is too difficult, the listener will not be motivated to help with the solution. It is imperative that the speaker present steps toward solving the problem and uses research to prove this solution is effective and doable. Using this strategy does not sound preachy because you are not blaming the audience for the problem, but enlisting their help to solve the problem. It is not gimmicky because the solutions are realistic and attainable.

Fourth, the speaker should help the audience visualize the results of solving the problem, whether it is the benefits of successfully solving the problem or consequences if the problem is NOT solved. This strategy involves connecting with the audience so they can see the vision of solving the problem as something that actually can happen.

Fifth, the speaker will need to challenge the audience to become an integral part of the solution. The Appeal to Action portion of the Persuasion Speech is the moment where the speaker challenges the audience with such passion and enthusiasm that the audience members are motivated to begin work that very moment to solve the problem that has been described. If the speaker has indeed influenced the values, beliefs, attitudes, and behaviors of the audience members, they will feel compelled to help the speaker solve the problem and they will want to begin immediately!

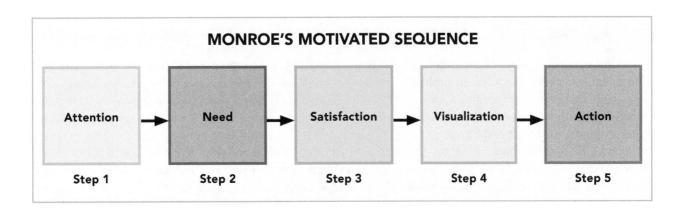

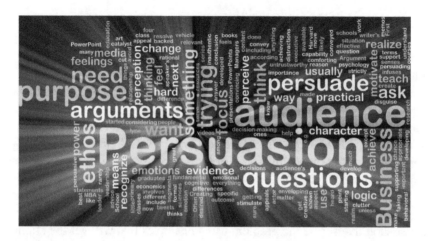

When choosing a topic for a persuasion speech, avoid choosing topics that are too controversial. Topics that are overly controversial can alienate your audience and you might find yourself in an unpleasant and hostile situation. In the few short minutes you have been given to present a Persuasion Speech, you will never be able to persuade an audience to completely change their way of thinking. Remember, people spend years deciding how they feel about things, whether it is religion, politics, personal rights, or simply things they like and dislike. Since people have very strong feelings about things, your topic will automatically be met with support or with opposition. Most speakers do not choose to cover a topic that would make most of the audience members angry. Even if your topic is not overly popular, you can motivate your audience to think about your topic in a different way. That is why following Monroe's Motivated Sequence is the best way to influence and motivate audience members to action!

What is a **Persuasion Speech**? This is a type of speech in which the speaker provides useful information and supporting research that will motivate the listener to action. When crafting a persuasion speech, the speaker will need to answer questions of fact, value, and policy. Let's take a moment to look at all three of these areas.

Questions of Fact: During the problem statement, it is important to answer questions of fact by using credible research for support. Choose one side or the other as your topic. This is not a good time to "sit on the fence." If your speech is titled, "Don't Text and Drive," then you will want to motivate your audience to never text and drive—ever! If you say it is allowed to text while you are at a traffic light, then you are defeating your point. Your audience needs to know you are 100% committed to the topic you are covering; otherwise, you will destroy your credibility as a speaker for the topic and will not be able to motivate the audience to help solve the problem you describe.

Questions of Value: The problem statement will also need to cover questions of value. For most of us, this involves whether something is moral or immoral, whether it is just or unjust, whether it is good or bad. Choose the moral argument to cover and then offer appeals that will tug at the hearts of your audience members. A good strategy for this is to use arguments that will strengthen the audience's attitudes or beliefs toward the topic.

Questions of Policy: The questions of policy are answered during the portion in the speech where you offer a realistic solution to solve the problem. Solutions often involve changing laws or enforcing existing laws or revising procedures that are not working effectively. The speaker should focus on offering solutions that are something that any person in the audience can do. Audience members will not be able to change a law and many of them are also not in the position to enforce an existing law. Many of us are not in the position to revise procedures that are no longer working. So, what can we do to solve a problem? We can talk to those in our circle of friends and family about the problem. We can volunteer to help in areas that will impact the problem. We can contact or write the mayor, Governor of our state, County Commissioner, or State Representative. We can let those people know that we want to see a solution to the problem, a change to laws, or the enforcing of existing laws. THAT is something we can do and this will answer questions of policy.

PERSUASION SPEECH BRAINSTORMING WORKSHEET

Speech Category: Persuasion Speech
Speech Title: Give your speech a clever title. _____
Specific Purpose: Write a full sentence to show the purpose of your speech.

_____

_____

Introduction:
Attention Step: Consider how you will get your audience's attention. Write all you plan to say using full sentences.

_____

_____

Establish Need/Relevance: Explain why this persuasion speech topic should interest the listener. Write all you plan to say using full sentences.

_____

_____

Establish Credibility: Explain why YOU are credible to speak about this topic. Write all you plan to say using full sentences.

_____

_____

Thesis (Preview) Statement: Write a full sentence and clearly state the three points you will cover:

_____

Point #1: Description of the Problem: _____

Point #2: Proposed Solution to the Problem: _____

Point #3: Visualization of the Results of Solving the Problem or the Consequences if the Problem Is NOT

Solved: _____

Body:

Transition Sentence: Write a full sentence to transition from the Introduction Step to the first main point.

_____

_____

   I. The Problem:
      A. Discuss the problem you are covering.
         1. Support the problem with research.
         2. Support the problem with a personal example.
      B. Why is there a need for change?
         1. Who or what is negatively affected by this problem?
         2. Use logical and emotional Appeals.

Transition Sentence: Write a full sentence to transition from the first main point to the second.

   II. Solution to the Problem:
      A. Offer a realistic, detailed solution which solves the problem.
         1. Explain how the audience can help to solve the problem.
         2. Provide personal examples and research to support your solution.
      B. Answer questions of policy.
         1. The solution affects values, beliefs, attitudes, and behaviors.
         2. Use logical and emotional appeals.
         3. Support points with credible research.

Transition Sentence: Write a full sentence to transition from the second point to the third point.

   III. Visualization of Results
      A. Benefits of Solving the Problem
         1. Does it answer questions of value?
         2. Use descriptions to help audience members visualize benefits.
      B. Consequences if the Problem is Not Solved
         1. Use imagery to show the consequences of not solving the problem.
         2. Use personal examples and vivid descriptions.

Transition Sentence: Write a full sentence to transition from the third main point to the conclusion.

Conclusion:

Summary: Write a full sentence to summarize your three main points.

_____

Point #1: The Problem _____

Point #2: The Solution to the Problem _____

Point #3: Visualization of Results _____

Appeal to Action: Leave your audience challenged to help solve the problem. End with a **BANG!**

(NOTE: Be sure to add a Works Cited Page as a page separate from the Outline. Include all sources used.)

Works Cited

(Note: If you use Visual Aids, please include a Visual Aid Explanation Page as a page separate from the Works Cited Page and separate from the Outline.)

Visual Aid Explanation Page

PERSUASION SPEECH OUTLINE TEMPLATE

First Name/Last Name
Persuasion Speech
Day Month Year

Speech Category: Persuasion Speech
Title:
Purpose:

Introduction:
Attention Step:
Establish Need/Relevance:
Establish Speaker Credibility:

Thesis: Today, I want to share three points about (Topic): (1) The Problem with _____,

(2) Possible ways to solve the problem _____, and (3) a Visualization of the world if

this problem is solved _____.

Body:

Transition/Link: First, I will start at the beginning by sharing a little about (Point #1).
    I. First Main Point—Problem
        A. Sub-point
        B. Sub-point

Transition/Link: I've shared (Point #1) with you, now I'd like to tell you about (Point #2).
    II. Second Main Point—Solutions
        A. Sub-point
        B. Sub-point

Transition/Link: You've heard about (Point #1 and Point #2), now I'll cover (Point #3).
    III. Third Main Point—Results
        A. Sub-point
        B. Sub-point

Transition/Link: My purpose today was to (insert purpose and add a statement about the topic).
Conclusion:

Summary: Today, I shared with you three points: (1) Point #1 _____,

(2) Point #2 _____, and (3) Point #3 _____.

Appeal to Action: As I conclude this speech, (End with a BANG).

(NOTE: Be sure to add a Works Cited Page as a page separate from the Outline. Include all sources used.)

Works Cited

(Note: If you use Visual Aids, please include a Visual Aid Explanation Page as a page separate from the Works Cited Page and separate from the Outline.)

Visual Aid Explanation Page

EXAMPLE: PERSUASION SPEECH OUTLINE

Waddell 1

Penny J. Waddell
Political Rally
30 June 2017

Speech Category: Persuasion Speech
Title: Support America
Purpose: The Purpose of this speech is to persuade my audience to support America.

Introduction:
Attention Step: Arnold Whittaker, Tom Malcolm, Buck Brownlee. What do these three men have in common? They all are from Georgia and they all are World War II Veterans who defended our country's freedom and came back home to raise families and make an impact on their communities, their state, and their country! But, there are also differences.
Establish Need/Relevance: At a time in our country where the political parties are at odds with each other, it is important for us to realize that we are all members of one country. Regardless of our political beliefs, regardless of whether we are Democrat, Republican, or Independent, we are ALL Americans!
Establish Speaker Credibility: As an Independent American, I am credible to speak to you about how importance it is for our countrymen and women to stand together first as Americans. Also, the three men that I mentioned in the beginning of this speech were all very dear to me. I loved them, all.
Thesis: Today, I plan to share with you (1) the problem of a country divided, (2) solutions to this problem, and (3) help you visualize a future where we all stand together as one country.

Body:

Transition/Link: The first point that I'll share is about the problem we have with divided political parties.
    I. The Problem: Divided Political Parties in America (Pennock 203)
        A. Democrat Party
        B. Republican Party
        C. Independent Party

Transition/Link: I've shared with you the Problem of divided political parties in our country, but there is a solution.
    II. The Solution
        A. One Country: Bi-partisan Solutions (O'Neil 158)
        B. Working together as one country

Transition/Link: You've heard about the problem of divided political parties in our country, and you've heard about a solution where we all choose to work together to find bi-partisan solutions to a divided problem.
    III. Visualization of Results
        A. Results: see other party's views and work together for a solution (Dalton 191)
        B. Consequences: We will continue divided

Transition/Link: My purpose today was to motivate you to consider a world where we all work together to find the best solutions for America.

Conclusion:

Summary: Today, I shared three points: (1) the problem of a country divided, (2) solutions to this problem, and (3) helped you to all visualize a future where we all stand together as one country.

Appeal to Action: As I close this speech, the three WWII heroes that I mentioned to you did have ONE thing in common. They are all Americans. They also had differences. One was a Democrat. One was a Republican. One was an Independent. However, they did not let that stand in their way when they stormed the beaches of Normandy and fought to preserve the freedoms that so many of us hold dear. All three men have recently passed away. The last one, Mr. Brownlee, just passed away this year. They all three left behind families and friends who are enjoying the freedoms we have every day simply because they chose to overlook differences and worked together to make sure YOU are free. Free to worship, work, and live the way you choose. You can do the same. Will you stand with me today as an American? Not as a political party, but as an American? God Bless America!

(Note: The Works Cited page is a separate page from the Outline).

Works Cited

Dalton, Russell J. *Citizen Politics: Public Opinion and Political Parties in Advanced Industrial*

    Democracies. 6th ed. Washington DC: CQ Press, 2014.

O'Neil, Patrick H. *Essentials of Comparative Politics.* 5th ed. International Student. 2015.

Pennock, James, Roland. *Democratic Political Theory.* Princeton: Princeton University Press, 2016.

(Note: The Visual Aid Explanation page should be placed on a separate page from the Outline and Works Cited page).

Visual Aid Explanation Page

PowerPoint Presentation
Slide #1: Introduction—Title of Speech and pictures of the three men
Slide #2: The Problem—Pictures of each Political Party
Slide #3: The Solution—Picture of an American Flag
Slide #4: The Results—Picture of American Flag with Citizens
Slide #5: Conclusion—Picture of Soldiers and Their Families with American Flag

Handout
Tri-Fold Brochure—American Flag on the front
Inside Left—Definition of Republican Party
Inside Center—Definition of Democratic Party
Inside Right—Definition of Independent Pary
Back—Center—Research Citations for Further Reading

Special Occasion Speech

EVERYBODY LOVES A PARTY!

See how happy they are? This group of students just finished toasting each other and you can tell how much fun they had! There is always an abundance of laughter and mouths frozen into happy smiles as friends come together to celebrate! This is why we have Special Occasion Speeches. Although there are many reasons and occasions for Special Occasion Speeches, not all of them are the happy celebration that you see above. Some are more formal and subdued. Others are informal and spontaneous. Whether formal or informal, it is always a great opportunity to share your expertise at presenting a Special Occasion Speech as long as you understand the occasion and make a presentation your audience will remember fondly!

Most Special Occasion Speeches are not very lengthy. They are usually short and to the point, so they need to pack a punch! The words used during this type of speech need to be carefully chosen and precisely delivered to achieve the results that you want. Tribute speeches are delivered with dignity, grace, and sincerity. Ceremonial speeches will involve pomp and circumstance. Roasts and toasts can be delivered with humor. All Special Occasion Speeches will take on the personality of the occasion. With this in mind, it is important that you understand the different types of Special Occasion Speeches so you can choose the right one for your special occasion.

The three basic types are (1) work-related speeches, (2) ceremonial speeches, and (3) social occasion speeches. Most of these speeches will last three to seven minutes. A Keynote Address, Eulogy, Commencement, or Commemoration could last between twenty to forty minutes. As with any speech, you should always check with the host who invites you to speak and ask for the time frame the host requires. A good rule to remember is that you should always end your speech before the final time that you are given. A three- to seven-minute speech should last five minutes. A twenty- to forty-minute speech should last no longer than thirty-five minutes.

Work-Related Speeches

- **Keynote Address:** Consider yourself a good speaker if you have been chosen to deliver the Keynote Address of a meeting or conference. This honor is usually reserved for established speakers with an impressive résumé. The first order of business is to establish a connection or bond with the audience and then welcome them to the event. Make sure that you thoroughly research the event, audience members, and organization sponsoring the event so that your speech will reflect the values, attitudes, beliefs, and behaviors of audience members. Choose a topic that will set the tone for the meeting or conference. Realizing the participants at this meeting or conference are already quite knowledgeable about the purpose for the gathering, your topic will need to be on-point to add to their existing knowledge and create value for each participant.

- **Announcement:** Regardless of the organization, you can bet there will be announcements delivered at each meeting. If asked to make the announcement, plan to deliver a brief explanation and address the announcement in a speech that is short and to the point. Having notes for this speech is a good idea so you do not leave out pertinent information which might lead to the need for a second announcement.

- **Public Relation:** This type of speech is made to inform the audience about aspects that are designed to improve a problem. It may deal with attendance, insurance changes, policy, procedure adjustments, or changes in protocol. This speaker will need to establish goodwill and a positive atmosphere prior to delivering the required information. It is important to set a stage that will encourage the audience to accept the information you are sharing. Public Relation Speeches are not always met with approval; therefore, it is important that you have the audience in your corner before giving the information needed.

- **Report:** The purpose of presenting a report is to communicate information to the audience. This information will not be entertaining and usually involves numbers, charts, and data as a vehicle for the information. Audience members will appreciate a visual aid to see a visual report in the form of charts or graphs as you provide the information. Keep your visual aids simple, but include all necessary material for a complete report. This report is short, to the point, and detail oriented.

- **Nomination:** Corporations and Clubs that follow Roberts' Rules of Order will allow formal nominations to nominate people for positions or to make a motion to consider a change or alteration of a policy or procedure. This is usually not considered a formal speech, but will need to be treated as such as the person making the nomination will need to offer verbiage that is concise, clear, and complete.

Ceremonial Speeches

- **Installation:** Installations usually take place during a ceremony, but are also delivered in workplace situations. The purpose of this type speech is to install a person into a particular office or position. Once installed, the person who is installed will usually offer a few, well-chosen words of thanks to those who might have made the decision for the installation. This speech usually lasts two to three minutes.

- **Presenting an Award:** The actual presentation of an award is an extremely short speech. This involves referring to the occasion, acknowledging the contributions of the recipient, and then presenting the award with dignity and grace. This is a solemn presentation and care must be made to correctly name the award and to pronounce the recipient's name correctly.

- **Accepting an Award:** Often, the recipients of the awards will not know ahead of time that they are receiving an award. In this impromptu type situation, it is important that the recipient understand the gravity of the honor and accept the award in such a manner that the presenter of the award feels they made a good choice. The recipient should show sincere appreciation for receiving the award, delivering the acceptance speech with dignity and grace and should acknowledge the organization presenting the award. If advance notice is given, the recipient could add personal stories that led to the award and could thank individuals who contributed to the presentation of the award.

- **Dedication:** Dedication ceremonies happen at the birth of new babies, and for the opening of new buildings, parks, or monuments. This type speech is short and to the point. The person or object being dedicated is the focal point of the speech and allows those gathering to honor the occasion. The person chosen to present the Dedication Speech is usually someone quite close to the child being dedicated or to the organization or person who initiated the building, park, or monument. The speaker will need to establish a connection with the audience in the beginning before completing the formal dedication service.

- **Eulogy:** A Eulogy is a ceremony delivered with the purpose of honoring or paying tribute to the deceased. Some people say they are *paying respects* to the person. Culture dictates how this speech presentation will be handled. The length of this speech will vary according to the culture of those attending and the circumstances to which the group has gathered. Often the speaker who has this task will recount personal experiences and stories of times spent with the person being honored.

- **Commemorative:** This type of ceremony is appropriate when a group wishes to celebrate a person or event and is most often delivered as a tribute speech. The speaker will need to emphasize people or history involved with the subject being commemorated. Accurate data and stories are necessary to present the information with dignity and honor. The speaker will need to correctly pronounce the person's name or the subject of the commemoration.

- **Commencement:** Everyone enjoys attending the graduation of a loved one, but no one enjoys a Commencement Speech that is long and boring! Therefore, it is important that the speech focuses on the actual event and those who are graduating, offers words of encouragement and motivational stories for the graduates, and keeps the speech short and to the point. It is a good idea to include research data and facts of positive employment trends that will give hope and encouragement to the graduates and their families.

I would like to propose a toast to all the SpeechSharks in our world!
To those of you who said you would never give a speech
and to those of you who are great at sharing your thoughts and feelings with others,
*I invite ALL of you to raise your glasses high as I wish you **oceans of success**.*
May you be as stealthy and goal driven as a shark
and may all of your speeches be delivered with ease and finesse.
Cheers!

Social Occasion Speeches

- **Toast:** While not everyone at your event may drink alcohol, a Toast is a wish that can be shared with everyone. Always make sure the glasses are filled prior to making the Toast. Raise your glass to eye level as you present the Toast. Plan your Toast ahead of time making sure to put a great deal of thought into the sentiment so that it truly means something to the person you are honoring. Memorize the Toast (it isn't cool to read notes at a Toast). Acknowledge those present in the room and those who are not there to share the moment. Show emotion and passion for the moment. Keep the Toast short, light, and meaningful. As you finish, raise the glass above your head as a symbol of extending the wish.

- **Welcome:** This is another speech that could easily move over to the Work-Related speeches; however, it is also appropriate to list it with the Social Occasion Speeches. The Welcome Speech is presented at the beginning of a social event. This should be used as a point to welcome those who are attending the event and should be short, light, and to the point. This also may be the time to introduce the agenda for the day and to introduce the next speaker or event on the agenda.

- **Farewell:** There are two different ways to offer a Farewell Speech. It can be presented by someone who is leaving or it can be presented by a person who is remaining and chooses this opportunity to honor the person who is leaving. It can be work-related or socially-related. Again, this is a speech that is offered in less than two minutes and offers regards with kindness, grace, and dignity. The Farewell can also be delivered as a Toast. There are lots of options here, but it is always important that it is brief and that every word is carefully chosen to say the things that need to be said.

- **Retirement:** There are distinct similarities with the Farewell and the Retirement Speech, in that the speech can be presented by the person who is retiring or by a person from the organization who would like to honor the person who is retiring. This should be a short presentation that highlights the accomplishments of the person retiring and delivered with kindness, grace, and dignity.

- **Roast:** Full disclaimer about this type of speech . . . we saved this one for last because it truly is one of our favorites. Also, this type speech is BEST when combined with a Toast at the end of the Roast. This type of speech has become quite popular recently and creates a stand-alone event where people attend just to hear and participate in the Roast. Usually this type of gathering begins as a dinner and ends with the Roast as the after-dinner entertainment. A traditional Roast will involve several speakers and might focus on just one person or can focus on many people. Each speaker will take three to five minutes to Roast the guest of honor and the purpose is to have lots of laughter. Research is not always necessary for this type of speech, but if research is used, please make sure that you correctly cite the source in the outline and include a Works Cited page to show the complete citation. My speech class always ends the semester with a Roast followed by a Toast. During the assignment, the students are asked to Roast the people who are in their class. Often, they will Roast the three or four people in their Speech Groups providing one funny item about each person; however, they can also choose to Roast one person in the class and include three areas of humorous events about that one person. We tell the students that they have a full semester to gather material for the Roast that is held the last day of class. The result is three hours of non-stop laughter and an opportunity for the classmates to bid farewell to each other. They all conclude their speech by ending with a well-designed Toast to the person or persons that they just roasted.

Each Special Occasion Speech should be planned according to the occasion where the speech will be presented. Since the Roast and Toast is our favorite Special Occasion Speech, we will provide an example to help as you plan your next Roast and Toast! Use the Brainstorming Worksheet as you plan for your own Special Occasion Speech!

SPECIAL OCCASION SPEECH BRAINSTORMING WORKSHEET

Speech Category: Special Occasion Speech

Identify whether your speech will be Work-Related, Ceremonial, or Social: _____

Identify which category you will cover: _____

Speech Title: Give your speech a clever title: _____

Specific Purpose: Write a full sentence to show the purpose of your speech.

_____

_____

Introduction:

Attention Step: Consider how you will get your audience's attention. Write all you plan to say using full sentences.

_____

_____

Establish Need/Relevance: Explain why this topic should interest the listener. Write all you plan to say using full sentences.

_____

_____

Establish Credibility: Explain why YOU are credible to speak about this topic. Write all you plan to say using full sentences.

_____

_____

Thesis (Preview) Statement: Write a full sentence and clearly state the three points you will cover:

_____

Point #1: _____

Point #2: _____

Point #3: _____

Body:

Transition Sentence: Write a full sentence to transition from the Introduction Step to the first main point.

_____

_____

    I. First Main Point:
       A. Sub-Point.
       B. Sub-Point.
Transition Sentence: Write a full sentence to transition from the first main point to the second.

_____

_____

    II. Second Main Point
       A. Sub-Point.
       B. Sub-Point.
Transition Sentence: Write a full sentence to transition from the second point to the third point.

_____

_____

    III. Second Main Point
       A. Sub-Point.
       B. Sub-Point.
Transition Sentence: Write a full sentence to transition from the third main point to the conclusion.

_____

_____

Conclusion:

Summary: Write a full sentence to summarize your three main points.

_____

Point #1: _____

Point #2: _____

Point #3: _____

Toast: Plan a Toast to leave with your audience as you conclude the speech. Toasts can be original or you may use one that has been passed down for years and years. If you use a Toast that has a copyright, be sure to cite the source and include a Works Cited page.

(NOTE: Be sure to add a Works Cited Page as a page separate from the Outline. Include all sources used.)

Works Cited

(Note: If you use Visual Aids, please include a Visual Aid Explanation Page as a page separate from the Works Cited Page and separate from the Outline.)

Visual Aid Explanation Page

SPECIAL OCCASION SPEECH OUTLINE TEMPLATE

Last Name 1

First Name/Last Name
Special Occasion Speech
Day Month Year

Speech Category: Special Occasion Speech
Title:
Purpose:

Introduction:
Attention Step:
Establish Need/Relevance:
Establish Speaker Credibility:

Thesis: Today, I want to share three points about (Topic): (1) _____,

(2) _____, and (3) _____.

Body:
Transition/Link: First, I will start at the beginning by sharing a little about (Point #1).
    I. First Main Point
        A. Sub-point
        B. Sub-point

Transition/Link: I've shared (Point #1) with you, now I'd like to tell you about (Point #2).
    II. Second Main Point
        A. Sub-point
        B. Sub-point

Transition/Link: You've heard about (Point #1 and Point #2), now I'll cover (Point #3).
    III. Third Main Point
        A. Sub-point
        B. Sub-point

Transition/Link: My purpose today was to (insert purpose and add a statement about the topic).
Conclusion:

Summary: Today, I shared with you three points: (1) Point #1 _____,

(2) Point #2 _____, and (3) Point #3 _____.

Appeal to Action: As I conclude this speech, (End with a BANG).

(NOTE: Be sure to add a Works Cited Page as a page separate from the Outline. Include all sources used.)

Works Cited

(Note: If you use Visual Aids, please include a Visual Aid Explanation Page as a page separate from the Works Cited Page and separate from the Outline.)

Visual Aid Explanation Page

EXAMPLE: SPECIAL OCCASION SPEECH OUTLINE

Penny J. Waddell
Roast and Toast
15 May 2017

Speech Category: Special Occasion Speech
Title: Out of the Frying Pan and Into the Fire: An Opportunity to ROAST my Students!
Purpose: The purpose of this speech is to Roast and Toast my speech students on the last day of class.

Introduction:
Attention Step: Have you ever opened the oven while you have potatoes roasting and felt the heat that comes from the oven? Well, that is nothing compared to the heat all of you might feel today as I take you out of the frying pan and throw you into the fire of an authentic Speech Roast and Toast!
Establish Need/Relevance: We have spent 16 weeks together in the speech class and today will be our last class of the semester. This will be a perfect time for us to have fun with each other before we part ways.
Establish Speaker Credibility: Since I have had the pleasure of being your instructor this semester and I have graded every homework assignment, every speech, every outline, and every Chapter Quiz, I find myself completely qualified to Roast and Toast all of you today!
Thesis: There are three main points I would like to cover during this good-natured Roast, (1) E-mails and Frantic Phone Calls, (2) Outlines and Visual Aids, and (3) Speech Day Attire.

Body:

Transition/Link: Let's begin with the first point, E-mails and Frantic Phone Calls the morning of speech assignments.
    I. E-mails and Frantic Phone Calls
        A. Yes, Students, due dates are due dates!
        B. All assignments are given to students the first day of class.
        C. Heartburn and Antacids are in your future, if you don't work ahead!

Transition/Link: I've shared stories of e-mails and frantic phone calls the morning of speech assignments, now I'd like to tell you about the Outlines and Visual Aids
    II. Outlines and Visual Aids
        A. Outlines – Did you see the example I left for you in the textbook?
        B. Visual Aids – Are you going for "Hall of Fame" and "Hall of Shame"!

Transition/Link: You've heard about the e-mails and frantic phone calls the morning of speech assignments, the outlines and visual aids that I saw this semester, now, I would like to talk to you about the way you dressed for speeches.
    III. Speech Day Attire
        A. Yes, I would hire you, if you dress as if you are going to an interview.
        B. Oops, you are fired, if you show up in Blue Jeans, T-Shirt that says, "Bite Me," and Flip-Flops!

Transition/Link: My purpose today was to Roast all of my speech students who gave speeches this semester that can only be defined as, "The Good, The Bad, and The Ugly"—No, Really, I would call them, "The Best Speeches I've Ever Heard!"
Conclusion:
Summary: Today, I shared with you three points: (1) E-mails and Frantic Phone Calls, (2) Outlines and Visual Aids, and (3) Speech Day Attire.
Appeal to Action: I would like to propose a Toast to all the SpeechSharks in this class! To those of you who said you would never give a speech and to those of you who are great at sharing your thoughts and feelings with others, I invite ALL of you to raise your glasses high as I wish you oceans of success. May you be as stealthy and goal driven as a shark and may all of your speeches be delivered with ease and finesse. Cheers!

(Note: Research was not used for this speech, so a Works Cited page was not necessary. The Visual Aids Explanation page is a separate page from the Outline).

Visual Aids Explanation Page

PowerPoint Presentation:

Slide #1: Title of Speech—Out of the Frying Pan and Into the Fire
   Picture of the Class (Group)
Slide #2: (Point #1): E-mails and Frantic Phone Calls
   Picture of Teacher at a Computer (hair frazzled and talking on the phone)
Slide #3: (Point #2): Outlines and Visual Aids
   Picture of the Textbook
Slide #4: (Point #3): Speech Day Attire
   Picture of Professionally Dressed Student/Picture of a Student in Jeans and Flip-Flops
Slide #5: Picture—Champagne Glasses Raised in a TOAST with the word—CHEERS!

Group Presentation

The task of presenting a Group Presentation is not always met with enthusiasm. That is because most of us have had the experience of working with a group and doing a majority of the group work on our own to make sure the project was completed on time and in good shape. We often think of group projects gone south when we think of group work in college. However, I can assure you that group work can also be a struggle in the corporate world. We wanted to cover Group Presentations in this book because you will be met with this task more often than you would like and it is a good idea to understand what is involved with a Group Presentation!

Everyone in a group is unique. That can be a bonus for your presentation, if you are able to use the strengths present within your group. As with any presentation, you should conduct an audience analysis, consider the purpose of the presentation and develop a topic that will enhance the knowledge of your audience members.

There are advantages for presenting a project as a Group Presentation. First, realize that you cannot possibly know everything. Working with a group will allow the opportunity to expand the knowledge base and will cause you to add to your own knowledge of the subject your group will be covering.

Avoid disagreements regarding the division of labor by verbally acknowledging the value brought to the group by your group members. This also builds a feeling of teamwork among group members and fosters collaboration for the project.

Brainstorming is always much more effective when you can include more brains! This will also cause more active discussions to erupt which in turn will spark more ideas for the topic. Since each group is unique and there are many diverse cultures and thoughts present in a group, this will allow the group to incorporate different speech styles during the presentation.

Finally, speakers who are a bit shy usually feel more confident when they realize they are not alone on the stage making a presentation, but surrounded by their peers who are working together for a positive result.

Use this checklist when planning a Group Presentation:

Things to Consider	Explanation
Know Group Members	☐ Introduce yourself to the group. ☐ Exchange names and contact information. ☐ Discover strengths and weaknesses of group members. ☐ Determine a meeting schedule that works with everyone. ☐ Record information and distribute it to group members.
Discuss Group Expectations	☐ Ask questions. Answer questions. ☐ Divide tasks equally among group members. ☐ Be realistic with due dates and job responsibilities. ☐ Indicate group member responsibilities. ☐ Exercise accountability/responsibility duties. ☐ Establish consequences if a group member does not follow through.
Understand the Task	☐ Research the topic. ☐ Learn the time requirement for the presentation. ☐ Know what is expected. Do you need a visual aid? ☐ Do you need handouts? ☐ Create a timetable for responsibilities. ☐ What order will group members speak? ☐ Is there a Question/Answer segment during the presentation? ☐ Will you have a group moderator to introduce and conclude the speech? ☐ How will you be evaluated?
Respect Diversity	☐ Keep an open mind for other ideas. ☐ Encourage members to speak without reservation. ☐ Allow opportunities for members to interject opinions for the project.
Communicate Effectively	☐ Use effective listening skills. ☐ Speak clearly and make yourself heard. ☐ Ask for clarification, if you do not understand something. ☐ Use positive communication skills with group members.
Rehearsals	☐ Plan rehearsal dates. ☐ Rehearse together as a group. ☐ Assign a Tech Team member to manage the visual aids. ☐ Assign a Tech Team member to distribute handouts. ☐ Rehearse using visual aids for the presentation.

During the presentation, there is a protocol that should be followed. Here is the plan to follow for a Group Presentation:

1. **Moderator:** The moderator will open with an attention step, establish a need/relevance for the group presentation topic, establish speaker credibility for the group by introducing each speaker (first name and last name) and provides a clear thesis and list a brief description of each main point identifying the group member designated to cover. The moderator will then transition to the first speaker by again stating the speaker's first and last name along with the topic they will cover. *One thing to note: the moderator will be responsible to keep the presentation flowing. If at any time there is an awkward moment, the moderator has the responsibility of keeping the presentation advancing in a positive direction.*

2. **Speaker #1:** The first speaker will thank the moderator for the introduction and then will proceed to cover the main point. This will include an introduction, body, and conclusion of the point. Speaker #1 will then transition to the second speaker by stating the speaker's first and last name along with the topic the second speaker will cover.

3. **Speaker #2:** The second speaker will thank Speaker #1 for the introduction and then will proceed to cover the next main point. This will include an introduction, body, and conclusion of the point. Speaker #2 will then transition to the third speaker by stating the speaker's first and last name along with the topic the third speaker will cover.

4. **Speaker #3:** The third speaker will thank Speaker #2 for the introduction and then will proceed to cover the next main point. This will include an introduction, body, and conclusion of the point. Speaker #3 will then transition to the fourth speaker. If there is not a fourth speaker, then Speaker #3 will transition back to the Moderator using his or her first and last name.

5. **Moderator:** The Moderator will thank the last speaker and will proceed to summarize the three main points covered listing each Speaker's first and last name with the summary. Next, the Moderator will open the floor for a question and answer session. During the Q & A, the Moderator is responsible for keeping the conversation flowing, directing questions to different group members, and making sure that not one member monopolizes the conversation. If questions from the audience are all directed to one or two members, the Moderator can call for the audience that may have a question for the Speaker who has not been questioned. After a few questions and answers, the Moderator can then close the Q & A and thank the audience for their attention as they discussed the topic and participated in the Q & A session. Finally, the Moderator will again thank the group speakers, one at a time before closing the speech with a prepared Appeal to Action, which should be designed to keep the audience thinking about the group presentation topic.

NOTE: Research will be needed to support the individual points. The Moderator and each of the Group Speakers are responsible for conducting research to provide credible support of the points covered. Personal stories and personal experiences are also very helpful to support the points and to bring in a personal touch regarding the topic.

For a Group Presentation to be successful, the group needs to work together as a cohesive unit to make one presentation. They should choose a topic with the audience in mind, make a plan to achieve the purpose, decide on tasks and work divisions, create visual aids and handouts, set times for completion dates, individually work on identified tasks which includes research for the point to which the group member is assigned, evaluate progress, rehearse as a group and then of course, present the Group Presentation.

Group Presentations may not be the easiest presentations on the schedule, but they can be very effective because the group has different levels of knowledge about the topic and can also bring diverse thoughts and ideas to the table for discussion.

How does the Moderator Handle the Question and Answer Sessions?

The way the Moderator handles the Q&A session will have a direct impact on the success of the group presentation. First, ask the audience members who want to ask a question to stand, identify themselves by first and last name, and then direct the question to a specific group member. The audience member should remain standing while the question is answered. Following the delivery of the answer, the audience member should thank the group member and then take their seat.

Group members should make sure the audience member has finished asking the question before they begin to answer the question. A good rule of thumb is to thank the audience member for the question and then repeat the question as mental preparation before answering. This step is important because it will mean that the group member will be answering the question that was asked. It also gives the speaker a moment to formulate the answer that will be given. After the question is answered, the speaker should say to the audience member, "I hope this has answered your question." The audience member can give a verbal or non-verbal response prior to sitting down so that the next question can be asked. Depending upon the time allotted for the Group Presentation, the Moderator can choose to take three to five questions or more.

The Question and Answer (Q & A) Session takes on the model of an impromptu speech. As the group member responds to unrehearsed questions and attempts to further add knowledge regarding the point, it is great to use the PREP model that is reserved for impromptu speeches and interview type situations. Here is how you PREP to prepare for any question!

P.R.E.P.

P = Point. Restate the question asked because that is the POINT. As you restate the question, it helps you to hear the question again and formulate the answer in your mind. Before you answer the question, be sure to follow the next step!

R = Relevance. Thank the person who asked the question for asking the question. Then, explain why the question is important because that is the RELEVANCE. After you cover the importance, then it is time to answer the question.

E = Example. Give a clear EXAMPLE as a follow-up to the answer of your question to make sure the audience has an understanding of the POINT. There is only one thing left to do, now!

P = Point. All good speeches will offer a summary and an impromptu speech requires the same. As you conclude, be sure to restate the question because that is the POINT and ask if you completely answered their question. If you get a head-nod or an affirmation, then you are good to go!

Group Presentations will use a different type of outline than other speeches because it involves information that will be covered by several people. We suggest using a One Point Outline for this type of presentation.

Here is a Brainstorming Worksheet to help you plan and an example of a One Point Outline for the Group Presentation.

GROUP PRESENTATION BRAINSTORMING WORKSHEET

Speech Category: Group Presentation

Identify Group Members:

Moderator: _____

Group Member #1: _____

Group Member #2: _____

Group Member #3: _____

Speech Title: Give your speech a clever title _____

Specific Purpose: Write a full sentence to show the purpose of your speech.

_____

_____

Introduction—This will be covered by the Moderator: _____

Attention Step: Consider how you will get your audience's attention. Write all you plan to say using full sentences.

_____

_____

Establish Need/Relevance: Explain why this topic should interest the listener. Write all you plan to say using full sentences.

_____

_____

Establish Credibility: Explain why the group is credible to speak about this topic. Write all you plan to say using full sentences. Introduce each group member and establish their credentials.

_____

_____

Thesis (Preview) Statement: Write a full sentence that clearly states the three points you will cover:

_____

Point #1: Name of Group Member and The Point to be Covered: _____

_____

Point #2: Name of Group Member and The Point to be Covered: _____

_____

Point #3: Name of Group Member and The Point to be Covered: _____

_____

Body:

Transition Sentence: Write a full sentence to transition from the Introduction Step to the first main point.

_____

_____

    I. **First Main Point (Covered by Name of Group Member):**
       A. **Sub-Point.**
       B. **Sub-Point.**

Transition Sentence: Write a full sentence to transition from the first main point to the second.

_____

_____

II. Second Main Point (Covered by Name of Group Member):
   A. Sub-Point.
   B. Sub-Point.

Transition Sentence: Write a full sentence to transition from the second point to the third point.

_____

_____

III. Third Main Point (Covered by Name of Group Member):
   A. Sub-Point.
   B. Sub-Point.

Transition Sentence: Write a full sentence to transition from the third main point to the conclusion.

_____

_____

Conclusion—This will be covered by the Moderator

Summary: Write in full sentence format a summary of your three main points. Identify the name of each Group Member covering each point.

_____

Point #1: _____

Point #2: _____

Point #3: _____

Moderator: Opens the floor for the Question and Answer Session.

Moderator: Concludes the speech with Appreciation and a Wrap-Up: _____

_____

(NOTE: Be sure to add a Works Cited Page as a page separate from the Outline. Include all sources used.)

Works Cited

(Note: If you use Visual Aids, please include a Visual Aid Explanation Page as a page separate from the Works Cited Page and separate from the Outline.)

Visual Aid Explanation Page

GROUP PRESENTATION ONE POINT OUTLINE TEMPLATE

Group Name 1

List All Group Members' Names Alphabetically
First Name/Last Name
Group Presentation
Day Month Year

Speech Category: Group Presentation
Title:
Purpose:

Introduction:
Attention Step:
Establish Need/Relevance:
Establish Speaker Credibility: Introduce each group member by first and last name.

Thesis: Today, I want to share three points about (Topic): (1) _____,

(2) _____, and (3) _____.

Body:

Transition/Link: First, I will start at the beginning by sharing a little about (Point #1).
    I. First Main Point—Presented by _____
        A. Sub-point
        B. Sub-point

Transition/Link: I've shared (Point #1) with you, now I'd like to tell you about (Point #2).
    II. Second Main Point—Presented by _____
        A. Sub-point
        B. Sub-point

Transition/Link: You've heard about (Point #1 and Point #2), now I'll cover (Point #3).
    III. Third Main Point—Presented by _____
        A. Sub-point
        B. Sub-point

Transition/Link: My purpose today was to (insert purpose and add a statement about the topic).
Conclusion:
Summary: Today, I shared with you three points—include each group member's name:

(1) Point #1_____, (2) Point #2 _____, and

(3) Point #3 _____.
Appeal to Action: As I conclude this speech, (End with a BANG).

(NOTE: Be sure to add a Works Cited Page as a page separate from the Outline. Include all sources used.)

Works Cited

(Note: If you use Visual Aids, please include a Visual Aid Explanation Page as a page separate from the Works Cited Page and separate from the Outline.)

Visual Aid Explanation Page

EXAMPLE: GROUP PRESENTATION ONE POINT OUTLINE

Group #5 1

Ruth Joyner, Travice Obas, Bonnie Smith, Penny Waddell, Cassandra West
Group Presentation
1 August 2017

Speech Category: Group Presentation
Title: Preparing Students for Success
Purpose: The purpose of this group presentation is to provide the audience with useful tips to prepare students for the workplace.

Introduction: (Presented by the Moderator: Ruth Joyner)
Attention Step: Would you like to take your students from stress to success? How about from scared to prepared?
Establish Need/Relevance: Student success is a relevant topic as we all work to prepare students for the workforce. It is important, as educators, that you hear this presentation and learn tips for student success.
Establish Speaker Credibility: Realizing that experience is the best teacher, we have compiled a group of instructors with practical and experiential knowledge from elementary, middle, high school, and college settings.
Thesis: Today, I want to share four points about preparing students for success: (1) Travice Obas will share information about Time Management Skills, (2) Bonnie Smith will talk about Teamwork, (3) Penny Waddell will be covering Effective Communication Skills, and (4) Cassandra West will explore Cooperation.

Body: (Each point will be covered by an assigned group member)

Transition/Link: First, Travice Obas will share tips for Time Management Skills.
  I. **(Presented by Travice Obas) Time Management Skills**
      A. Managing Time
      B. Setting Priorities

Transition/Link: I've shared tips to encourage Time Management, now Bonnie Smith will tell how to foster Teamwork.
  II. **(Presented by Bonnie Smith) Teamwork**
      A. T.E.A.M. Acronym
      B. Tips for Teams

Transition/Link: You've heard about Teamwork, now Penny Waddell will cover effective Communication Skills.
  III. **(Presented by Penny Waddell) Communication Skills**
      A. Verbal Communication Skills
      B. Non-Verbal Communication Skills

Transition/Link: Verbal and Non-Verbal Communication Skills are essential for success, now Cassandra West will cover tips to encourage Cooperation.
  IV. **(Presented by Cassandra West) Cooperation**
      A. Respect Peers and Management
      B. Develop a "Do Whatever It Takes" Attitude

Transition/Link: Our purpose today was to share information with you to help you prepare students for success. At this time, I will relinquish the stage back to our Moderator, Ruth Joyner.
Conclusion: (Presented by the Moderator: Ruth Joyner)

Summary: Today, we shared with you four important work ethic skills to help your students find success: (1) Travice Obas shared information about Time Management Skills, (2) Bonnie Smith talked about Teamwork, (3) Penny Waddell covered Effective Communication Skills, and (4) Cassandra West helped us explore Cooperation.

Question and Answer Session: At this time, we would like to invite the audience to participate in a Question and Answer Session. Please stand to be recognized, provide your full name, address the group member by name and ask your question. (The Moderator will call on audience members one at a time and will conclude the session according to an established time by saying...) That is all the time we have for questions tonight. Thank you for attending. If you have further questions, please contact any of our group members by using the contact information supplied in your program. We challenge you to take your students from scared to prepared and from stress to success by encouraging strong work ethic skills in the classroom and in the workforce!

NOTE: For this outline example, research was not used; therefore, a Works Cited page is not included. However, if you do use research for your own group presentation, please add parenthetical citations in the outline and a Works Cited page following the outline on a separate page.

The same is true if you use visual aids for a group presentation. Add a separate page that details the visual aids you plan to use and a description of each.

Sales Presentation

Sales Presentations follow much of the same strategies as Persuasion Speeches; therefore, we suggest that you review the Persuasion Speech section in this book. Pay close attention to the section about motivation. The purpose of your sales pitch is to motivate the audience to purchase an item or service that you are selling! To do this you will need to motivate and influence **values, beliefs, attitudes, or behaviors**.

Consumers today are quite different from consumers in the past and the sales force has changed from strictly face-to-face interactions to include Internet, telephone, videos, photographs, and social media. If you truly want to be a great salesperson, you will soon realize the importance of walking a fine line to create a balance between being persuasive, but not too pushy. This takes planning and practice. Once you can establish a solid strategy that works for your personality, then you will begin to close more deals.

Here are proven strategies to help you find success in sales:

1. **Identify the decision maker:** Whether you are making a sales pitch to a company or to a couple, you must first know the person that will ultimately make the decision to buy. Once you identify the decision maker, you can customize your sales presentation to the person. This is where it is important to use good listening skills. Listen carefully to understand the needs of the individual or the corporation so that you can provide what the customer needs.

2. **Care for the best interest of the customer:** Instead of working hard to sell the one product your boss is pushing, try to provide the product or service that your customer truly needs. Let the customer know that you care about their business and that your first priority is to help them solve the problem they are having by providing the product or service they need. The "deal" should not be more important to you than their satisfaction with the product or service. This is the way to foster repeat customers.

3. **Identify the deadline:** Again, you need to be a good listener. When do they need this product or service? Does your organization have a special price deal that is or will be available for the product or service they need? Can you help them make the right choice at the right time to save money or time?

4. **Overcome obstacles:** This is the time to focus on the problem which is motivating customers to make this purchase. Do they need to purchase the car you are selling by a certain date to meet a deadline? Is this a seasonal purchase? What potential objections might slow down the decision-making process? What questions or concerns may the customer have? If you can think ahead to prepare for problems or obstacles that could slow down or stop the sale, then you will have time to find a solution and close the sale!

5. **Know your competitors:** Depending upon the product or service you will be selling, you should understand that competition can be tough! Why is your product superior, less expensive, or more effective than the competition? If you want to make the sale, you need to conduct research on any competitors that might waltz in and take your business. Take time to prepare your sales presentation, conduct research to learn about any and all markets that may stand in your way, and make sure that you are providing something that your competitor will not, such as customer service and care for your customer. It has been proven time and again that customers return to the same salesperson if they feel like the salesperson has their best interest at heart.

6. **Create a positive reputation:** Say what you mean and mean what you say! If you tell your customer you will do something, make sure you do it. Even if it is a simple phone call to provide additional information. Make sure your conversations stay on the product or service that the customer wants. Customers don't want to hear about your problems, your bad cold, or your car that will not start. The customer is there because they are in the market for a product or service that your organization may be able to provide. They are not there to visit. Keep conversations professional and to the point. Create a reputation of caring for your customers, having their best interest at heart, and making the sales transaction a fast and enjoyable experience.

7. **Close the Sale:** Do you remember the Kenny Rogers song with the lyrics, "You've got to know when to hold 'em, know when to fold 'em, know when to walk away, know when to run!"? I wouldn't advise singing this song out loud around your customers, but it is good advice. If you are an effective listener, then you will know your customer's deadline for purchasing the product or service you represent and you should know when to make the pitch, when to back off and let the customer consider what you have shared, and then know when to provide a sense of urgency to purchase the product or service. Many salespeople are not successful because they simply do not know how to close the sale. A good salesperson will tell you that closing the sale is a matter of knowing when to encourage the customer to make the decision. The customer has a problem to solve. You can solve the problem with the product or service your organization provides. It is your job to convince the customer that the money charged is a deal and the time to purchase is now.

Here are some good phrases to use as a closer:

- If our company can provide a solution to your problem, would you make this purchase?
- When would you like to get started?
- Is there anything I can do to help you with this decision?
- It looks like we have two options for what you need. Would you prefer to choose A or B?
- It is against our policy to push an item on a customer that they really do not need; however, it appears that this (product or service) has exactly what you are looking for and the price is competitive with all others on the market. Are you ready to complete the paperwork?
- During our first meeting, you mentioned that you needed this product or service by July 1st. If you make this decision by Friday of this week, we will be able to meet your deadline and help solve your problem. Does this date sound like something to which you can commit?
- Are you ready to get started? I'll be happy to start the paperwork.
- We have a special price on this product or service that will begin next Monday. Do you want me to save that price for you?

Closing strategies are important, but there are no magic words or phrases that will work every time. That is why you must begin by listening to your potential customer and help the customer identify needs, wants, budget, and deadline to purchase the product or service.

Be a SpeechShark and not a sales shark! There are differences. No one enjoys a slicked-up salesperson whose only concern is the commission they will put in their own pocket. When it is time to make a purchase, customers want an honest salesperson who has their best interest in mind and will help them search to find the right product for the right price and available at the right time. Now, that is a sales strategy that will win every time. And, you will enjoy the benefits of having repeat customers!

Use the Sales Presentation Brainstorming Worksheet to help create your best sales pitch:

SALES PRESENTATION BRAINSTORMING WORKSHEET

Speech Category: Sales Presentation

Speech Title: Give your speech a clever title _____

Specific Purpose: Write a full sentence to show the purpose of your presentation—what are you trying to sell?

_____

_____

Introduction:

Attention Step: Consider how you will get your customer's attention. Write all you plan to say using full sentences.

_____

_____

Establish Need/Relevance: Explain why this product or service should interest the customer. Write all you plan to say using full sentences.

_____

_____

Establish Credibility: Explain why YOU are credible to sell this product or service. Write all you plan to say using full sentences.

_____

_____

Thesis (Preview) Statement: Write a complete sentence that clearly states the three points you will cover:

_____

Point #1: Describe the problem with the product or service the customer has now:

_____

Point #2: Identify the new product or service that will solve the customer's problem:

_____

Point #3: Visualization of the results of solving the problem or the consequences if the problem is NOT solved:

_____

Body:

Transition Sentence: Write a full sentence to transition from the Introduction Step to the first main point.

_____

_____

    I. The Problem:
        A. Discuss the problem they are having.
            1. Support the problem with research.
            2. Support the problem with examples.
        B. Explore the need for purchasing the new product or service.
            1. Identify who or what is negatively affected by this problem.
            2. Use logical and emotional Appeals.

Transition Sentence: Write a full sentence to transition from the first main point to the second.

_____

_____

    II. Solution to the Problem—the product or service you plan to sell:
       A. Offer a realistic, detailed explanation of the product or service as a solution to the problem.
         1. Explain how the customer can help to solve the problem.
         2. Provide examples and research to support your solution.
       B. Does your solution solve the problem?
         1. Does your solution affect values, beliefs, attitudes, and behaviors?
         2. Use logical and emotional Appeals.

Transition Sentence: Write a full sentence to transition from the second point to the third point.

_____

_____

    III. Visualization of Results
       A. Describe the benefits of using the new product or service.
         1. Does it answer questions of value?
         2. Use descriptions to help audience members visualize benefits.
       B.   Consequences if the product or service is not purchased
         1. Use imagery to show the consequences of not purchasing the product or service.
         2. Use examples and descriptions.

Transition Sentence: Write a full sentence to transition from the third main point to the conclusion.

_____

_____

Conclusion:

Summary: Write in full sentence format a summary of your three main points.

Point #1: The Problem _____

Point #2: The Solution to the Problem _____

Point #3: Visualization of Results _____

Appeal to Action: Leave your customer challenged to purchase the product or service and CLOSE THE SALE!

(NOTE: Be sure to add a Works Cited Page as a page separate from the Outline. Include all sources used.)

Works Cited

(Note: If you use Visual Aids, please include a Visual Aid Explanation Page as a page separate from the Works Cited Page and separate from the Outline.)

Visual Aid Explanation Page

SALES PRESENTATION OUTLINE TEMPLATE

Last Name 1

First Name/Last Name
Group Presentation
Day Month Year

Speech Category: Sales Presentation
Title:
Purpose:

Introduction:
Attention Step:
Establish Need/Relevance:
Establish Credibility:

Thesis: Today, As you consider making this purpose, first consider these points: (1) _____,

(2) _____, and (3) _____.

Body:

Transition/Link: First, let's begin with (Point #1).
    I. First Main Point—The Problem with the existing product or service.
        A. Sub-point—examples/research
        B. Sub-point—examples/research

Transition/Link: I've shared (Point #1) with you, now I'd like to tell you about (point #2).
    II. Second Main Point—Identify the new product or service that will solve the customer's problem.
        A. Sub-point—values, beliefs, attitudes, behaviors
        B. Sub-point—logical and emotional appeals

Transition/Link: You've heard about (Point #1 and Point #2), now I'll cover (Point #3).
    III. Third Main Point—Visualization of results
        A. Sub-point—benefits of using the new product or services
        B. Sub-point—consequences of not using the new product or services

Transition/Link: My purpose today is to give you information about (Topic).
Conclusion:
Summary: Today, I shared with you three important points about (Topic):

(1) Point #1_____, (2) Point #2 _____, and

(3) Point #3 _____.

Closing the Sale: End with a strong appeal/closing statement.

(NOTE: Be sure to add a Works Cited Page as a page separate from the Outline. Include all sources used.)

Works Cited

(Note: If you use Visual Aids, please include a Visual Aid Explanation Page as a page separate from the Works Cited Page and separate from the Outline.)

Visual Aid Explanation Page

Types of Speeches

After reading this chapter, you will be able to answer the following questions:

1. What are the three basic purposes/types of speeches? _____

   _____

   _____

2. What are Informative Speeches? _____

   _____

   _____

3. What are Entertaining Speeches? _____

   _____

   _____

4. What are Motivational Speeches? _____

   _____

   _____

5. What is a good organizational strategy for introducing yourself? _____

   _____

   _____

6. What is an Informative Speech often called? _____

_____

_____

7. When would you choose to present a Demonstration Speech? _____

_____

_____

8. What three points should be covered in a Demonstration Speech? _____

_____

_____

9. What are the four areas you might consider influencing during a Persuasion Speech? _____

_____

_____

10. Explain values: _____

_____

_____

11. Explain beliefs: _____

_____

_____

12. Explain attitudes: _____

_____

_____

13. Explain behaviors: _____

_____

_____

14. Who developed the Motivated Sequence Theory? _____

_____

_____

15. What three main points should be covered when using the Motivated Sequence Theory?

_____

_____

16. List the types of Work-Related Speeches: _____

_____

_____

17. List the types of Ceremonial Speeches: _____

_____

_____

18. List the types of Social Occasion Speeches: _____

_____

_____

19. What are six things to consider when involved with planning a Group Presentation?

_____

_____

20. Who conducts the Question and Answer session of a Group Presentation? _____

_____

_____

21. What strategy works best for a Sales Presentation? _____

_____

_____

22. List seven strategies important for making the sale: _____

_____

_____

23. What Special Occasion Speech would you most enjoy presenting? _____

_____

_____

24. What Special Occasion Speech would you least enjoy presenting? _____

_____

_____

25. What is a One-Point Outline and when would you use this? _____

_____

_____

Shark Bites

BRAINSTORMING A TOPIC

Let's work on a Clustering and Webbing strategy to help you brainstorm your next speech. Start with the speech topic. What three points will you cover? How will you begin the speech? How will you close the speech? Brainstorm the speech organization by filling in each bubble or use your new SpeechShark app to do this for you!

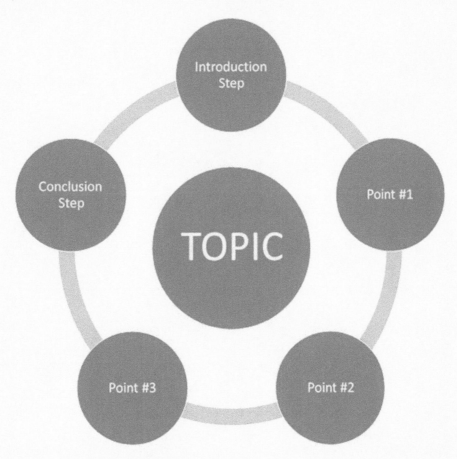

Chapter Four
Methods of Delivery

METHODS OF DELIVERY

Effective delivery does not just happen. You have to plan for it. Delivery is the ability to convey your ideas clearly without distracting the audience. The most effective delivery combines elements of formal oratory skills along with the best attributes of conversational quality—directness, spontaneity, animation, vocal and facial expressiveness, and a sense of lively communication.

To attain effective speech delivery, it is important to relate methods of delivery concepts and skill. You can become a skilled speaker by following a set of guidelines and PRACTICE! You've heard it said, "Practice makes perfect!" Although there is no such thing as a perfect speech, discussed in this chapter are basic delivery guidelines to get you started in the right direction.

When planning your speech, concentrate on such basics as speaking intelligibly, avoiding distracting mannerisms, and establishing eye contact with the audience. Once you get these elements under control and begin to feel fairly comfortable in front of an audience, you can work on polishing your delivery to enhance the impact of your ideas.

METHODS (MODES) OF DELIVERY

There are four basic methods of delivering a presentation: (1) reading from a manuscript, (2) reciting from memory, (3) speaking impromptu, and (4) speaking extemporaneously.

MANUSCRIPT

Certain speeches must be delivered word for word, according to a meticulously prepared manuscript. One example would include the State of the Union address delivered by the president. In this situation, absolute accuracy is essential. Every word of the speech will be analyzed by the press and leaders from other nations. In the case of the president, a misused phrase could lead to an international incident.

Although it looks easy, delivering a speech from manuscript requires great skill. Some people do it well, they sound vibrant and conversational, while those lacking in skill come across as boring and artificial. They falter over words, pause in the wrong places, read too quickly or too slowly, speak in a monotone voice, or march through the speech without even glancing at their audience. In this instance, they come across as reading to their listeners, rather than talking to them.

If you are in a situation where you must speak from a manuscript, practice out loud to make sure the speech sounds conversational. Work on establishing eye contact with your listeners. Be certain the final manuscript is legible at a glance. Above all, reach out to your audience with the same directness and sincerity that you would if you were speaking extemporaneously.

MEMORIZED

Actors are known for the practice of presenting the longest and most complex content and dialogue entirely from memory. It is no longer necessary to memorize shorter speeches—toasts, congratulatory remarks, acceptance speeches, introductions, and so on.

If you are giving a speech of this kind and want to memorize it, by all means do so. However, be sure to memorize it so thoroughly that you will be able to concentrate on communicating with the audience, not on trying to remember the words. Speakers who gaze at the ceiling or stare out the window trying to recall what they have memorized are no better off than those who read from a manuscript.

IMPROMPTU

An impromptu speech is delivered with little or no immediate preparation. Few people choose to speak impromptu, but sometimes it cannot be avoided. In fact, many of the speeches you give in life will be impromptu. You might be called on suddenly to "say a few words" or provide feedback during a class discussion.

When such situations arise, don't panic. No one expects you to deliver a perfect speech on the spur of the moment. If you are in a meeting or discussion, pay close attention to what the other speakers say. Take notes of major points with which you agree or disagree. In the process, you will automatically begin to formulate what you will say when it is your turn to speak.

When speaking impromptu, present your speech in these simple steps: First, begin with some type of attention grabber. Second, state the point(s) you wish to make. Third, support your point with appropriate material. Fourth, summarize/conclude your point. This simple method will help you organize your thoughts quickly and clearly.

If time allows, construct a quick outline of your remarks on a piece of paper before you rise to speak. This will help you remember what you want to say and will keep you from getting off topic.

If the situation calls for you to speak from a podium, walk to it calmly, take a deep breath or two (not a visible gasp), establish eye contact with your audience, and begin speaking. No matter how nervous you are inside, do your best to look calm and assured on the outside.

Once you begin speaking, maintain eye contact with the audience. Help the audience keep track of your ideas with signals such as "My first point is . . . ; second, we can see that . . . ; in conclusion, I would like to say . . . " By stating your points clearly and concisely, you will appear organized and confident.

As with other kinds of public speaking, the best way to become a better impromptu speaker is to practice. You can do this on your own. Simply choose a topic on which you are already well informed and give a one- or two-minute impromptu talk on some aspect of that topic. Any topic will do, no matter how serious or frivolous it may be. For practice, you don't need an audience—you can speak to an empty room. You could even record the speech and review it to assess how you sound. The purpose is to gain experience in pulling your ideas together quickly and stating them succinctly.

EXTEMPORANEOUS

An extemporaneous speech is carefully prepared and practiced in advance. In presenting the speech, the extemporaneous speaker uses only a brief set of notes or a speaking outline to jog the memory. The exact wording is chosen at the moment of delivery.

This format is particularly effective for first-time presenters and college students. Once you have your outline (or notes) and know what topics you are going to cover and in which order, you can begin to practice the speech. Each time you rehearse, the wording will be slightly different. As you practice the speech over and over, the best way to present each part will emerge and stick in your mind.

The extemporaneous method has several advantages. It gives more precise control over thought and language than does impromptu speaking, it offers greater spontaneity and directness than does speaking from memory or from a full manuscript, and it is adaptable to a wide range of situations. It also encourages the conversational quality audiences look for in speech delivery.

"Conversational quality" means that no matter how many times a speech has been rehearsed, it still sounds spontaneous. When you speak extemporaneously—and have prepared properly—you have full control over your ideas, yet you are not tied to a manuscript. You are free to establish strong eye contact, to gesture naturally, and concentrate on talking with the audience.

Methods of Delivery

After reading this chapter, you will be able to answer the following questions:

1. What is the most important concept to consider when achieving effective speech delivery?

_____

_____

2. What are the critical elements of effective speech delivery?

_____

_____

3. What are the four methods/modes of speech delivery?

_____

_____

4. How are Impromptu and Extemporaneous speeches different?

_____

_____

5. What type speech is used when the speech must be presented word for word?

_____

_____

Shark Bites

An excellent way to improve your delivery skills is to read out loud selections from works that require emphasis and feeling. You could select one of your favorite poems or plays that falls into this category.

1. Practice reading the selection out loud. As you read, utilize your voice to make the selection come alive. Vary your volume, rate, and pitch. Find the appropriate places for pauses. Underline the key words or phrases you think should be stressed. Modulate your tone of voice and use inflections for emphasis and meaning. Following these strategies will go a long way toward capturing and keeping the interest of your listeners. If possible, practice reading the selection and record it. Listen to the playback. If you are not satisfied with what you hear, practice the selection and record it again.

2. Listen to a presentation. You could also watch a speaker via TED Talk, or other channels to complete the assignment. Prepare a brief report on the speaker's delivery.

First, analyze the speaker's volume, pitch, rate, pauses, vocal variety, pronunciation, and articulation. Then evaluate the speaker's personal appearance, bodily action, gestures, and eye contact. Explain how the speaker's delivery added to or detracted from what the speaker said. Finally, note at least two techniques of delivery used by the speaker that you might want to try in your next speech.

SpeechSHARK™

Unit #3:

Planning the Speech

Conducting an Audience Analysis

Defining the Purpose

Choosing a Topic

Conducting Research

Understanding Speech Outlines

Constructing the Outline

Key Terms to Know

Chapter 5—Conducting and Audience Analysis

- Ethos
- Logos
- Pathos

Chapter 6—Defining the Purpose

- General Purpose
- Opportunities
- Specific Purpose
- Strengths
- SWOT Analysis
- Threats
- Weaknesses

Chapter 7—Choosing a Topic

- Category
- Narrow
- Point
- Topic
- Type

Chapter 8—Conducting Research

- APA
- Blogs
- Citations
- Closed Question
- CMS
- CSE
- GALILEO
- Information Gathering Interview
- Internet
- Interview
- Job Interview
- Key Words

- MLA
- Open Question
- Paraphrasing
- Performance Review
- Plagiarism
- Probing Question
- Problem-Solving Interview
- Public Domain
- Research
- Wikis

Chapter 9—Understanding Speech Outlines

- Bibliography
- Causal Order
- Chronological Order
- Delivery Cues
- Main Points
- Preparation Outline
- Problem-Solution Order
- Spatial Order
- Speaking Outline
- Strategic Organization
- Supporting Materials
- Topical Order

Chapter 10—Constructing the Outline

- Connective
- Credibility
- Goodwill
- Internal Summary
- Preview Points
- Rhetorical Question
- Signpost
- Transition

Chapter Five

Conducting an Audience Analysis

In this chapter:

Will you SINK or SWIM?

How will you plan, prepare, and present a speech?

How do you conduct an audience analysis?

What should you understand about your speaking environment?

How can you show respect for diversity in your speech?

WILL YOU SINK OR SWIM?

Preparation is the key to success! It is the difference between success and failure and will make the difference in whether you will sink or swim! Never forget that the buck stops with YOU! When facing the task of making a speech presentation, it is your job to plan, prepare, and present the speech. These simple steps to SUCCESS will help you to swim with the sharks!

Even with a great tool, like the SpeechShark app, you still have to make time to work through the plan. The first thing that a speaker should do before planning a speech is to conduct an audience analysis and gain an understanding about the speaking environment.

Once you understand **WHO** is in your audience and **WHERE** you will be speaking, you will be able to make a better decision regarding **WHAT** content to include in the speech.

The following worksheet offers several key questions that you need to ask yourself as you begin the planning process. Take time to answer each of these questions every time you plan for a speech. The questions will lead you to the topic and main points that you should cover.

Conduct an Audience Analysis and Understand the Speaking Environment

Questions to Consider:	Answers to Help Plan:
What is the purpose of the speech?	
When will the speech be presented? (Date/Time of Day)	
Do you have a time limit for the speech?	
Is this speech being directed to a particular type of audience? (Example: Senior Citizens, High School Glee Club, Community Volunteers, etc.)	
What is the occasion for this speech?	
Is there a stage?	
Will you have a lectern for notes?	
Will you need visual aids?	
Will you require a Tech Team for sound, lights, setup, breakdown?	
Will you need a microphone?	
Will someone introduce you or will you introduce yourself?	
How many people will attend the speech?	
How many women will attend?	
How many men will attend?	
Is there a large gender gap?	
What is the average age of audience members?	
Is there a large age gap?	
What is the cultural background of the audience?	
Is there a large cultural gap?	
Are there political and religious differences to consider? If so, explain.	
What is the educational status of the audience?	
Are there restrictions which might limit your topic?	
Will the audience enjoy your topic?	
Will the audience be receptive to you as the speaker?	
What does your audience expect from you?	
What kind of information should you share with your audience?	
What type of clothing should you wear for this audience? Are there certain types of clothing and/or jewelry items that would distract your audience?	
Is this audience formal or casual?	
Are there other factors to consider?	

Once you answer these questions, you have entered the planning stage. All that you have to do at this point is to take a deep breath and dive in. There will be no sinking here—you will swim and you will swim with ease!

All of these steps may seem time-consuming, but if you want to SWIM and not sink, these are details that cannot be overlooked or ignored.

Here is a diagram to help you understand the planning process better:

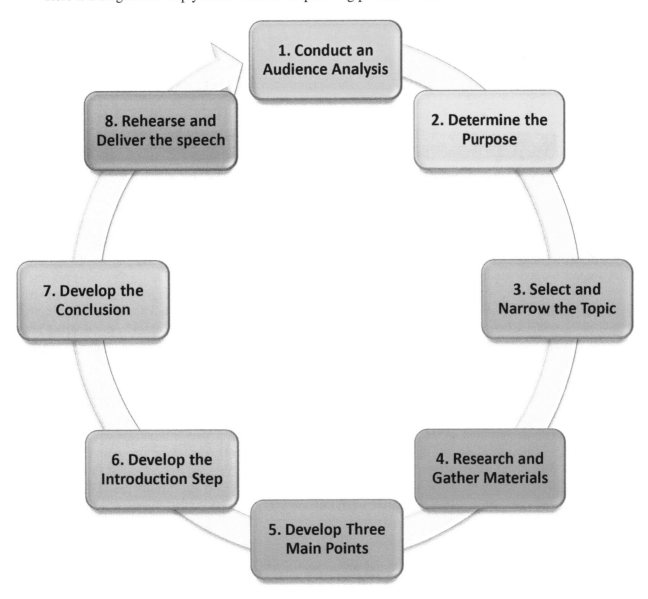

RESPECT DIVERSITY

Since all of us are unique in our own way, it is important that your presentation should be designed to respect everyone in your audience. Most likely, there will be diversity in religious and political beliefs, cultures, genders, age, educational levels, and a multitude of other pre-conceived notions held by each audience member. The larger your audience, the more diversity plays into the way you plan a speech.

Make no assumptions about the beliefs of your audience members and remain ethical by keeping this in mind as you plan presentations. Ethical issues should be considered as you speak and as you listen to the speeches of others. Establish positive ethos by being the kind of person the audience thinks you are based upon what you say and how you project yourself as a speaker.

You've heard the terms ethos, pathos, and logos. These are defined as follows:

Ethos is an appeal to ethics. This is answered as you establish credibility in the introduction section of your speech.

Pathos is an appeal to emotion. This happens as you appeal to the audience's passions or emotions and as you create an emotional response through story telling or argument.

Logos is an appeal to logic. We do this as we reason with our audience and provide logical uses of examples and research to support points we are making in the speech.

The combination of all three (ethos, pathos, and logos) are incorporated as we show respect to our diverse audience members. Know your audience so that you are sure to accomplish these appeals and exhibit respect. Avoid stereotyping and consider situations which might surface. As a speaker, seek to maintain the highest standards of ethics because you are responsible for the content you share with others. As you do this, you will show respect for your audience and they in turn will respect you.

Be aware of the non-verbal cues that are being sent your way during the speech and be flexible enough to change your plan if you notice that audience members are uncomfortable with your topic. A good speaker should never push his/her own agenda on the audience. Show respect for your audience by considering their views and incorporate them into your speech. This will show your audience that you are striving to meet them where they are.

Every person in your audience will have different perspectives, backgrounds, and experiences. We each see, hear, and respond to the world in our own way. It is because of this that we need to learn ways to embrace differences that we have and find common ground to connect with each person in our audience. Your primary responsibility as a speaker is to understand that differences between your audience members will exist. Therefore, you will need to consider every aspect in planning the speech so that your speech will be well received by the majority of people in your audience. In other words, for speaking situations you may need to adapt to others who are different than you and overcome barriers which tend to spotlight our differences.

Before I end this section about diversity, I would like to ask you to go to the Internet and in your search engine bar, type in: TED Talks: Chimamanda Ngozi Adichie: *The Danger of a Single Story.* For your convenience, I will post the URL Address and a link:

https://www.ted.com/talks/chimamanda_adichie_the_danger _of_a_single_story

You've all heard of TED Talks and I'm sure you have spent time watching great speeches through this venue. All of the topics offered in TED Talks are fascinating to me, but this one struck a different chord because of the honesty shared. In less than twenty minutes, this amazing young woman tells a story of the dangers of knowing only one story and not seeing the whole picture.

As I watched this speech, I realized just how guilty **all** of us are. For the most part, we understand our own cultures and we think we understand the cultures of others, but often we do not. It is our own assumptions and perceptions that dictate our innermost thoughts about others from different cultures. Whether we are talking about a culture of gender, age, race, ethnicities, locations, political or religious beliefs, or any number of other categories that we seem to box ourselves and others into, we need to be aware that we may only view that culture as a single story. And, that is wrong. To reach a diverse audience population means that we must look further than the box or category that we perceive as the only story to realize there are always more stories to uncover and more perceptions to understand. Please watch this video and let me know if it also helps you to think in a broader term when planning for your diverse audience members!

What are the most common mistakes beginning speakers make?

The speaker may be confident, have a beautiful voice, and great delivery skills; however, the speech will fall flat if the speech does not contain usable and credible content that will add value to the audience's current knowledge of the topic. Know what your audience needs to know, but also know their current level of understanding about your topic. Choose a topic in which you are the expert and then add to the audience's knowledge base.

How can we avoid these mistakes?

Three simple steps can help avoid mistakes: Plan, Prepare, and Persevere! Plan what you want to say by keeping the audience in mind and understanding the purpose of your speech. Prepare by conducting credible research and including examples that will paint a picture for your audience. Persevere by rehearsing several times until you know your content is being delivered in a manner that is clear, concise, and to the point. The common denominator here is to make sure you conduct an audience analysis. Know your audience and make your plans with them in mind. If you do this, you will be successful!

Conducting an Audience Analysis

After reading this chapter, you will be able to answer the following questions:

1. Why should a speaker conduct an audience analysis? _____
   _____
   _____

2. What are the eight steps for planning a speech? _____
   _____
   _____

3. What is the definition of ethos? _____
   _____
   _____

4. What is the definition of pathos? _____
   _____
   _____

5. What is the definition of logos? _____
   _____
   _____

6. What does the combination of ethos, pathos, and logos do? _____

_____

_____

7. What are the most common mistakes beginning speakers make? _____

_____

_____

8. What are three simple steps to help avoid speaking mistakes?_____

_____

_____

9. What should you consider first when planning a speech? _____

_____

_____

10. What should you do before developing the three main points? _____

_____

_____

Shark Bites

CONDUCTING AN AUDIENCE ANALYSIS

Challenge: Learn who is in your audience and find out what they want/need to know.

Task: If you have been asked to speak for an event, contact the event manager and ask questions about the audience. If possible, get an e-mail or telephone contact list. Send a short message to welcome the potential attendees to the event and to briefly introduce yourself. Invite them to answer the following questions:

1. What is your purpose for attending this event?

2. What is it that you would like to learn?

3. How much do you already know about the subject?

4. Are there any pressing questions that you have about the advertised topic? If so, please list the questions.

Challenge Accepted: Craft your speech by including your audience in every aspect. Give your audience what they want or need to know. Answer the following questions:

1. Does your content address positive ethos, pathos, and logos?

2. Does your topic respect the diversity of audience members?

3. Did you seek to understand the audience's perspectives, backgrounds, and experiences?

4. Did you consider all aspects of the speaking event and choose a topic to add to the audience's knowledge base?

Chapter Six
Defining the Purpose

In this chapter:

How do I define the purpose of my speech?

How do I set goals for my speech presentation?

What strategies are most effective?

What is the expected length of time for my speech?

DEFINING THE PURPOSE

Strategic planning is needed for speeches. Once you understand who will be in your audience, your next step is to define the purpose of the speech. Size up the situation and use this information to make choices to help you reach your goal. Strategic planning includes knowing when to speak, what topics to cover, how to phrase your points, how to explain, how to demonstrate a process or procedure, how to defend a point or motivate your audience to solve a problem, how to organize the message and relate the message to the audience. Making choices are important for strategic planning!

Your speech will have two purposes: a general purpose and a specific purpose. The **general purpose** is the type speech you will present. Are you speaking to inform, entertain, motivate, or perhaps all three? This is your general purpose. The **specific purpose** is more detailed. As you determine the purpose for a speech presentation, you are actually creating a plan to achieve a particular goal. Determining the purpose helps the speaker know what information to share in the body of the speech, how to introduce the topic, and how to conclude the speech.

Here is an example of how this might look on your speech outline:

General Purpose: Inform
Specific Purpose: The purpose of this speech is to inform my audience about the dangers of texting while driving.

General Purpose: Motivate
Specific Purpose: The purpose of this speech is to motivate my audience to give blood at the Red Cross Blood Drive at City Hall next week.

General Purpose: Entertain
Specific Purpose: The purpose of this speech is to entertain my audience as I Roast and Toast our volunteers at the annual end of the year celebration.

GOALS

Having a clear understanding of the purpose of your speech presentation will help you to achieve your speaking goals, develop strategies for a successful presentation, and stay within the time frame that has been offered.

Some use the SWOT strategy to define speaking goals: **S**trengths, **W**eaknesses, **O**pportunities, and **T**hreats. Work through each area analyzing the area and recording your responses. Consider each area as they pertain to the specific speech type that you will be presenting. Each speech is different. Each audience is different. With this in mind, you will want to revisit the SWOT strategy each time you plan a speech.

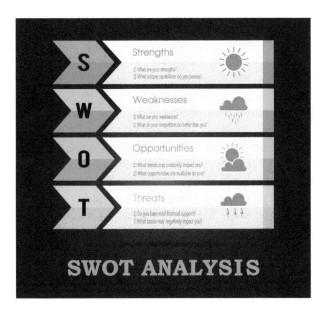

This table will help you understand the goal to achieve a general and specific purpose for each type of speech. Plan to use these suggestions for your general and specific purpose.

Type of Speech	General Purpose	Specific Purpose
Introduction Speech	Inform	The purpose of an Introduction Speech is to introduce yourself or someone else to the audience.
Informative Speech	Inform	The purpose of an Informative Speech is to inform the audience about a topic.
Demonstration Speech	Inform and Entertain	The purpose of a Demonstration Speech is to demonstrate a process or a product.
Persuasion Speech	Motivate	The purpose of a Persuasion Speech is to motivate the audience to solve a problem.
Special Occasion Speech	Inform and/or Entertain	The purpose of a Special Occasion Speech is to inform or entertain an audience through work-related, social, and ceremonial occasions.
Group Presentation	Inform, Entertain, Motivate	The purpose of a group presentation is to present a topic as a group effort with each member taking equal responsibility to inform, entertain, or motivate the audience according to the topic.
Sales Presentation	Motivate	The purpose of the sales presentation is to motivate a buyer to purchase a product or service.

STRATEGIES

Develop a timeline for creating and presenting the speech. Start with the date for the speech and work backward from there. Allow time to conduct the audience analysis, determine the purpose, and select the topic. Critical thinking skills are used during this stage as you plan the topic with the audience and purpose in mind. Once your topic has been selected, narrow the topic and begin conducting research to develop and support your points. Add personal stories and experiences along with research to appear more credible to your audience. Create the presentation outline by starting with the three main points of the body, build the introduction step, and finally, draft the conclusion. Once the outline has been completed, it is time to create a visual aid and handout to support the speech and make presentation notes. The final part of the task is to Rehearse, Rehearse, Rehearse to prepare for a successful presentation. Don't forget to pack supplies for your speech and meet with your Tech Team to make sure all is ready for your presentation! This is the easiest part, Sharks! This is where you are confident because you have taken the time to plan and prepare!

TIME

When asked to speak, make sure you meet with the organizer of the event and find out exactly how much time the organizer needs for you to speak. Plan your speech according to the time frame allotted. Many times, your speech will not be the only point of interest for the event. The organizer will appreciate knowing that you will stay on time because that will mean that her event will also end on time.

Time each rehearsal and take an average of each rehearsal time to get a good idea of the length of time for your speech. If you find that you are going "over time" you will need to cut some of your sub-points. If you find that you are going "under time" you will need to add sub-points. Now, you are almost ready! These details will not "just happen" and it is up to you to make sure that they do happen and at the time that you choose.

The SpeechShark app has a handy timer built in. Simply choose the amount of time you will need to complete your speech and the app will remind you when you need to move from one point to the next. Just another way that you can swim with ease through murky waters!

Defining the Purpose

After reading this chapter, you will be able to answer the following questions:

1. What two purposes should be written for the speech? _____

   _____

   _____

2. Define the general purpose: _____

   _____

   _____

3. Define the specific purpose: _____

   _____

   _____

4. What is the SWOT strategy? _____

   _____

   _____

5. What is the goal of the Introduction Speech? _____

   _____

   _____

6. What is the goal of the Informative Speech? _____

_____

_____

7. What is the goal of the Demonstration Speech? _____

_____

_____

8. What is the goal of the Persuasion Speech? How is the Persuasion Speech and Sales Presentation

   similar? _____

_____

_____

9. What is the goal of the Special Occasion Speech? _____

_____

_____

10. What is the goal of the Group Presentation? _____

_____

_____

Shark Bites

PRACTICE WRITING PURPOSE STATEMENTS

Challenge: You will need to introduce yourself to the board members of a new organization that you have recently joined. Please complete the following purpose statements for this situation:

General Purpose:

_____

_____

Specific Purpose:

_____

_____

Challenge: The topic of your Informative Speech is about organ donations. Please complete the following purpose statements for this situation:

General Purpose:

_____

_____

Specific Purpose:

_____

_____

Challenge: The topic of your Persuasion Speech is about texting and driving. Please complete the following purpose statements for this situation:

General Purpose:

_____

_____

Specific Purpose:

_____

_____

Chapter Seven
Choosing a Topic

In this chapter:

How do I begin searching for a topic?

What is the process for narrowing the topic?

Who can answer my questions?

What are some topic suggestions?

SEARCHING FOR A TOPIC?

Now that you have conducted an audience analysis and determined the purpose of your upcoming presentation, you can begin to think of a topic that will interest your audience and a topic for which you have experience and prior knowledge! This can be an overwhelming task and you might feel like you are a shark circling the waters for just the right target. Truthfully, that is not too far from reality.

When asked to speak for a particular event, you may not have the luxury of choosing a topic because it may be assigned to you; however, you still have the freedom to plan, develop, and add your own personal touch to the topic. For this type situation, it is a good idea to meet with the organizer of the event and ask about their expectations. Some speakers have been known to make phone calls to random audience members to ask what topic they would like to hear and to pinpoint information that is relevant for their personal or professional situations.

If you are still having trouble settling on the topic for your presentation, look through books or magazines for inspiration. Meet with friends and colleagues to brainstorm possible topic choices. Listen to news stations or read news articles to pick up on trending topics. Dive into the Internet and search "Speech Topics" to see what you find. There are billions of topics. Choose the one that is right for your audience and the one that is right for you! Once you have your topic, you will be able to choose three main points, sub-points in the form of research, personal stories, and examples, and create your message to make it memorable for your audience!

NARROWING THE TOPIC

Narrowing the topic is one part of the process involved with choosing a topic. In a short five- to ten-minute speech, you will not be able to cover everything there is to say about the topic. With this in mind, it becomes necessary to narrow the topic to a manageable size.

Here is an example: You LOVE sports, so you are thinking about giving a speech about sports. But, sports is a huge topic and can't be covered in less than ten minutes. Choose one type of sport. Do you want to talk about baseball, basketball, tennis, soccer, racquetball, swimming, skydiving, biking, golf, running, boating, parasailing, skydiving, zip lining, or—Oh My Goodness! Do you see the problem with this? There are so many sports and I love them, ALL! How do I choose? Well, it is obvious you can't speak about all of them in less than ten minutes.

Settle on one **type** of sport and then from that category, narrow the large topic down to a smaller manageable **category**. You are still not finished. Break that down again into a **point** about that sport that is interesting. Almost done . . . Narrow that point into three clear **points**! Aha, now you are swimming and thinking like a SpeechShark!

Here is a way to narrow a topic:

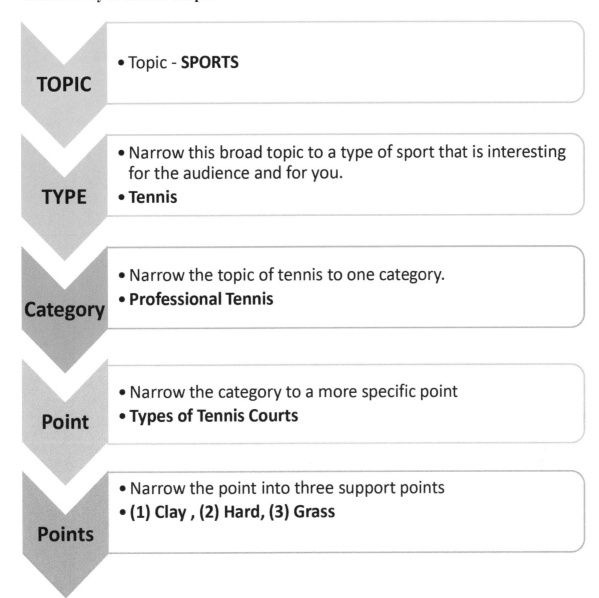

Does this help you understand the process? Often people try to make speeches without really thinking about the points they will cover. It's time to get to the point. Think of specific and clear points that will add information to your audience's existing knowledge.

Why not give this a try with your own topic for the next speech? Write your answers here:

Topic
- Topic

Type
- Narrow the broad topic to a type

Category
- Narrow the type to a category

Point
- Narrow the category to a point

Points
- Narrow this into three points
- 1.
- 2.
- 3.

If you are using the SpeechShark app (www.SpeechShark.com), there is a section early in the development stage where you will be prompted to share the topic of your speech. Before you begin that process, make sure you know the answer!

Whether you have been given a topic or if you can choose a topic, you will want to answer important questions to create a strategic plan.

Here is a guide to help choose the topic for your next speech.

Write Your Topic Choice Here: _____ Answer These Questions:	YES	NO
Does your topic satisfy the general purpose for the presentation?		
Is your topic narrow enough to be completed within your allotted time?		
Will your audience relate to the topic?		
Will this topic be meaningful to the audience?		
Can you add information about the topic that your audience may not already know?		
Is this topic appropriate for your audience? Consult your audience analysis again and examine the topic as it will appeal to diverse audiences.		
Is the topic you have chosen controversial?		
Will your audience be receptive to a controversial topic?		
Are you passionate about this topic?		
Are you excited about sharing this topic with others? Remember, enthusiasm is contagious. If you are excited and enthusiastic about the topic, there is a good chance that your audience will "catch" your enthusiasm.		
Can you choose three points to develop for this topic? List the three points here: 1. 2. 3.		
Do you need to conduct research to support your topic?		
What type of research do you need?		
Do you have personal stories and experience about this topic to share?		
Can you provide simple examples of your main points that are clear and easily understood?		
Will you need to supply your audience with a handout after the speech?		
Will you need to create a PowerPoint or Prezi Presentation as a visual aid?		
Will you have a Tech Team to handle your visual aids?		
Can you think of a creative way to introduce this topic to your audience?		
Is the setting for the speech conducive to this topic?		

Topic Suggestions to Get You Thinking

Informative Speech Topics:	
Bargain Shopping	Learning Disabilities
Body Piercings	Learning How to Knit
Carpooling Tips	Meditation
Cloning	Privacy Rights
College Requirements	Recycling
Coping with Online Courses	Rescuing Pets
Dressing for Success	Smoking Policies
Facebook Security	Television Viewing Habits
Finding Balance	To Tweet or Not to Tweet?
Going Green	Volunteering in Homeless Shelters
Home-schooling	Wikis are Wonderful
Healthcare Options	Working from Home
Kid-Friendly Activities	Would you like to go Skydiving?
Labor Unions	Zip-Lining in Costa Rica
Learning a Foreign Language	Zoo Animals at Risk

Demonstration Speech Topics – Notice They All Begin with "How to . . ."	
How to Arrange Flowers	How to Light a Fire
How to Ask for a Date	How to Make Ice Cream
How to Bake a Cake	How to Make a Mojito
How to Belly Dance	How to Pack a Suitcase
How to Change a Tire	How to Plan a Party
How to Clean Shoes	How to Rearrange Your Closet
How to Fold a Flag	How to Sew on a Button
How to Grate Carrots	How to Sing a Lullaby
How to Hang Christmas Lights	How to Tune a Guitar
How to Juggle Three Balls	How to Write a Speech

Persuasion Speech Topics – Notice the Topics All Begin with an Action Word	
Adopt a Grandparent	Go Back to School
Avoid Artificial Sweeteners	Grow a Vegetable Garden
Apply for Scholarships	Invest in Your Future
Ban Beauty Pageants	Join a Club
Be a Mentor	Join a Community Theater
Become a Vegetarian	Learn to Cook
Buy Organic	Learn to Play
Care for Your Elders	Lose Weight
Donate Blood	Lower the Drinking Age
Don't Text and Drive	Make a "Bucket" List
Dress for Success	Practice Safe Sex
Eat Healthy	Prayer in Schools
Exercise	Register to Vote
Keep Prayer in Schools	Save Money
Search Your Family History	Support the Arts
Make a Bucket List	Teach Children to Save Money
Freedom of Speech	Train Your Dog

Group Presentation Topics:
Choosing a College (Report on different aspects: history, courses, sports, campus life, cost)
Creating a Bucket List (travel, adventure, learning a new skill, volunteering)
Health Benefits of Exercising (heart, lungs, muscles, mental)
Making Money (time involved, benefits, getting started, mentor/mentee)
Movies to Remember (categories, story lines, themes, genres)
Plan a Meal (include recipes: appetizers, soup, salad, main course, desserts, beverages)
Plan a Trip (who, when, where, how)
Report on a Country (culture, foods, government, sports, traditions)
Sales Presentation (product, demonstration, costs, benefits)
Volunteer Opportunities (time, money, benefits, getting started)

Choosing a Topic

After reading this chapter, you will be able to answer the following questions:

1. If given the chance to choose a topic for a speech presentation, what strategies might help with this

   task? _____

   _____

   _____

2. Why is it important to narrow your topic? _____

   _____

   _____

3. What is a good strategy for narrowing your topic? _____

   _____

   _____

4. What are five steps for narrowing your topic? _____

   _____

   _____

5. What questions should you answer when considering a topic for your next speech? _____

   _____

   _____

6. What is an Informative Speech topic that interests you? _____

_____

_____

7. What is a Demonstration Speech topic that interests you? _____

_____

_____

8. What is a Persuasion Speech topic that interests you? _____

_____

_____

9. Why is the title of the speech important? _____

_____

_____

10. What is a good Informative Speech title for a speech about volunteering in your community? _____

_____

_____

Shark Bites

LET'S CHOOSE A TOPIC

To choose a topic, you first need to understand the culture of your audience and choose a topic that will interest them and add to their knowledge base. Choose a topic with which you have experience.

Make a list of possible topics and indicate reasons this topic may work well for your audience. Use this list to help make the right choice! If you can't think of a good reason why the topic may work for your audience, cross it out and go back to the drawing board!

Possible Topics	Reasons This Topic May Work Well
Example: Packing for a Trip to Italy	The audience is made of adult members who belong to a travel club.

Chapter Eight
Conducting Research

In this chapter:

What do I need to know about conducting research?

What is plagiarism?

What guidelines and methods should I consider when conducting research?

How do I include a personal interview in my research plan?

What are citation guidelines?

CONDUCTING RESEARCH

Now that you have chosen a topic for your speech, it is time to develop your understanding of the topic by conducting research. During the research process, speakers will often refine three main points or use research they have gathered to craft sub-points. Information found during research can be used as the attention step, the conclusion, or as support for main points within your speech.

Research can come in the form of data, statistics, opinions, or ideas, but can also be as simple as someone's experience or a story that supports your topic. It is up to you to decide what type of research will be most effective for your particular topic. Speakers also use videos, music, art, photography, and other mediums to support points or create visual aids to support the speech topic. In all cases, if it does not belong to you, it is necessary to cite the source.

Research is defined as the process for finding support materials and credible information. This information will be added to your already vast knowledge of the topic you have chosen to cover. One mistake people often make is to use a base search engine on the Internet to find support material. While this is a simple way to conduct research, it does not always promise credible results.

Read the research guidelines and methods in this chapter to learn the best way to use online resources to support your topic. Credible research will help you appear more credible as a speaker. On the other hand, weak research choices can undermine your speaker credibility and may create confusion, especially if sources are not vetted and reviewed.

As you begin to conduct research, please follow these simple checkpoints:

✔ Use research that is current: preferably less than five years old.

✔ Use research that is credible. Avoid using Wikis, blogs, advertisements, or Web pages.

✔ Use research that will support the topic and your view of the topic.

✔ Use research that will clarify the topic.

✔ Use research that will expand your knowledge of the topic.

✔ Use research that has been written or published by recognizable credible sources.

In years past, the only way that someone could conduct research was to visit a brick-and-mortar library and spend hours looking through books and reference materials. Once the desired article or data was found, the research would need to be photocopied or typed into a document. Thankfully, finding credible research now is simply a click away as most of us conduct research using the Internet. If you do choose to visit a library to conduct research, you will be pleasantly surprised by the amount of online materials available through the library and also by the helpfulness of local librarians to help narrow down sources to find the most useful and productive sources for your topic.

Whether you conduct research online or at the library, you may find it helpful to create a speech materials file to store articles which may prove helpful as you plan your speech. Online articles can be e-mailed to yourself and digital files can be created to store quotes, data, brainstorming ideas, anecdotes, or stories to support your topic. This will be helpful as you sift through possible sources searching for the two or three best sources to serve your needs.

Plagiarism

We can't talk about research without including tips to avoid plagiarism. The interesting thing about plagiarism is that it can occur verbally as well as in writing, so make sure you cite everything you use that is not your own. **Plagiarism** is the act of using someone else's ideas or work as if they are your own. In essence, this is stealing and in the educational and professional arena, plagiarism is an act which may lead to immediate dismissal. Copyright laws are in place to protect authors of written works.

The best way to avoid plagiarism charges is to verbally or in writing cite everything that belongs to someone else. Turnitin.com is a Web site that checks for plagiarism. Many colleges and universities use this site regularly to check students' work for plagiarism. In the corporate world, a plagiarism charge can harm your reputation and career. Just to be safe, always verbally and in writing cite the source of research and give proper credit. Citation guidelines are noted toward the end of this chapter.

Guidelines

How do you know if a source of research is credible? Blogs on the Internet can appear to be quite credible. They can be written and posted by someone with a Ph.D., but even that will not determine if the source is credible. Often blogs or Wikis will provide interesting or amusing information, but that also does not determine if the source is credible. Interesting or amusing does not equal credible. With this in mind, I always warn the speech students that I coach to never use a blog, Wiki, or advertisement link—no matter how legitimate it may sound. The point is to evaluate the research and make decisions regarding whether or not the source is credible and offers information you can use to support your speech.

Use credible research owned, reviewed, and monitored by reputable organizations, government sources, newspapers, journals, books, and magazine sources. Stay away from blogs, Wikis, and advertisements which might link to credible sources, but are not credible in their own rights.

Use the following checklist to determine if the source is credible:

☐ Would my audience recognize the source?

☐ Does the source list an author?

☐ Does the author have credentials to verify his/her credibility?

☐ Does the source list copyright information?

☐ Was this source published within the past five years?

☐ Is the content clear and helpful? Is the content accurate and unbiased?

☐ Does the content offer opposing viewpoints?

☐ Does the content support my topic?

Research Methods

Gathering materials online has never been easier than it is right now. Through the Internet, online research has become the primary source for gathering information for college students and professionals. The Internet can be an incredible source for locating great information, but it is also a source for spreading misinformation! Take care to choose sources of research from credible sources and confirm that the information you share with your audiences is something that will clarify the topic and not confuse your audience.

The **Internet** is one of the most popular go-to sources for people who want to conduct research for any topic in the world. Online search engines like Google, Bing, Yahoo, and Google Scholar have become quite popular. Do not rely solely upon Google; however, if you search Google Scholar, it is possible to find credible research for your speech. Print materials from periodicals, newspapers, encyclopedias, dictionaries, journals, and books are also available through the Internet in digital formats.

Many states offer credible online search engines for a small fee. A student in any of the state of Georgia high schools, technical colleges, community colleges, and university systems are able to use the well-known virtual library called GALILEO (Georgia, Library of Learning Online). Everything in GALILEO is credible. Students are able to search, save, e-mail sources, and get citation help through this easy to navigate system. Many of the sites found in GALILEO offer audio versions of articles, as well as translations into many other languages. Other states have programs similar to GALILEO to help with student research.

Through various search engines, we are able to use key words in a search window to limit the search and to make the research process simpler. The downside is that search engines usually provide a broad expanse of materials, all of which are not credible or relevant for the topic you have chosen. Directories, on the other hand, allow people to link with key words or matches regarding the topic and are manned by a librarian who chooses the prospective sites based upon the quality of that site.

Here are other options:

- **Government and survey sites** such as the Gallup Polls offer reliable information that can be used as support materials.

- **Libraries** often have resources that cannot be found online; therefore, you may want to visit your local library as you conduct research for your speech.

- **Magazines and journals** are the most common forms of research and are readily available in hard copy and online.

- **Television and radio programs** provide transcripts of trending stories that can be used as support for speeches.

- **Newspapers**, available in hard copy and online, offer current and trending information about topics of interest.

- **Books** are an excellent source of information, but readers should understand that it takes months for books to be published and the information contained in a book may not be the very latest information released to the public. Be sure to check the copyright date before using a book.

- **Interviews** are a perfect way to get stories and personal experience about your topic. Just make sure your interviewee is a credible source for your topic.

When using **key words** to initiate a search, take care to spell the key words correctly, use nouns and avoid using more than six words per search. If your search is not successful, try using different key words. As you type in key words into the search box, you will notice that other popular searches will pop up. Sometimes following the pop-up trails will lead to sources that are useful, but other times they will not.

Research is a way to find the answers you need to support points and explore facts that will make you appear more credible to your audience.

Just remember that conducting research is a process. It's like fishing. You have to bait a lot of hooks before you catch the prize fish. With research, you have to review a lot of sources before you find the right data, anecdote, or information to support the point you want to make!

Interviews

Interviews are often used as a source of experiential research to support speech topics. For example, you may choose to integrate an interview with credible print or electronic research to support your topic. We often associate interviews as part of a job-search process and that is true; however, interviews can provide information to help further your knowledge about a subject. An **interview** is defined as the asking of specific questions with the intent to gather information from the person being interviewed. All interview types follow the same basic formula. Prepared questions are chosen depending upon the purpose. Questions are asked and answers are provided. Here are the different types of interviews:

- **Information gathering interviews** are often conducted with many people responding to a question asked.
- **Job interviews** are structured conversations with a goal to discover if a person is suitable for an open position within a company.
- **Problem-solving interviews** are designed to bring peace or solve grievances between two parties. A mediator is usually present in the event of a problem-solving interview.
- **Performance reviews** are considered interviews and are initiated by management authorities in a company to review the performance of employees.

There are three parts to every interview: opening, body, and closing.

The **opening** sets the stage for the type of interview and is usually a time where the interviewer creates a rapport with the interviewee to establish open communication lines in the hope of having a positive interaction between the two.

The **body** of the interview includes questions that are asked. There are different types of questions used for interviews. The most appropriate question to use during the interview is the **open question**. These are broad questions that cannot be answered with a simple "yes" or "no" answer. These questions open the interviewee to answer in-depth thereby adding knowledge for your topic.

Probing questions are good questions to use during an interview because these questions encourage the interviewee to elaborate about the topic.

Avoid asking **closed questions**, as this limits the responses you might receive and will also limit the amount of information you are able to gather about the topic. Closed questions are usually answered by a "yes" or "no."

The **closing** of the interview is an opportunity to summarize the interview and to close on a positive note. Each person, the interviewer and the interviewee, has a responsibility to the other.

Audio or video recording an interview is a good idea, especially when you will be writing and presenting a transcript of the interview. After the introductions and before beginning the interview, ask your interviewee if he/she would mind if you record the interview. You can decide if you want to audio or video record the session. Most electronic devices, whether it is your phone, tablet, or iPad, have the audio and video recording feature, making this an easier task. If the interviewee agrees to the interview, place your electronic device in full view of the interviewee and pointed toward the speaker so that it will pick up both of your voices. If by chance the interviewee does not allow the recording, then it will be your responsibility to repeat back the interviewee's answers to make sure that your note-taking skills are accurate and that you are able to fully understand the interviewee's response.

The purpose of this unit is to work through expectations so that your next interview will be successful. E-mail, telephone, and Skype interviews are sometimes appropriate; however, face-to-face interviews yield the most promising results.

There are advantages and disadvantages of both types of interviews:

Advantages:	Disadvantages:
E-mail, telephone, and Skype interviews take less time than a personal visit.	You cannot be sure who is replying to your e-mail or phone questions.
E-mail questions are efficient and provide a paper trail.	A breakdown in communication can happen with phone conversations.
E-mail questions allow the interviewee time to formulate a response.	Skype interactions rely on Internet connections and contact could be disrupted.
E-mail responses are useful if the interviewee lives in another time zone.	E-mail restricts your ability to question the response.
E-mail, telephone, and SKYPE are more convenient for both parties.	E-mail and telephone interviews cannot communicate non-verbal cues.

To include experiential research as support for your upcoming speech, here is a convenient checklist to make sure you are prepared:

BEFORE the Interview
☐ Decide who you will interview.
☐ Prepare interview questions.
☐ Craft open-ended questions that cover your topic.
☐ Contact the interviewee.
☐ Request an appointment.
☐ Pack a recording device.
☐ Arrive ten minutes early.
☐ Dress professionally.
☐ Have note-taking materials.
☐ Introduce yourself to the receptionist.
☐ Wait to enter until you are invited into the office.

DURING the Interview
☐ Behave professionally.
☐ Shake hands with the interviewee.
☐ Smile and make eye contact.
☐ Wait to sit until you are invited by the interviewee.
☐ Ask permission to audio record the interview.
☐ Ask questions clearly and one at a time.
☐ Wait patiently for answers.
☐ If necessary, clarify the questions.
☐ After all questions, stand and extend your hand for a handshake.
☐ Thank the interviewee for his time.
☐ Invite him to hear your speech.
☐ Provide the day/time/location.
☐ Do not overstay.
☐ Thank the receptionist for her assistance.

AFTER the Interview
☐ Write a thank you note or e-mail as soon as you return from the interview.
☐ Include an invitation to hear the speech.
☐ Using the audio recording, write a transcript of the interview.
☐ Include the entire conversation in the transcript.
☐ Using the transcript, include the research in your outline and speech.
☐ Correctly cite the interview source verbally and in writing.

A thank you note following the interview should follow standard letter-writing guidelines.

Example of Thank You Letter:

Name
Address, City, State, Zip Code
Phone Number
E-mail Address

Date of the Interview

Interviewee's Name
Interviewee's Address

Dear Mr./Ms./Dr. Last Name:

Thank you for taking time to meet with me and answer questions I had about (enter the topic of your speech). I appreciate your time. The information you supplied will be used as research to support my speech.

I would like to invite you to attend the speech that will be given at (time) on (date) and held at (location). It would be an honor to have you as a guest.

Thank you again!

Sincerely,
(Add your signature)
Type Your Full Name

Type the interview transcript using this template:

Example of the Interview Transcript

Interviewer:
Name
Address, City, State, Zip Code
Phone Number
E-mail Address

Interviewee:
Name
Address, City, State, Zip Code
Phone Number
E-mail Address

Interviewee's Credentials: Provide details regarding why you chose to interview this person as a source of research for your speech topic. What experience have they had with this topic that would prove credibility for the topic?

Interview Date/Time:
Interview Location:

Question #1:
Interviewee's Response:

Question #2:
Interviewee's Response:

Question #3:
Interviewee's Response:

Question #4:
Interviewee's Response:

Question #5:
Interviewee's Response:

WRITTEN CITATIONS OF RESEARCH

Let's talk about citation of sources, since this is a big responsibility for the speaker! First, you should know that there are different ways to cite research. The most frequently used citation styles are APA, MLA, CSE, and CMS. With each style, you will notice a specific set of rules and guidelines established to indicate the author, title, publishing source, date of publication, and page numbers of the source.

Additionally, you will notice there are different ways to cite each type of source, whether it is a book, e-book, dissertations, Web sites, radio or television episodes, videos or film clips, magazines, journals, or newspaper articles, music, art, or pictures.

How do you know which style to use and what makes each style unique? Each style is formulated for a particular discipline. If you are not tasked with using one specific guideline, then please follow the notations below to make sure you are using the style most suited for the topic you are covering. We have also included the links to their Web sites so that you can go directly to the source to see clear instructions regarding how to cite the source of research in your outline or document.

Here is a breakdown of styles, a notation of when they should be used, and the link to their Web sites:

APA is known as the American Psychological Association style of citing research. Disciplines that cover psychology, sociology, social work, criminology, education, business, and economics may use the APA style of citing research. For APA Guidelines, please visit their website at http://www.apastyle.org/.

MLA is known as the Modern Language Association style of citing research. Documents using research for literature and language will use this style of citing research. Since you are learning about public speaking and crafting speeches to inform, persuade, and entertain, you will need to cite your sources of research using the MLA Guidelines for source citations. We'll provide examples of MLA citations in this book. For MLA Guidelines, please visit their website at https://www.mla.org/MLA-Style.

CSE citations follow the guidelines established by the Council of Science Editors and are used primarily when the writer or speaker is citing research in the applied sciences areas. These will include biology, chemistry, physics, astronomy, and earth science. For CSE Guidelines, please visit their website at https://www.councilscienceeditors.org/publications/scientific-style-and-format/.

CMS is known as the Chicago Manual of Style. These guidelines are used to cite research that involve the arts and humanities. For CMS Guidelines, please visit their website at http://www.chicagomanualofstyle.org/home.html.

VERBAL CITATIONS OF RESEARCH

Whether in writing or verbally, any source of research used must be cited. To avoid plagiarism charges during your speech, cite every source you use. In recent news, we learned of a case where one prominent politician plagiarized the words and ideas of another. The words used were so identical that the news reporters and commentators had a field day reporting how this one person blatantly used the very same words as the other. It was quite embarrassing for the politician, who then made a formal statement apologizing for the error. Make sure that you do not find yourself in the same situation.

When you are speaking to an audience and you want to support your point with a credible source of research, it is important to give a verbal indication that you are using someone else's work, ideas, or opinions. The best way to do this is to lead into the research and then indicate whether you are offering a direct quote of the research or paraphrasing the information. Audience members cannot see when the research begins or ends as they do when reading your written document and having the benefit of a parenthetical citation. For this reason, it is the speaker's responsibility to clearly detail the research verbally.

Transition into the research using a signal word which offers a cue for your audience that you are going to cite a source. Vary the signal words you use as the transition and use words that move nicely into the information you are sharing. Here is a short list of signal words that you might use: said, claims, asserts, denies, disputes, expresses, generalizes, implies, lists, maintains, offers, states, suggests, responds, replies, reveals, acknowledges, advises, or believes. Here is an example of how you might use these words:

> **Example of a verbal citation of a direct quote:** In his 2013 New York Times Bestseller book titled *Cooked*, Michael Pollan said this about bread, and I quote, "One way to think about bread—and there are so many . . . is simply this: as an ingenious technology for improving the flavor, digestibility, and nutritional value of grass." End quote.

This process will involve indicating the author's name, the title of the article or the title of the book, and the publication date—not necessarily in that order. If it is a direct quote, you will add the words, ". . . and I quote." Following the direct quote, you will end with the words, ". . . end quote."

PARAPHRASING

If paraphrasing, you will indicate the author's name, the title of the article or the title of the book and the publication date, just as you would for a direct quote. Then you will announce that you are paraphrasing the content. This allows your listener to know where your research begins and where it ends. The listener will know which words belong to the author of the source and which words belong to you. This can be a bit tricky, but with a little practice, you will find that inserting this information as you use a source of research will also help you to appear more credible for your audience. It is easier to paraphrase thoughts, opinions, or ideas, such as the following:

> **Example of a verbal citation of a paraphrased quote:** I would like to paraphrase a unique perception held by Michael Pollan in his 2013 New York Times Bestseller book titled *Cooked*. As the author was talking about bread, he explained how a great recipe can produce something extremely delicious, even though it is nothing more than grass.

Notice in the paraphrase example, the speaker still needed to transition to the research material, supply the author's name, the title of the book, and then paraphrase the idea of the information read in the book.

Some research can NOT be paraphrased. This would include information that includes numbers, dates, proper names, and places. For example, you cannot paraphrase the number 12,643,279. That number is too precise to be paraphrased. For the same reason, you cannot paraphrase June 30, 1935. To paraphrase these, you will need to generalize the information. You can do that by saying "over twelve million" or for the date you could say toward the middle of 1935. The same is true for a person's name or the name of a place. For example, you cannot paraphrase Savannah, Georgia. What do you think you would say, if you needed to paraphrase a person's name? How you would paraphrase the name of a city and state? When do you think paraphrasing would be appropriate?

CITING PRESENTATION AIDS

Citations also need to be included in your visual aids. The only time you will not need to cite visual aids will be if the visual aid belongs to you or if it is considered **public domain**. Merriam-Webster's Online Dictionary defines public domain as "the realm embracing property rights that belong to the community at large, are unprotected by copyright or patent, and are subject to appropriation by anyone" *("Public Domain")*. Here is an example of a PowerPoint slide with a picture that belongs to me and therefore does not need to be cited:

Here is an example of using a picture that does not belong to me and is <u>not</u> public domain. In this case, I included a full citation on the PowerPoint slide where the picture is shown. It is not good to have a Works Cited slide at the end of your PowerPoint Presentation because the audience will not know which citation goes with which picture. Cite the picture in the footer area of the slide where the picture is shown.

ADDING PERSONAL STORIES

Storytelling, personal stories, anecdotes, even hypothetical examples are ways to add interest to your speeches. While it is good to have credible sources to support points, don't forget to always add the human element by including stories. Whether they are your own personal stories or stories from some of your friends or family, including this into your speech will make your topics so much more interesting for the audience.

This is a good time to use material discovered while conducting a personal interview with an interviewee who has experience with your topic. Asking questions and receiving personal stories and information from the interviewee will provide strong material to support points during your speech. Don't forget to also verbally cite the sources for your stories!

Example of a verbal citation of an interview: Last week I was able to interview Mr. Thaddeus Nifong, who is a public speaking instructor and advises a college Toastmasters International Club. During the personal interview, I asked Mr. Nifong what is one of the biggest challenges of advising a college club? Mr. Nifong revealed, and I quote, "The biggest challenge of advising a college Toastmasters International Club is to continually recruit officers and members. College members are going to graduate, transfer to other colleges, and sometimes life just gets in the way. It is because of this that our club officers and members are continuously recruiting and spreading the word about this great club on our campus! With that said, yes, there are challenges, but the rewards far outweigh the challenges when you can become involved as a college club advisor." End quote.

As you can see, when verbally citing a personal interview, it is important to use a transition to lead into the quote, include the interviewee's name, tell your audience why you chose to interview this person based upon his experience, and set the stage for the response. Here is another way to think about it:

1. Transition to citation
2. State the interviewee's full name
3. State the interviewee's credentials
4. Share the question asked
5. Share the response

If you are including a direct quote, preface the quote with . . . "and I quote" before sharing the quote. Following the quote, it is important to conclude with . . . "End quote." In doing this, the audience will clearly differentiate between the words said by the interviewee and your own words. When paraphrasing content within the interview, include all of the information shown above, but indicate that you are paraphrasing instead of using a direct quote.

Conducting Research

After reading this chapter, you will be able to answer the following questions:

1. Define the process of research. _____

   _____

   _____

2. Why should you use credible research? _____

   _____

   _____

3. What are the preferred research checkpoints? _____

   _____

   _____

4. What is plagiarism? _____

   _____

   _____

5. How can you avoid being charged with plagiarism? _____

   _____

   _____

6. Are blogs considered credible research sources? _____

_____

_____

7. How can you determine if the source is credible? _____

_____

_____

8. What does the acronym GALILEO stand for? Do you have something like this in your state? What is it

called? _____

_____

_____

9. What is the purpose of conducting an interview as a source of research? _____

_____

_____

10. What are the different types of interviews? _____

_____

_____

11. What are the three parts to every interview? Explain each part. _____

_____

_____

12. What is the difference between open questions and closed questions? _____

_____

_____

13. What are the advantages and disadvantages of e-mail interviews? _____

_____

_____

14. What should you do to prepare yourself before the interview? _____

_____

_____

15. What is expected from the interviewer during the interview? _____

_____

_____

16. What is expected from the interviewer following the interview? _____

_____

_____

17. What are the four most frequently used citation styles? _____

_____

_____

18. How do you know which of the four styles of citations to use? _____

_____

_____

19. What is an example of using a signal word when verbally citing research? _____

_____

_____

20. How do you paraphrase research? _____

_____

_____

21. What research cannot be paraphrased? _____

_____

_____

22. Where do you cite pictures/photographs on PowerPoint or Prezi slides? _____

_____

_____

23. Do personal interviews need to be verbally cited in the speech? _____

_____

_____

24. What are the steps involved with citing a personal interview? _____

_____

_____

25. Let's practice! Hypothetically, how would you verbally cite a personal interview between you and a mechanic at a local auto shop about the informative speech topic of properly maintaining your car?

_____

_____

_____

Shark Bites

CITING RESEARCH SOURCES

Find one source of research about your topic from the following sources: newspaper, book, journal, interview. Cite the source below using MLA Guidelines for citations.

Written Citation of a Newspaper Article:

Verbal Citation of the Newspaper Article:

Written Citation of a Book:

Verbal Citation of Book:

Written Citation of a Journal Article:

Verbal Citation of a Journal Article:

Written Citation of a Personal Interview:

Verbal Citation of a Personal Interview:

Chapter Nine

Understanding Speech Outlines

In this chapter:

How do I organize my speech?

What are the different methods of arranging main points?

What are the different types of speech outlines?

How do I create useful notes?

ORGANIZATION IS IMPORTANT

There are many studies that show the importance of organization in effective speechmaking. Your audience will expect a cohesive and coherent presentation, so you the presenter must be sure the audience will be able to follow the progression of ideas in your presentation from start to finish. This requires that speeches be organized strategically. They should be put together in particular ways to achieve particular results with particular audiences.

Speech organization is important for other reasons as well. It is closely connected to critical thinking. When you work to organize your speeches, you gain practice in the general skill of establishing clear relationships among your ideas. In addition, using a clear, specific method of speech organization can boost your confidence as a speaker and improve your ability to deliver a message fluently.

STRATEGIC ORDER OF MAIN POINTS

Once you establish your main points, you need to decide the order in which you will present them. The most effective order depends on three things—your topic, your purpose, and your audience. Below are the five basic patterns of organization used most often by public speakers.

Chronological Order: Speeches arranged chronologically follow a time pattern. They follow a series of events in the sequence in which they happened. Chronological order is also used in speeches explaining a process or demonstrating how to do something.

Topical Order: Topical order results when you divide the speech topic into subtopics, each of which becomes a main point in the speech.

Spatial Order: Speeches arranged in spatial order follow a directional pattern or geographical location. That is, the main points proceed from top to bottom, left to right, east to west, or some other route.

Casual Order: Speeches arranged in causal order organize main points so as to show a cause-effect relationship. When you put your speech in causal order, you have two main points—one dealing with the causes of an event, the other dealing with its effects. Depending on your topic, you can deal first with the effects and then with the causes.

Problem-Solution Order: Speeches arranged in problem-solution order are divided into two main parts. The first shows the establishment of a problem. The second presents a workable solution to the problem.

KEYS FOR MAIN POINTS

1. Keep main points separate
2. Use the same pattern of wording for main points
3. Balance the amount of time devoted to main points

Because your main points are so important, you want to be sure you allow sufficient time to develop each main point. This is not to say that all main points must receive exactly equal emphasis, but only that they should be roughly balanced. The amount of time spent on each main point depends on the amount and complexity of supporting materials for each point.

As you can see, clear organization is vital to speechmaking. Audience members demand coherence. They get only one chance to grasp the presenter's ideas, and they have little patience for presenters who ramble aimlessly from one idea to another. A well-organized speech will enhance your credibility and make it easier for the audience to understand your message.

The process of planning the body of a speech begins when you determine the main points. You should choose them carefully, phrase them precisely, and organize them strategically. Because audience members cannot keep track of a multitude of main points, most speeches should contain no more than two to five.

Supporting materials are the backup ideas for your main points. When organizing supporting materials, make sure they are directly relevant to the main points they are supposed to support.

Organize main points in various ways, depending on your topic, purpose, and audience. Chronological order follows a time pattern, whereas spatial order follows a directional pattern. In causal order, main points are organized according to their cause-effect relationship. Topical order results when you divide your main topic into subtopics. Problem-solution order breaks the body of the speech into two main parts—the first showing a problem, the second giving a solution.

Research studies confirm that clear organization is vital to effective public speaking. Your audience must be able to follow the progression of ideas in a speech from beginning to end.

Outlines are essential to effective speeches. It allows you to see the full scope and content of your speech. By outlining, you can determine if each part of the speech is fully developed, whether you have adequate supporting materials for your main points, and if the main points are properly balanced.

You will likely utilize two kinds of outlines for your speeches—one very detailed, for the planning stage (Preparation Outline) and one very brief, for the delivery of the speech (Presentation or Speaking Outline).

TYPES OF OUTLINES

The **preparation outline** is just what its name implies—an outline that helps you prepare the speech. Writing a preparation outline means putting your speech together—deciding what you will say in the introduction, how you will organize the main points and supporting materials in the body, and what you will say in the conclusion.

GUIDELINES FOR THE PREPARATION OUTLINE

A relatively uniform system for preparation outlines is explained below; however, you should check with your instructor to see what format you are to follow.

State Purpose of Your Speech

The purpose statement should be a separate unit that comes before the outline itself. Including the purpose makes it easier to assess how well you have constructed the speech to accomplish your purpose.

Label the Introduction, Body, and Conclusion

If you label the parts of your speech, be sure that you have an introduction and conclusion and have accomplished the essential components of each. Generally, the names of the speech parts are placed in the middle of the page or in the far left margin.

Use a Consistent Pattern of Symbolization and Indentation

In the most common system of outlining, main points are identified by Roman numerals and are indented equally so as to be aligned down the page. **Sub-points** (components of the main points) are identified by capital letters and are also indented equally so as to be aligned with each other. Here is an example of how your main point should look:

I. Main point

   A. Sub-point

   B. Sub-point

      1. Sub-sub-point

      2. Sub-sub-point

As outlines are essential to speechmaking, develop an outline to help ensure that the structure of your speech is clear and coherent. Once you have organized the body of your speech, identify the main points. The most important ideas (main points) are farthest to the left. Less important ideas (sub-points, sub-sub-points, and so on) are progressively farther to the right. This pattern reveals the structure of your entire speech.

Use sub-points and sub-sub-points, as necessary, to support the main points. Stating your main points and sub-points in full sentences will ensure that you develop your ideas fully.

Label Transitions

One way to make sure you have strong transitions is to include them in the preparation outline. Usually they are not incorporated into the system of symbolization and indentation but are labeled separately and inserted in the outline where they will appear in the speech.

Attach a Bibliography or Works Cited Page

Include with the outline a bibliography or Works Cited page depending upon the citation guideline you follow that shows all books, magazines, newspapers, and Web sources you consulted, as well as any interviews or independent research you conducted.

The two major bibliographic formats are those developed by the Modern Language Association (MLA) and the American Psychological Association (APA). Both are widely used by communication scholars; ask your instructor which he or she prefers.

Preparation Outline Checklist:

- Have I stated the purpose statement?
- Have I labeled the introduction, body, and conclusion?
- Are my main points and sub-points written in full sentences?
- Have I labeled transition sentences?
- Does my outline follow a consistent pattern of symbolization and indentation?
- Does my bibliography identify all the sources I consulted in preparing the outline?
- Does the bibliography follow the format required by my instructor?

The Speaking Outline (also called a Presentation Outline) is a condensed version of your preparation outline. The goal of your speaking outline is to help you remember what you want to say. It should only contain key words or phrases to jog your memory, as well as essential content you don't want to forget. But it should also include material not in your preparation outline, such as cues to sharpen your delivery. See the basic guidelines below.

GUIDELINES FOR THE SPEAKING OUTLINE

- Your speaking outline should use the same framework as your preparation outline.

- Make the outline legible.

- Your speaking outline must be instantly readable at a distance.

- As you work on your outline, organize it into three main points, each with two supporting points. Compose an outline that organizes the points in this manner. Some presenters opt to place speaking notes on index cards. It is best to select either 3 × 5 size or 4 × 6 size.

- Keep the outline brief. If your notes are too detailed, you will have difficulty maintaining eye contact with your audience. A detailed outline will tempt you to look at it far too often.

Keep your speaking outline as brief as possible. Most presenters use too many notes. You do not need all of them to remember the speech, and will find that too many notes can actually interfere with the presentation. Limit information to key words or phrases to help you remember major points and connectives. The best rule is that your notes should be the minimum you need to jog your memory and keep you on track.

Creating Useful Notes for Delivering the Speech

An effective speaking outline reminds you not only of what you want to say but also of how you want to say it. It is imperative to include in your speaking outline delivery cues—directions for delivering the speech. One way to do this is by highlighting key ideas that you want to be sure to emphasize. Then, when you reach them in the outline, you will be reminded to stress them. Another way is to jot down on the outline explicit cues such as "pause," "repeat," "slow down," "louder," "breathe," etc.

Outlines are essential to effective speeches. By outlining, you make sure that your thoughts flow from one to another, and that the structure of your speech is coherent. You will probably use two kinds of outlines for your speeches—the detailed preparation outline and the brief speaking outline.

In the preparation outline, you state your purpose, label the introduction, body, and conclusion, and designate transitions and connectives. You should identify main points and sub-points by a consistent pattern of symbolization and indentation.

The speaking outline should contain key words or phrases to jog your memory. Be sure your speaking outline is legible and includes cues for delivering the speech.

Outline Organizing Basics

After reading this chapter, you should be able to answer the following questions:

1. Why is it important that speeches be organized clearly and coherently? _____

_____

_____

_____

2. How many main points will your speeches usually contain? Why is it important to limit the number of

main points in your speeches?_____

_____

_____

_____

3. What are the five basic patterns of organizing main points in a speech? _____

_____

_____

_____

4. What are three tips for preparing your main points? _____

_____

_____

_____

5. What is the most important thing to remember when organizing supporting materials in the body of

your speech? _____

_____

_____

_____

6. Why is it important to outline your speeches? _____

_____

_____

_____

7. What is a preparation outline? _____

_____

_____

_____

8. What are the guidelines discussed for writing a preparation outline? _____

_____

_____

_____

9. What is a speaking outline? _____

_____

_____

_____

10. What are the guidelines for your speaking outline? _____

_____

_____

_____

Shark Bites

What organizational method (or methods) might you use to arrange main points for speeches with the following specific purpose statements?

1. Teaching Piano Skills _____

   _____

   _____

2. Evolution of Mustangs _____

   _____

   _____

3. Advantages of Eating Yogurt _____

   _____

   _____

4. Life and Death of Princess Diana _____

   _____

   _____

5. Legalization of Marijuana _____

   _____

   _____

Chapter Ten
Constructing the Outline

In this chapter:

What are the parts of an outline?

How do I begin planning the body (main points)?

What is involved with planning the introduction step?

What is involved with planning the conclusion step?

How do I include transitions (links) in my outline?

The first step in constructing an outline is to master the three basic parts of a speech—introduction, body, and conclusion—and the strategic role of each. We will focus on the body of the speech, in addition to the introduction and the conclusion.

There are good reasons for talking first about the body of the speech. The body is generally the longest and most important part. Also, you will prepare the body first. It is easier to create an effective introduction after you know exactly what you will say in the body. The process of organizing the body of a speech begins when you determine the main points.

MAIN POINTS (BODY)

The main points are the central features of your speech. You should select them carefully, phrase them precisely, and arrange them strategically.

How do you select your main points? Sometimes they will be evident from your specific purpose statement. Your main points may not be so easy to determine. Often, they will emerge as you conduct research and evaluate content to include in your presentation.

NUMBER OF MAIN POINTS

You will not have time during your speeches to develop more than four to five main points, and most speeches will contain only two or three. Regardless of how long a speech might last, if you have too many main points, the audience will have a difficult time keeping track of them in your presentation.

The Introduction

First impressions are important. A poor first impression may alienate the audience, so the presenter getting off on the correct foot is vital.

In most speech situations, the introduction has four objectives: (1) gain the attention and interest of your audience, (2) reveal the topic of your speech, (3) establish your credibility and goodwill, and (4) preview the body of the speech.

GAIN ATTENTION AND INTEREST

A presenter can lose an audience if they do not utilize the introduction to gain attention and interest. Gaining the initial attention of your audience is usually easy; however, keeping the attention of your audience once you start talking is more difficult. Discussed below are the most common methods utilized in presentations. Whether you choose to incorporate them individually or in combination, they will assist with engaging the audience in your speech.

Startle the audience: One way to arouse interest quickly is to startle your audience with an intriguing statement. This technique is highly effective and easy to implement. Be sure the startling introduction relates directly to the content of your presentation.

Arouse curiosity of the audience: People are curious. One way to draw them into your speech is with a series of statements that progressively engage their curiosity about the content of the speech. By building suspense about a subject, the presenter pulls the audience into the speech.

Question the audience: Asking a rhetorical question is another way to get your audience thinking about your presentation. Sometimes a single question will do. The audience will answer mentally, not out loud.

In other circumstances, you may want to pose a series of questions. When utilizing this technique, be sure to pause for just a moment after each question. This will give the question time to sink in. The audience could respond with a verbal response, or with a show of hands.

Begin with a quotation: Another way to arouse the interest of your audience is to start with an attention-getting quotation. You don't need to use a famous quotation. Generally, quotations are relatively short. Opening your speech with a lengthy quotation can bore your audience.

Tell a story: We all enjoy hearing stories, particularly if they are dramatic and have us on the edge of our seats. You can also use stories based on your personal experience. In some cases, this will expose your vulnerability, however it is worth it. Be sure to use vivid language to tell the audience members a story that they may or may not have experienced.

Relate topic to the audience: People pay attention to things that impact them directly. If you can relate the topic to your audience, they are much more likely to be interested in it.

State importance of your topic: This technique can be utilized when discussing social and political issues such as poverty, endangered species, and domestic violence, but it is appropriate for other topics as well. Whenever you discuss a topic whose importance may not be clear to the audience, you should think about ways to demonstrate its significance in the introduction.

Speech Introduction Checklist:

- Have I gained the attention and interest of my audience by using one or more of the methods discussed in this chapter?

- How do I relate the speech topic to my audience?

- How do I establish my credibility to speak on this topic?

- Have I defined any key terms that will be necessary for the audience to understand my speech?

- Have I provided a preview of the main points to be covered in the body of the speech?

- Is my introduction limited to ten to twenty percent of my entire speech?

- Have I practiced the delivery of my introduction so I can present it fluently, confidently, and with strong eye contact?

As you work on your presentations, work to craft an introduction that will capture the attention of your audience. It should arouse the interest of the audience and allow them to become emotionally invested in the speech.

The effectiveness of any introduction, particularly with a personal one, will rely on the presenter's delivery as well as on the content. The methods discussed are the ones used most often by speakers to gain attention and interest. Other methods include referring to the occasion, inviting the audience to participate, using a video or audio clip, visual aids, and beginning with humor. For the presentation, choose the method that is most suitable for the topic, the audience, and the occasion.

REVEAL THE TOPIC and ESTABLISH RELEVANCE FOR THE TOPIC

In the process of gaining attention, be sure to state clearly the topic of your speech. This is a basic point—so basic that it may hardly seem worth mentioning.

ESTABLISH CREDIBILITY

Besides getting attention and revealing the topic, you will need to establish your credibility in your introduction. Credibility is a matter of being qualified to speak on a certain topic, or being perceived as qualified by your audience.

Your credibility does not simply need to be based on firsthand knowledge and experience. It can come from research, from professionals, from interviews, from friends, etc. Whatever the source of your expertise, be sure to let the audience know.

CLEARLY STATE THREE MAIN POINTS (THESIS)

After you have gotten the attention of your audience, established relevance for the topic, established your credibility as a speaker for the topic, be sure to clearly detail the three or four main points that you will be covering during the speech. This needs to be crystal clear so the audience knows the direction you are taking and will be able to follow along.

TIPS FOR THE INTRODUCTION

Keep the introduction relatively brief. Under normal circumstances it should not constitute more than ten to twenty percent of your speech. Be creative in devising your introduction. Experiment with two or three different openings and choose the one that seems most likely to get the audience interested in your speech.

Don't worry about the exact wording of your introduction until you have finished preparing the body of the speech. After you have determined your main points, it will be much easier to make final decisions about how to begin the speech.

Work out your introduction in detail. You can write it out word for word, or outline it. Whichever method you use, practice the introduction over and over until you can deliver it smoothly from a minimum of notes and with strong eye contact.

When you present the speech, don't start talking too soon. Establish eye contact with the audience, smile, and then begin the presentation.

The Conclusion

Your closing remarks are your final impressions and will probably linger in your audience's minds. Be sure to craft your conclusion with as much care as your introduction.

No matter what kind of speech you are giving, the conclusion has two major functions:

1. To let the audience know you are ending the speech.
2. To reinforce the audience's understanding of main points.

SIGNAL END OF THE SPEECH

It may seem obvious that you should let your audience know you are going to stop soon. However, you have heard presentations in which the presenter concludes so abruptly that you are caught off guard. Too sudden an ending will leave the audience confused.

How do you let an audience know your speech is ending? One way is through what you say: "In conclusion," "To wrap things up," "Let me end by saying,"—these are all brief cues that you are getting ready to stop. Successful presenters craft their conclusions to leave a strong impression. The final words fade like the spotlight, bringing the speech to a definitive close.

Summarize Your Speech

Restating the main points is the easiest way to end a speech. The summary clearly restates all main points one last time. Once you have summarized your speech, leave the audience with a closing statement that will keep them thinking about your speech long after the speech is over.

Here are some examples of effective closing statements:

End with a quotation: A quotation is one of the most common and effective devices to conclude a speech. The closing quotation is particularly effective if it can perfectly capture your presentation's overall purpose.

Make a dramatic statement: Rather than using a quotation, you may want to devise your own dramatic statement to rivet your audience with a dramatic concluding statement.

Refer to the introduction: An excellent way to conclude your presentation is to refer to ideas in the introduction.

Summarizing the speech, ending with a quotation, making a dramatic statement, referring to the introduction—all these techniques can be used separately. But you have probably noticed that presenters often combine techniques. One other concluding technique is making a **direct appeal to your audience for action**. The techniques covered are appropriate for all types of presentations.

Conclude with a bang. Be creative in devising a conclusion that will capture the hearts and minds of your audience. Work on several possible endings and select the one that seems likely to have the greatest impact. **Try to be succinct.** The conclusion generally accounts for five to ten percent of your overall presentation.

Don't leave anything in your conclusion to chance. Work it out in detail, and give yourself plenty of time to practice delivering it. You may choose to write out the conclusion word for word. Make your last impression as forceful and as favorable as you can.

Speech Conclusion Checklist

- Did I signal that my speech is coming to an end?
- Have I summarized the main points of my speech?
- Is the conclusion limited to five to ten percent of my entire speech?
- Have I worked out the language of my conclusion in detail?
- Have I practiced the delivery of my conclusion so I can present it fluently, confidently, and with strong eye contact?

First impressions are important. So are final impressions. This is why speeches need strong introductions and conclusions. In most speaking situations, you need to accomplish four objectives with your introduction—get the attention and interest of the audience, reveal the topic of your speech, establish your credibility, and preview the body of the speech. Gaining attention and interest can be done in several ways. You can show the importance of your topic, especially as it relates to your audience. You can startle or question your audience or arouse their curiosity. You can begin with a quotation or a story.

Be sure to state the topic of your speech clearly in your introduction so the audience knows where the speech is going. Establishing credibility means that you tell the audience why you are qualified to speak on the topic. Previewing the body of the speech helps the audience listen effectively and provides a smooth lead-in to the body of the speech.

The first objective of a speech conclusion is to let the audience know you are ending. The second objective of a conclusion is to reinforce your main purpose. You can accomplish this by summarizing the speech, ending with a quotation, making a dramatic statement, or referring to the introduction.

CONNECTIVES

Many presenters, when speaking to an audience, often will rely on "filler words" unconsciously during the presentation. Example words like "alright" or "like" or "uhm" are utilized each time the presenter moves from one thought to the next. After awhile, the audience will begin keeping count. By the end of the presentation, most audience members are too busy waiting for the next filler word, rather than paying attention to the presenter's message. In most cases, presenters are unaware of the overuse of verbal fillers, and those simply pop out when they are unsure of what to say next in the presentation.

When a plethora of verbal fillers are utilized in a presentation, generally what is lacking are strong connectives—words or phrases that join one thought to another. Without connectives, a speech is disjointed and uncoordinated.

We all have stock phrases that we use to fill the space between thoughts. In casual conversation, they are not as much of an issue. However, in speechmaking they distract the audience by calling attention to themselves.

Three types of speech connectives are transitions, internal summaries, and signposts.

Transitions are words or phrases that indicate when a presenter has just completed one thought and is moving on to another. Here is an example: "Now that we have discussed this, let me discuss . . ." This phrase reminds the audience members of the thought just completed, as well as reveal the thought about to be developed.

INTERNAL SUMMARIES

Internal summaries let the audience members know what is coming up next or remind the audience of what they have just heard. Such summaries are an excellent way to clarify and reinforce main points. By combining them with transitions, you can also lead your audience smoothly into your next main point.

SIGNPOSTS

Signposts are very brief statements that indicate exactly where you are in the presentation. You can use signposts to indicate where you are in the speech, or focus attention on key ideas. You can do this with a simple phrase, as in the following example(s):

1. Be sure to keep this in mind . . .
2. This is crucial to understanding the rest of the speech . . .
3. Above all, you need to know . . .

Depending on the needs of your speech, you may want to use two, three, or even all four kinds of connectives in combination. The important thing is to be aware of their functions. Properly applied, connectives can make your presentation more unified and coherent.

Connectives help tie a speech together. They are words or phrases that join one thought to another and indicate the relationship between them. The four major types of speech connectives are transitions, internal previews, internal summaries, and signposts. Using them effectively will make your speeches more unified and coherent.

The new SpeechShark app available in the Apple Store for iOS users and in GooglePlay for Android users makes short work out of writing speech outlines. Just answer the questions and this amazing app does the work for you! Check it out at www.SpeechShark.com.

Constructing the Outline

After reading this chapter, you should be able to answer the following questions:

1. What are the four objectives of a speech introduction?

   _____

   _____

2. What are some methods you can use in the introduction to get the attention and interest of your audience?

   _____

   _____

3. Why is it important to establish your credibility at the beginning of your speech?

   _____

   _____

4. What are six tips for your introduction?

   _____

   _____

5. What are the major functions of a speech conclusion?

   _____

   _____

6. What are two ways you can signal the end of your speech?

_____

_____

7. What are four tips for your conclusion?

_____

_____

8. What are the four kinds of speech connectives? What role does each play in a speech?

_____

_____

Shark Bites

Think of a speech topic (preferably one for your next speech in class). Create an introduction for a speech dealing with any aspect of the topic you wish. The beginning, or introduction, prepares audience members for what is to come. In your introduction, be sure to gain the attention of the audience, reveal the topic to the audience, establish your credibility, and preview the body of the speech.

_____

_____

_____

_____

Using the same topic as above, create a speech conclusion. The conclusion ties up the speech and alerts audience members that the speech is going to end. Be sure to let your audience know the speech is ending, recap the major points, and make the conclusion vivid and memorable.

_____

_____

_____

_____

SpeechSHARK™

Unit #4:

Visual Aids

Creating Presentational Aids

Working with a Tech Team

Key Terms to Know

Chapter 11—Creating Presentational Aids

- Bar Graph
- Chart
- Font
- Graph
- Line Graph
- Pie Graph

Chapter 12—Working with a Tech Team

- Scripts
- Tech Team

Chapter Eleven

Creating Presentational Aids

In this chapter:

What type of visual aids should I use in my speech?

What do I need to know about table displays?

How do I create and manage handouts?

What do I need to know about fonts and graphics?

Generally, an audience will find a presenter's message more effective when it is presented visually as well as verbally. If utilized properly, visual aids should enhance each aspect of the presentation. A presenter who utilizes visual aids will appear better prepared, more credible, and more professional. **Visual aids** should heighten audience interest, shift attention away from the presenter, and give the presenter greater confidence in the presentation as a whole.

Visual aids should add value to your presentation and help your audience to retain the information you share.

Let us look first at the kinds of visual aids you are most likely to use, then at guidelines for preparing visual aids, and finally at guidelines for using visual aids.

OBJECTS

Bring an object related to your presentation, it can be an excellent way to clarify your ideas. If your presentation covers information related to skydiving, why not bring the skydiving equipment to class to show your audience? Or suppose you want to inform your classmates about the art of candle making. Bring several candles to class to display and explain how they were made.

TABLE DISPLAYS

A table display should be visible to the entire audience. It is appropriate to have a table cover, and ensure the table cover is not wrinkled and placed neatly. When creating a table display, only include a collection of props that you plan to refer to in your presentation. Mishaps can be averted if you plan what to include well in advance. Make sure your audience can see everything on your table display. Avoid laying items flat on the table. Instead use easels or boxes to lift items for a clear display. Don't forget the audience members who sit in the back row. Make sure they also have a clear view of items used on your table display.

PHOTOS AND DRAWINGS

Photos make excellent visual aids if they are large enough to be seen easily by your audience. Normal-size photos are generally too small to be seen clearly without being passed around, which only diverts the audience from what you are saying.

The most effective way to show photos is to include them on a PowerPoint or Prezi slide.

GRAPHS

Your audience may have trouble grasping a complex series of numbers. You can ease their difficulty by using graphs to showcase statistical trends and patterns.

A **pie graph** can be used to show the parts of a whole. A pie graph should ideally have from two to five segments.

The **bar graph,** like the one shown on the right, is a particularly good way to show comparisons among two or more items. It also has the advantage of being easy to understand.

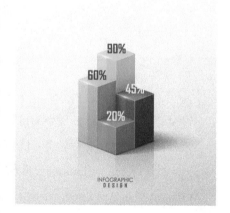

CHARTS

Charts are particularly useful for summarizing large blocks of information. By listing them on a chart, the presenter makes it easier for the audience to retain information. The biggest mistake presenters make when using a chart is to include too much information. Visual aids should be clear, simple, and uncluttered. Lists on a chart should rarely exceed seven or eight items, with generous spacing between items. If you cannot fit everything on a single chart, make a second one.

HANDOUTS

Handouts are used to help the audience retain information supplied during the speech. It is best to create your own handout rather than use a handout designed and distributed by an organization. Usually organizations design handouts for marketing purposes and their material will include company branding and contact information that is not appropriate for a speech, unless you are making a sales presentation for that organization.

Handouts can be anything from an object with a tag, to printed designed handouts that support your speech. A good handout for a cooking demonstration would be a recipe card. If your topic is to motivate your audience to spay or neuter pets, a tri-fold color brochure with information about the process may be more appropriate. If creating brochures, recipe cards, or business card handouts, be sure to use heavy card stock. Color is always a bonus, but if you find the ink costs are too expensive, try printing information on color paper instead of printing with color ink.

Since most speeches for a speech course are not sales presentations, avoid distributing handouts that market one particular company, product, or organization. However, if you are making a sales presentation, your handout should reflect the information, company, and product that you are trying to sell.

As with any visual aid, please make sure fonts and colors are consistent throughout the handout. Check for spelling and grammatical errors prior to printing and distributing the handout.

Distribute handouts before your speech if you need your audience to do something with the handout during your speech. Distribute after your speech if the purpose of the handout is to promote audience retention about the topic.

For a more professional presentation, appoint tech team members to distribute the handout for the speaker, and give clear instructions regarding the time and manner in which the handouts are distributed.

VIDEO CLIPS and MUSIC SOUNDBITES

Adding video clips or music to a speech should be conducted carefully and expertly. First, make sure the clip is not too long. While a 30–45-second video can illustrate your ideas in a memorable way, anything much longer will distract attention from the speech itself. Second, make sure the video or music is cued to start exactly where you want it. Third, if necessary, edit the video or music to the precise length you need so it will blend smoothly into your speech. The last step is to rehearse with your visual aids and with your Tech Team.

YOURSELF

Sometimes you can use your own body as a visual aid—by showing how to perform a skill, talent, and so forth. In addition to clarifying a presenter's ideas, doing some kind of demonstration helps keep the audience involved. It also can reduce a presenter's nervousness by providing an outlet for extra adrenaline. Doing a demonstration will require special practice to coordinate your actions with your words and to control the timing of your speech.

PRESENTATION TECHNOLOGY

Presentation technology allows you to integrate a variety of visual aids—including charts, graphs, photos, and videos in the same presentation. The most commonly used presentation programs are PowerPoint and Prezi.

We will look at guidelines for planning and presenting visual aids effectively. We will also look at the pros and cons to consider and the following factors when thinking about including presentation technology in your speeches.

PLANNING TO USE PRESENTATION TECHNOLOGY

If you are going to employ presentation technology effectively, you need a clear idea of exactly why, how, and when to use it. Rather than putting everything you say on-screen for the audience to read, you need to choose which aspects of your speech to illustrate. This requires careful planning.

The first step is deciding where you can use PowerPoint or some other program to your best advantage. After you have finished developing the speech, think about places where you can incorporate well-developed slides that will genuinely enhance your message.

As you plan your speeches, think about how you can use presentation technology to enhance your ideas. At the same time, remember that too many visuals—or poor visuals—can do more harm than good. Be creative and resourceful without allowing technology to overpower your entire speech.

PROS AND CONS OF PRESENTATION TECHNOLOGY

When used well, presentation technology is a great asset to presentations. Unfortunately, it is not always used well. Too often speakers allow it to dominate their presentation, attempting to wow the audience with their technical proficiency, while losing the message in a flurry of sounds and images.

At the other extreme are mind-numbing presentations that gave rise to the phrase "Death by Power-Point." In such cases, the presenter virtually reads the speech to the audience as the words appear on-screen. This is no more effective than reading dully from a manuscript. Do this and I guarantee you that your audience will be snoozing or making a grocery list, but they will not be listening to your speech.

GUIDELINES FOR PREPARING VISUAL AIDS

Whether you are creating visual aids by hand or with PowerPoint, the following guidelines will help you design aids that are clear and visually appealing.

PREPARE VISUAL AIDS IN ADVANCE

Preparing visual aids well in advance has two advantages. First, it means you will have the time and resources to devise creative, attractive aids. Second, it means you can use them while practicing your speech. Visual aids are effective only when they are integrated smoothly with the rest of the speech. If you lose your place, drop your aids, or otherwise stumble around when presenting them, you will distract your audience and shatter their concentration.

KEEP VISUAL AIDS SIMPLE

Visual aids should be simple, clear, and to the point. They should contain enough information to communicate the presenter's point, but not so much as to confuse or distract the audience. Limit your slides to a manageable amount of information, and beware of the tendency to go overboard.

MAKE SURE VISUAL AIDS CAN BE SEEN

A visual aid is useless if no one can see it. Keep in mind the size of the room in which you will be speaking and make sure your aid is big enough to be seen easily by everyone. Check your visibility by moving to a point as far away from it as your most distant audience member will be seated.

If you are using a presentation program such as PowerPoint, make sure your text and images are easy for everyone in your audience to see. By making sure your visual aid is large enough, you will avoid having to introduce it with the comment "I know some of you can't see this, but . . ."

USE A LIMITED AMOUNT OF TEXT

When displaying text on visual aids, keep it simple. Succinct phrases containing only essential key words will help audience members grasp your basic point and process the information as you're speaking.

One of the biggest mistakes people make with presentation technology is putting too much text on a single slide. A general rule for slides that contain only text is to include no more than seven lines of type. If you are combining text with images, you may need to limit yourself to fewer lines to keep the text from getting too small. If you have a number of important points to cover, spread them out over multiple slides.

USE FONTS EFFECTIVELY: Not all fonts are suitable for visual aids. Using fonts effectively can make a huge difference in your slides. Keep the following guidelines in mind when selecting fonts:

- Select fonts that are clear and easy to read.
- Avoid using ALL CAPS because they are difficult to read.
- Do not use more than two fonts on a single slide—one for the title or major heading and another for subtitles or other text.
- Stay consistent with the same fonts on all your slides.
- Place titles and headings in at least 36- to 44-point type; make subheads and other text at least 24- to 30-point.

If you use one of the built-in themes in PowerPoint, you can be confident that the fonts, which have been preselected according to the design of the theme, are clear, legible, and consistent.

USE COLOR EFFECTIVELY

When used effectively, color can dramatically increase the impact of a visual aid. Some colors do not work well together. You can use either dark print on a light background or light print on a dark background, simply make sure there is enough contrast between the background and the text so the audience can see everything clearly.

Also, stick to a limited number of colors and use them consistently. Use one color for background, one color for titles, and one color for other text throughout all your slides. This consistency will unify the slides and give your speech a professional appearance.

USE IMAGES STRATEGICALLY

One of the benefits of presentation technology is the ease with which it allows you to include photos, charts, graphs, and other images, including video. Unfortunately, some presenters are prone to adding images simply because it is easy, rather than because it is essential for communicating the message. You should never add images of any sort to a slide unless they are truly necessary. There is a great deal of research showing that extraneous images distract audience members and reduce comprehension of the presenter's point.

In addition to keeping your slides free of extraneous images, keep these guidelines in mind:

1. Make sure images are large enough to be seen clearly.
2. Choose high-resolution images that will project without blurring.
3. Keep graphs and charts clear and simple.
4. In most cases, include a title above charts and graphs so the audience knows what they are viewing.
5. Edit videos and music sound bites so they are integrated seamlessly into your slides.

GUIDELINES FOR PRESENTING VISUAL AIDS

No matter how well designed your visual aids may be, they will be of little value unless you display them properly, discuss them clearly, and integrate them effectively with the rest of your presentation. Below are guidelines that will help you get the maximum impact out of your visual aids.

Presenting Visual Aids Checklist

1. Have I prepared my visual aids well in advance?

2. Are my visual aids clear and easy to comprehend?

3. Does each visual aid contain only the information needed to make my point?

4. Are my visual aids large enough to be seen clearly by the entire audience?

5. Do the colors on my visual aids work well together?

6. Is there a clear contrast between the lettering and background on my charts, graphs, and drawings?

7. Do I use line graphs, pie graphs, and bar graphs correctly to show statistical trends and patterns?

8. Do I limit charts to no more than eight items?

9. Do I utilize fonts that are easy to read?

DISPLAY VISUAL AIDS SO AUDIENCE CAN VIEW

Check the speech room ahead of time to decide exactly where you will display your visual aids. If you are displaying an object or a model, be sure to place it where it can be seen easily by everyone in the room. If necessary, hold up the object or model while you are discussing it.

Once you have set the aid in the best location, don't undo all your preparation by standing where you block the audience's view of the aid. Stand to one side of the aid, and point with the arm nearest it. You can also utilize a pointer, which will allow you to stand farther away from the visual aid, also preventing you from obstructing the view of the audience.

AVOID PASSING VISUAL AIDS AMONG THE AUDIENCE

Once visual aids get into the hands of your audience, they will be paying more attention to the aid than to you and are likely to spend a good part of the speech looking over the handout at their own pace, rather than listening to you. Although handouts can be valuable, they usually just create competition for novice presenters.

Here is a tip to help you understand WHEN to distribute handouts:

If you plan to use the handout during your speech, please ask your Tech Team to distribute the handouts before you take the stage to speak. If you plan to use the handout as a method of helping the audience remember your speech or to use as a point of reference after the speech is over, ask your Tech Team to distribute the handout after the speech is over and you have exited the stage. This will get the handout into your audience members' hands, but will not cause a distraction.

DISPLAY VISUAL AIDS ONLY WHILE DISCUSSING THEM

Just as circulating visual aids distracts attention, so does displaying them throughout a speech. If you are using an object or a model, keep it out of sight until you are ready to discuss it. When you finish your discussion, place the object or model back out of sight.

The same principle applies to PowerPoint slides. They should be visible only while you are discussing them. You can accomplish this by adding blank slides as needed, so the audience's attention will not be diverted by the prior slide. It is also a good idea to add a blank slide at the end of your presentation, so your last content slide will not continue to be exposed after you have finished discussing it.

EXPLAIN VISUAL AIDS CLEARLY

A visual aid can be of enormous benefit—but only if the audience member knows what to look for and why. Unfortunately, presenters often rush over their visual aids without explaining them clearly and concisely. Don't just say "As you can see . . ." and then pass quickly over the aid. Tell the audience what the aid means. Remember, a visual aid is only as useful as the explanation that goes with it. It should integrate into the speech smoothly and skillfully—and you should strive to maintain eye contact with the audience when you present visual aids in your presentation.

TALK TO THE AUDIENCE, NOT THE VISUAL AID

When explaining a visual aid, it is easy to break eye contact with your audience and talk to the aid. Of course, your audience is looking primarily at the aid, and you may need to glance at it periodically as you talk. But if you keep your eyes fixed on the visual aid, you will lose your audience. By keeping eye contact, you can also pick up feedback about how the visual aid and your explanation of it are coming across.

There are many kinds of visual aids. Most obvious is the object about which you are speaking. Photos should be large enough to be seen clearly by all your audience members. Graphs are an excellent way to illustrate any subject dealing with numbers, while charts are used to summarize large blocks of information. Videos can be useful as a visual aid, but it needs to be carefully edited and integrated into the speech. You can act as your own visual aid by performing actions that demonstrate processes or ideas.

If you use presentation technology, plan carefully why, how, and when you will utilize it. Rather than putting everything you say on-screen for your audience to read, use the technology only when it will genuinely enhance your message.

No matter what kind of visual aid you use, you need to prepare it carefully. You will be most successful if you prepare your aids well in advance, keep them simple, make sure they are large enough to be seen clearly, and utilize a limited amount of text. If you are creating visual aids utilizing presentation technology, use fonts, color, and images strategically and effectively.

In addition to being designed with care, visual aids need to be presented skillfully. Avoid passing visual aids among the audience. Display each aid only while you are talking about it, and be sure everyone can see it without straining. When presenting a visual aid, maintain eye contact with your audience and explain the aid clearly and concisely. If you are using presentation technology, make sure you check the room and equipment prior to the time of delivery. Above all, practice with your visual aids so they fit into your speech smoothly and expertly.

Visual Aids

After reading this chapter, you should be able to answer the following questions:

1. What are the major advantages of using visual aids in your speeches?

    _____

    _____

2. What kinds of visual aids might you use in a speech?

    _____

    _____

3. What factors should you consider when planning to use presentation technology in a speech?

    _____

    _____

4. What guidelines are given in the chapter for preparing visual aids?

    _____

    _____

Shark Bites

Watch a how-to television program (a cooking show, for example) or the weather portion of a local newscast. Notice how the presenter uses visual aids to help communicate the message. What kinds of visual aids are used? How do they enhance the clarity, interest, and retainability of the message? What would the presenter have to do to communicate the message effectively without visual aids?

_____

_____

_____

_____

Plan to use visual aids for your next speech. Be creative in devising your aids, and be sure to follow the guidelines discussed in the chapter for using them. After the speech, analyze how effectively you employed your visual aids, what you learned about the use of visual aids from your experience, and what changes you would make in using visual aids if you were to deliver the speech again.

_____

_____

_____

_____

Chapter Twelve

Working with a Tech Team

In this chapter:

How do I assign a tech team?

What do I need to know about rehearsing with a tech team?

ASSIGNING A TECH TEAM

As a speaker, you will notice there are many pieces to the speech puzzle and you will need help pulling it all together. To do this, you need a **tech team**. What is a tech team? This is a group of people qualified to help complete your speech presentation by setting up or breaking down, managing the PowerPoint/Prezi slides, managing lighting and sound requirements, and distributing handouts. Most speeches will require visual aids, handouts, lighting effects, sound, microphones, and backstage support. As with anything, the buck stops with you. The success of your speech depends upon you to cover every detail and that includes working with a tech team.

Never assume that your tech team will know what you want them to do. Consider yourself as a project manager and the speech is your project.

To accomplish the project, there are many strategies for getting the job done and according to expectations. Yet, these things do not just happen on their own. You have to plan for the success of your speech presentation.

First take a look at your speech plan. Answer the following questions:

1. What will you need to complete the speech project?

   _____

   _____

2. Who can help you reach your goals?

   _____

   _____

3. Is your tech team member qualified with the areas where you need help?

   _____

   _____

4. Did you supply a script for the tech team?

   _____

   _____

5. Can your tech team rehearse with you?

   _____

   _____

6. Do you have the materials and supplies needed for the tech team to do their jobs?

   _____

   _____

7. Can you count on your tech team member to be there and to be prepared?

   _____

   _____

Once you know what you need, you can begin assigning responsibilities for your tech team.

Ask questions! Make sure you KNOW that your tech team members understand how to run a simple PowerPoint or Prezi presentation. If they do not know, make plans to rehearse with them and show them how to do this. OR, fire that tech team member and appoint a new one!

Choose the number of tech team members you need for the speech. One or two tech team members may be enough, but if the presentation is complicated and involves multiple aspects, you will need to add tech team members.

Without a shadow of a doubt, you should be able to count on your tech team members to arrive on time and to be prepared. There is nothing in this world that can shake your speech-making resolve faster than to arrive for the speech and not see tech team members until five minutes before the speech begins! YIKES! That is when you will feel like a guppy navigating in murky waters and the results may not be pretty. Be a Speech-Shark and be prepared!

Use the following Tech Team Checklist to make sure you are prepared.

TECH TEAM CHECKLIST

Complete this form as you plan the use of visual aids so that you are prepared for the speech. Speakers who use visual aids will need to make use of a tech team. It is the speaker's responsibility to meet with the tech team ahead of time, provide a script, and rehearse with the tech team to make sure they understand what is needed. Visual aids are an important part of the speech and a direct reflection of your credibility as a speaker.

Date: _____ **Time of Speech**: _____

Type of Speech: _____

Description of Visual Aids:

_____

_____

_____

_____

Note: In the area below, please list each tech team member's name and assigned duties. Be sure to assign a member for the PowerPoint, sound, lights, setup, breakdown, and distribution of handouts. All duties may not be needed for all speeches.

Tech Team Member's Name: _____

Duties Assigned: _____

Tech Team Member's Name: _____

Duties Assigned: _____

Tech Team Member's Name: _____

Duties Assigned: _____

Tech Team Member's Name: _____

Duties Assigned: _____

_____

REHEARSING WITH A TECH TEAM

This part of your responsibility does not happen on its own. It is YOUR speech and it is YOUR responsibility to arrange the rehearsals with your tech team. Your speech will only be as good as your tech team! One slide out of place, one video that does not play as planned, one sound-bite or music segment that is not properly executed will affect your credibility as a speaker.

Now that you have identified tech team members, arrange at least two rehearsals with them prior to your speech. If possible, have the rehearsals in the place where you are going to make the presentation so that you can also become familiar with the stage, lights, and sound system.

As your tech team members arrive, shake their hands and tell them how much you appreciate their help with the presentation. Introduce the tech team members to each other and identify their responsibilities during the presentation. After the rehearsals and after your presentation, please make sure to thank each person who helped make your presentation spectacular! Even small details completed on your behalf add up to a big deal on speech day.

Distribute a script to each tech team member. Although you will have one basic script, it is a good idea to highlight and personalize each script so that it is clear what you want each tech team member to do during the presentation.

In the pages that follow, you will see a separate script for each of the three tech team members needed for the informative speech. Notice how each script is designed for the tech team member and highlights the job tasks needed for the speech.

EXAMPLE

SCRIPT: POWERPOINT PRESENTATION– TECH TEAM MEMBER #1

Penny J. Waddell
Toastmasters International Meeting
30 June 2017

Speech Category: Informative Speech
Title: How to Dress for an Interview
Purpose: The purpose of this speech is to inform my audience how to dress for an interview.

Introduction: As speaker is introduced, please have Slide #1 up.
Attention Step: (Show pictures on a PowerPoint Slide of different people dressed in different ways. One person is dressed in jeans, flip-flops, and a T-shirt; another is dressed in a short minidress with tattoos showing on her arms and legs; another is dressed business casual.) Take a look at the pictures of these three candidates who are about to interview for a job position at a Fortune 500 Company. Which candidate do you think will get the job?
Establish Need/Relevance: The truth is that any one of these candidates MAY get the job. The secret is knowing with which company the candidate is interviewing? If interviewing for a position at GOOGLE, the jeans and T-shirt may be appropriate. If interviewing for a position with The Coca Cola Company in Atlanta, the candidate dressed business casual may get the job. Before interviewing for a job position, be sure to know what type of dress is expected.
Establish Speaker Credibility: I am credible to speak to you today about dressing for an interview because I have recently interviewed for a job position and got the job! For the position, I needed to dress in an upscale suit, very little jewelry, and I needed to project extreme professionalism.
Thesis: Today, I will cover three points to inform you how to dress for an interview. (1) Research the company, (2) Understand the culture of the company, and (3) Put your best foot forward.

Body: During the transition sentence, please go to Slide #2—Research the Company.
Transition/Link: Let's begin with the first point, research the company.
    I. Research the Company
        A. What type of business does this company do?
        B. What type of work responsibilities are expected?

Transition/Link: I've shared the importance of researching the company with you, now I'd like to tell you how to understand the culture of the company. During the transition sentence, please go to Slide #3— Understand the Culture of the Company.
    II. Understand the Culture of the Company
        A. Make a trip to the company prior to the Interview (Quast).
        B. Watch to see how other employees dress.

Transition/Link: You've heard how to research the company and how to understand its culture, now I want to show you how to put your best foot forward. During the transition sentence, please go to Slide #4—Put Your Best Foot Forward.
    III. Put Your Best Foot Forward
        A. Choose clothing, shoes, and accessories that mirror how other employees in this company dress.
        B. Err on the conservative side, but don't forget to show your personality.

Transition/Link: Now you should understand a little more about how to dress for an interview.
Conclusion: During the transition sentence, please go to Slide #5—Quote.
Summary: Today, I shared with you three points: (1) Research the company, (2) Understand the culture of the company, and (3) Put your best foot forward.
Appeal to Action: As you interview for what might very well be the most important interview of your life, be sure to remember that "You never get a second chance to make a first impression" (Quast). With this quote, I want to challenge you to dress for success and make sure this interview is the one that will help you get your dream job!
Following the Appeal to Action, please go to slide #6—Blank Slide. After speaker leaves the stage, please take down the PowerPoint.

(Note: The Works Cited page should be added as a separate page following the Outline.)

Works Cited

Quast, Lisa. "8 Tips to Dress for Interview Success." *Forbes*. 2014. Accessed 12 March 2017.

(Note: The Visual Aids Explanation page is a separate page from the Outline and the Works Cited page.)

Visual Aids Explanation Page

PowerPoint Presentation:
Slide #1: Title of Speech—**How to Dress for an Interview**
    Pictures of Three People Dressed Differently
Slide #2: (Point #1): **Research the Company**
    Bullet Points:
      • Type of Business
      • Type of Work Responsibilities
Slide #3: (Point #2): **Understand the Culture of the Company**
    Picture of Business with Employees Entering the Door
Slide #4: (Point #3): **Put Your Best Foot Forward**
    Picture of Professionally Dressed Employee
Slide #5: **"You Never Get a Second Chance to Make a First Impression" (Quast)**
    Picture of a Group of Professionally Dressed Employees

EXAMPLE

SCRIPT: TABLE DISPLAY–TECH TEAM MEMBER #2

Penny J. Waddell
Toastmasters International Meeting
30 June 2017

Speech Category: Informative Speech
Title: How to Dress for an Interview
Purpose: The purpose of this speech is to inform my audience how to dress for an interview.

Introduction: Prior to introduction, please set up the Table Display—Table Cloth, Books/mannequin with suit and tie

Attention Step: (Show pictures on a PowerPoint Slide of different people dressed in different ways. One person is dressed in jeans, flip-flops, and a T-shirt; another is dressed in a short minidress with tattoos showing on her arms and legs; another is dressed business casual). Take a look at the pictures of these three candidates who are about to interview for a job position at a Fortune 500 Company. Which candidate do you think will get the job?

Establish Need/Relevance: The truth is that any one of these candidates MAY get the job. The secret is knowing with which company the candidate is interviewing? If interviewing for a position at GOOGLE, the jeans and T-shirt may be appropriate. If interviewing for a position with The Coca Cola Company in Atlanta, the candidate dressed business casual may get the job. Before interviewing for a job position, be sure to know what type of dress is expected.

Establish Speaker Credibility: I am credible to speak to you today about dressing for an interview because I have recently interviewed for a job position and got the job! For the position, I needed to dress in an upscale suit, very little jewelry, and I needed to project extreme professionalism.

Thesis: Today, I will cover three points to inform you how to dress for an interview. (1) Research the company, (2) Understand the culture of the company, and (3) Put your best foot forward.

Body:
Transition/Link: Let's begin with the first point, research the company.
    I. Research the Company
        A. What type of business does this company do?
        B. What type of work responsibilities are expected?
Transition/Link: I've shared the importance of researching the company with you, now I'd like to tell you how to understand the culture of the company.
    II. Understand the Culture of the Company
        A. Make a trip to the company prior to the Interview (Quast).
        B. Watch to see how other employees dress.

Transition/Link: You've heard how to research the company and how to understand its culture, now I want to show you how to put your best foot forward.
    III. Put Your Best Foot Forward
        A. Choose clothing, shoes, and accessories that mirror how other employees in this company dress.
        B. Err on the conservative side, but don't forget to show your personality.

Transition/Link: Now you should understand a little more about how to dress for an interview.
Conclusion:
Summary: Today, I shared with you three points: (1) Research the company, (2) Understand the culture of the company, and (3) Put your best foot forward.
Appeal to Action: As you interview for what might very well be the most important interview of your life, be sure to remember that "You never get a second chance to make a first impression" (Quast). With this quote, I want to challenge you to dress for success and make sure this interview is the one that will help you get your dream job!
Following the speech, please dismantle the table display and remove it from the stage.

(Note: The Works Cited page should be added as a separate page following the Outline.)

Works Cited

Quast, Lisa. "8 Tips to Dress for Interview Success." *Forbes.* 2014. Accessed 12 March 2017.

(Note: The Visual Aids Explanation page is a separate page from the Outline and the Works Cited page).

Visual Aids Explanation Page

PowerPoint Presentation:
Slide #1:   Title of Speech—**How to Dress for an Interview**
            Pictures of Three People Dressed Differently
Slide #2:   (Point #1): **Research the Company**
            Bullet Points:
              • Type of Business
              • Type of Work Responsibilities
Slide #3:   (Point #2): **Understand the Culture of the Company**
            Picture of Business with Employees Entering the Door
Slide #4:   (Point #3): **Put Your Best Foot Forward**
            Picture of Professionally Dressed Employee
Slide #5:   **"You Never Get a Second Chance to Make a First Impression" (Quast)**
            Picture of a Group of Professionally Dressed Employees

EXAMPLE

SCRIPT: HANDOUT DISTRIBUTION–TECH TEAM MEMBER #3

Penny J. Waddell
Toastmasters International Meeting
30 June 2017

Speech Category: Informative Speech
Title: How to Dress for an Interview
Purpose: The purpose of this speech is to inform my audience how to dress for an interview.

Introduction:
Attention Step: (Show pictures on a PowerPoint Slide of different people dressed in different ways. One person is dressed in jeans, flip-flops, and a T-shirt; another is dressed in a short minidress with tattoos showing on her arms and legs; another is dressed business casual.) Take a look at the pictures of these three candidates who are about to interview for a job position at a Fortune 500 Company. Which candidate do you think will get the job?

Establish Need/Relevance: The truth is that any one of these candidates MAY get the job. The secret is knowing with which company the candidate is interviewing. If interviewing for a position at GOOGLE, the jeans and T-shirt may be appropriate. If interviewing for a position with The Coca Cola Company in Atlanta, the candidate dressed business casual may get the job. Before interviewing for a job position, be sure to know what type of dress is expected.

Establish Speaker Credibility: I am credible to speak to you today about dressing for an interview because I have recently interviewed for a job position and got the job! For the position, I needed to dress in an upscale suit, very little jewelry, and I needed to project extreme professionalism.

Thesis: Today, I will cover three points to inform you how to dress for an interview. (1) Research the company, (2) Understand the culture of the company, and (3) Put your best foot forward.

Body:
Transition/Link: Let's begin with the first point, research the company.

    I. Research the Company
        A. What type of business does this company do?
        B. What type of work responsibilities are expected?

Transition/Link: I've shared the importance of researching the company with you, now I'd like to tell you how to understand the culture of the company.

    II. Understand the Culture of the Company
        A. Make a trip to the company prior to the Interview (Quast).
        B. Watch to see how other employees dress.

Transition/Link: You've heard how to research the company and how to understand its culture, now I want to show you how to put your best foot forward.

    III. Put Your Best Foot Forward
        A. Choose clothing, shoes, and accessories that mirror how other employees in this company dress.
        B. Err on the conservative side, but don't forget to show your personality.

Transition/Link: Now you should understand a little more about how to dress for an interview.

Conclusion:

Summary: Today, I shared with you three points: (1) Research the company, (2) Understand the culture of the company, and (3) Put your best foot forward.

Appeal to Action: As you interview for what might very well be the most important interview of your life, be sure to remember that "You never get a second chance to make a first impression" (Quast). With this quote, I want to challenge you to dress for success and make sure this interview is the one that will help you get your dream job!

Following the speech, please distribute the handouts. Make sure each person in the audience receives one.

(Note: The Works Cited page should be added as a separate page following the Outline.)

Works Cited

Quast, Lisa. "8 Tips to Dress for Interview Success." *Forbes.* 2014. Accessed 12 March 2017.

(Note: The Visual Aids Explanation page is a separate page from the Outline and the Works Cited page.)

Visual Aids Explanation Page

PowerPoint Presentation:

Slide #1: Title of Speech—**How to Dress for an Interview**
 Pictures of Three People Dressed Differently

Slide #2: (Point #1): **Research the Company**
 Bullet Points:
- Type of Business
- Type of Work Responsibilities

Slide #3: (Point #2): **Understand the Culture of the Company**
 Picture of Business with Employees Entering the Door

Slide #4: (Point #3): **Put Your Best Foot Forward**
 Picture of Professionally Dressed Employee

Slide #5: **"You Never Get a Second Chance to Make a First Impression" (Quast)**
 Picture of a Group of Professionally Dressed Employees

Working with a Tech Team

After you read this chapter, you will be able to answer the following questions:

1. What are the responsibilities of a tech team? _____

   _____

   _____

2. What should you provide to your tech team so they can complete the assigned tasks?

   _____

   _____

3. What will you need to do to plan a rehearsal with a tech team? _____

   _____

   _____

4. How many basic scripts are necessary? _____

   _____

   _____

5. What will you need to do to personalize each script?_____

   _____

   _____

6. How many tech team members are needed for a presentation? _____

_____

_____

7. Your next speech is coming up soon, what aspects are you including in your speech that may require a

tech team? _____

_____

_____

8. What time will your tech team need to arrive? _____

_____

_____

9. What will you need to do to make sure your tech team is prepared? _____

_____

_____

10. Whose responsibility is it to make sure your tech team is prepared? _____

_____

_____

Shark Bites

BUILDING YOUR TECH TEAM

List the visual aids and technical assistance that you will need for your speech. Assign a tech team member to each duty and set up a rehearsal schedule with them. Create the script for each tech team member.

Tech Team Member's Name:	Duty Assigned	Rehearsal Date Scheduled
	PowerPoint	
	Stage Setup	
	Lights	
	Sound/Microphone	
	Distribute Handouts	
	Stage Breakdown	

SpeechSHARK™

Unit #5:

Presenting the Speech

Presentation Skills

*Rehearsing the Speech and
Creating a Speech Day Checklist*

Evaluating the Speech

Specialty Speeches

Key Terms to Know

Chapter 13—Presentation Skills

- Albert Mehrabian
- Aromatherapy
- Body Language Cues
- Breathing
- Chronemics
- Color
- Dialects
- Eye Contact
- Facial Expressions
- Filler Words
- Gestures
- Haptics
- Head Tilting and Head Nodding
- Intimate Space
- Larynx
- Meditation
- Movement
- Non-Verbal Communication
- Pace
- Paralanguage
- Personal Space
- Physical Appearance
- Pitch
- Poise
- Posture

- Proxemics
- Public Space Rate
- Smiling
- Social Space
- Speech Anxiety
- Verbal Communication
- Volume

Chapter 14—Rehearsing the Speech and Creating a Speech Day Checklist

- Presentation
- Rehearse

Chapter 16—Specialty Speeches

- Competition Speeches
- Debates
- Humorous Speeches
- Improvisational Speeches
- Oral Interpretation
- PechaKucha Presentations
- Specialty Speeches
- Storytelling
- TED Talks

Chapter Thirteen
Presentation Skills

In this chapter:

Are you waiting for your ship to come in?

Who can answer my questions about presentation skills?

ARE YOU WAITING FOR YOUR SHIP TO COME IN?

If you are sitting around waiting for your ship to come in, then you really should take another look at details involved with achieving success.

Some people think they will find success as they sit in their sturdy little rowboat, master of their own ship, and armed with a strong work ethic and perhaps a few well-chosen tools (oars would be helpful). These people believe that they will row, row, row the boat toward their goals and ultimately find success! And, they may find success eventually and with a great deal of effort! But, that is not YOU!

Other people think they can sit back on their rickety old raft in a nice comfortable lounge chair with a glass of sweet Georgia tea close by and just follow the wind until, hopefully, success finds them! These dreamers believe they are so wonderful that sooner or later someone will notice how great they are and will drag them and their raft directly into the success stream! But, that is not YOU, either!

On the other hand, YOU stand at the helm of your stately sailboat with well-chosen officers on either side and a crew of qualified mates helping you to chart a course and carefully follow the route toward success. YOU have the vision to see what is beyond the horizon. Your loyal officers are paying attention to all details required to set manageable goals and your crew is determined to help you reach those goals. Yet, all of you realize that without the "wind in the sails," your sailboat will go nowhere. The wind is the motivation that comes from within! This is the force that will move this stately sailboat toward the goal. This is the catalyst that is needed to propel you, your officers, your crew, and passengers to success! Yes, this is YOU!

How did you arrive at this type of thinking? How do we know this is YOU? We know this because YOU are the person who sees the value in making good choices regarding your support staff! YOU are the kind of person who chooses to use a great app like SpeechShark to help draft and create speeches intended to reach your goals. YOU are the kind of person who reads a speech textbook to learn about extra tools needed to help you become the speaker you want to be.

You are the captain of your ship and you don't have to "wait for your ship to come in" because YOU are the one who is navigating the ship toward success! Whether you are making a point during a speech presentation with an audience or with your co-workers and colleagues, SpeechShark can help you verbally express your dreams and share enthusiasm for things that motivate and move you! Yes, this is YOU!

Questions? Yes, you will have lots of questions, but we have the answers. In the pages to follow, we have listed your questions about presentation skills and SpeechShark answers!

QUESTIONS AND ANSWERS ABOUT PRESENTATION SKILLS

What do you need to know about Verbal and Non-Verbal Communication Skills?

Verbal language transmits words and thoughts. Non-verbal language transmits feelings. Whether you realize it or not, your body is speaking volumes. What you DO speaks so loudly that I cannot hear what you say! Because of this, it is important to be aware of what you don't say. Body language is unconscious and it is the most honest form of communication we use. Our body language communicates true feelings even while we may be using words that communicate something entirely different!

In the communication field, Albert Mehrabian is a name often mentioned as we explore non-verbal communication skills. Mehrabian is a scholar who conducted non-verbal research and reported his findings in a book entitled *Silent Messages*. These findings were reported again in *Communication Theory*, edited by C. David Mortensen. Mehrabian's first findings were reported and tested again to show the very same results. In *Communication Theory*, published almost thirty years later, Mehrabian's findings are reported in a formula that many people are still trying to refute: "Total Impact 100% = .07 verbal + .38 vocal + .55 facial" (193).

Let me explain this in another way.

There are three primary areas of communication: verbal, vocal, and visual. 7% of our communication involves words (verbal), 38% of our communication involves how you say the words (vocal), and 55% of our communication is what others see (visual) while we are speaking. In other words, Mehrabian's findings suggest that 93% of all communication is actually non-verbal. Your body is speaking volumes!

Body language cues are communication signals that we send non-verbally. These cues help us to read the speaker's thoughts and feelings. While we are not mind readers, we do learn to read the cues sent to us. Here are five areas to consider about non-verbal communication: **paralanguage, kinesics, proxemics, chronemics, and haptics**. We'll discuss these areas one at a time.

What vocal cues are important for public speaking?

Paralanguage is the vocal part of speech and involves volume, rate, pitch, pace, and color. To have vocal variance, you will want to incorporate varying degrees of all these aspects. To create more emphasis or effects for your speech topic, you might choose to say some words louder or softer, some faster and others softer, some words with more emphasis showing energy for the topic, anger, or any other emotion.

Volume is the level at which a sound is heard. While it is important for the audience to hear your voice, your volume does not need to be so loud that it appears you are shouting. Speak at a volume that will allow everyone in the room to hear your message. You control this by the volume of air you project using your **larynx** or voice box. More air = louder volume. Less air = softer volume. If you normally have a softer voice, you might require a microphone to be heard comfortably by your audience. If this is the case, be sure to rehearse using the microphone prior to your speech so that you understand how to use it correctly.

Rate is the method we use to determine how fast or slow someone is speaking. Many speakers tend to speed up because their nerves often push them into overdrive. This is a normal result of adrenaline pumping through your body and causing your heart rate to rev up; resulting in faster speech. While this is not always a problem, it can cause your audience to have trouble following your message because they will not have time to comprehend everything that you say. What can you do to make sure your speech is presented at a comfortable rate? Rehearse your speech, video or audio record your rehearsal, and evaluate the rate at which you speak. Try to take notes of your speech as you listen to the recording. Do you have time to make notes? If not, then your speech rate may be too fast. Consciously make an effort to slow down your rate of speech. Is your rate too slow? Plan to speed up the speech to keep your audience sitting on the edge of their seats!

Pitch is determined by sounds produced by vocal cord vibrations. Faster vibrations result in higher pitches. Slower vibrations result in lower pitches. Typically, women and children have a higher pitch. Men normally have a lower pitch. While this is typical, it is not absolute. Women and children can slow the vocal cord vibrations to achieve a lower pitch and men can speed vocal cord vibrations to achieve a higher pitch when needed. Varying pitch is important to having good vocal variance. A constant pitch results in a monotone voice and this is truly one sure way to lose your audience because a monotone voice lacks interest, variety, and energy like the monotone teacher in Charlie Brown cartoons, "Mwa, mwa, mwa, mwa, mwa, mwa!"

Pace is the rate at which you say syllables in a word. For example, people from the southern states in America usually add a couple of extra syllables in words that folks from the northern states do not. Southerners tend to say the word, well, in two syllables. Here is an example of a typical slower pace to say, "Well, I don't think so!":

Color involves the energy, enthusiasm, feelings, and attitudes that are included in our message. It may have negative or positive implications and can extend to what we see as much as what we hear. Our voice can show color when we tell a story that describes our exhilaration about a new game or fear of the unknown. Color can also be added as we discuss our customs, habits, or describe a place or a person. We love to hear color in a speech. It is how a speaker can add a little spark to the speech!

Dialects often surface as we discuss paralanguage. Dialects are a form of language heard from people living in a particular region, but this term can also be used as we discuss language indigenous to people from specific social or cultural groups. You will hear dialects referred to as local speech, regional speech patterns, languages, linguistics, vernacular, or accents. Dialects may include variations of grammar, vocabulary, and pronunciations. For example, if someone described the man at the store as having a French accent, they would be describing the man's regional speech patterns that would lead the listener to think the man was from a French-speaking part of our world. A phonetic and/or cultural analysis can result in identifying the continent or region where the dialect is most often spoken.

Effective language skills also surface as we discuss paralanguage. It is not enough to have a great topic with research and stories to support the topic, speakers also need to use effective language skills to be a good communicator. In other words, make sure your language skills are clear, concise, and constructive! Here are some tips for using effective language skills:

- Use standard English grammar, mechanics, and language.
- Use concrete and specific language and avoid using vague or abstract language.
- Avoid using acronyms or descriptions that only select audience members will grasp. If you need to use an acronym, identify the full meaning of the acronym before going into detail.
- Create images using adjectives to describe situations or people.
- Eliminate filler words that do not serve a purpose.
- Use vocabulary and grammar that is easily understood by your audience to establish a sense of commonality with the audience.
- Use language that is on the educational level of audience members. Do not talk "above" or "below" your audience's level of understanding.

How do I avoid using "Filler Words"?

Well, you know, it is uhm, like, well, like totally the most annoying thing you can hear, you know, in somebody's well, uh, you know, their speech presentation. It's uhm, the words that people, uhm, well, you know, they add them to what they are uhm, trying to say, when well, you know what I mean, they are so darn aggravating, and you like, well you hear them literally all of the time. You know?

You are in good company because about six million other people have asked this question. **Filler words** are the types of phrases, sounds, or words that speakers use to fill in an awkward pause when trying to communicate a thought or make a speech presentation. Filler words are contagious and socio-linguistically, can be a tribal form of bonding. Filler words are heard in formal speeches and in social conversations. They are "like" everywhere and add no value to the sentence or thought being communicated.

Do you use filler words? Many people use these words without ever realizing how often they use them and how distracting they might be. Once you realize you are using them, you might discover that sometimes you use them more than other times. Often people use them as a filler when they can't think of the word or thought they are trying to share. We feel that the sound helps to soften the pause while we search for the right word. Truthfully, the sound distracts the listener from hearing the full meaning we are attempting to communicate.

Speakers use filler words when:

1. Searching for the right words

2. Filling an awkward pause

3. Making a sentence sound more passive

4. Making a sentence sound more active

5. Sharing what you are thinking

6. Bonding with a friend that speaks with fillers

7. Expanding the sentence to take more time

8. Sharing the idea/experience with the listener

While it is acceptable to use an occasional filler word, it is important that you do not overuse them. Pausing to think of an answer or to remember your next point is a much better option than uhm, well, you know, throwing in a word or two that well uhm, like basically stretches out the moment but not the meaning.

Here are the filler words that you hear most often: Like, ya know, okay, uhm, uh, er, hmmm, so, well, literally, totally, clearly, actually, basically, seriously, really, like, I mean, just, whatever, I guess or I suppose, very, right, but, sorry, anyway, and, uh huh, uh uh, and any combinations of the above. Whew, I'll bet you thought that sentence would never end!

So, well, like, what can do you do to like, totally, get rid of all the well, you know what I mean, those annoying filler words?

Become aware of your filler word habit! Prepare and practice before speaking opportunities. Video or audio-record your speech rehearsals. Count the number of filler words you have in your presentation, speech, audition, pitch, toast, and so forth, and keep working until you eliminate as many filler words as possible.

My friend, Audrey Mann Cronin, is an acknowledged and long-time communication expert in the technology industry. She is on a mission to help us all become better speakers and created *LikeSo: Your Personal Speech Coach,* a mobile app that helps you to talk your way to success. Using voice recognition technology, *LikeSo* is a fun and effective way to practice being a more confident and articulate speaker. Speak into the microphone of your smartphone and LikeSo captures your words and helps you train and remove all of those filler words that undermine your speech, weaken your meaning, and distract your listeners. *LikeSo* also measures pacing (150 wpm considered optimal) and allows you to set goals, reminders, and track your progress over time (day/week/month/year). It is like a "Fitbit for your speech." Just search the app store: http://Apple.co/1QBuByY or the Web site: https//sayitlikeso.com and for only 99 cents you can get your own personal speech coach that will help you to be a more powerful, persuasive, and articulate speaker.

I have the app and enjoy using it with students and speakers that I coach. It is so easy! Just choose "Free-Style," your open mic for any upcoming speaking opportunity, or "TalkAbout" a conversation game to practice speaking on the fly with topics including "The Job Interview," "Debate Team," and "Small Talk." Choose your talk time, the filler words you want to train against, and receive a Speech Fitness Report. You can also follow her on Facebook, Twitter, and Instagram at @LikeSoApp. Here is a picture so that you will recognize it in the Apple Store:

Now that we know how to avoid distracting fillers, let's take a look at other important non-verbal cues.

Kinesics are physical cues we see. Following Mehrabian's research, 55% of non-verbal communication is visual and covers the majority of cues we use to read a situation. We begin evaluating and making judgments based upon what we see from the moment the speaker enters the stage area. These judgments continue until the speaker leaves the stage. As we watch the speaker, we evaluate the credibility of the speaker using his physical appearance, posture, poise, gestures, facial expressions, eye contact, smiling, and body movements. Often, we establish a judgment about the speaker before the speaker ever utters the first word. Although we would like to argue that we are not quite so petty, Albert Mehrabian's research findings prove the opposite. So, what do we need to learn from this? Take care that you are putting your best foot forward. Plan to show positive physical cues for your audience.

What type of appearance is expected during a speech?

Appearance is a non-verbal cue. Whether you are in a public speaking environment or a social arena, be very aware of the cues you are sending. The clothes and shoes you wear, the jewelry you choose, the type briefcase or bag you carry all speak to your brand. Take a look at the way you see yourself. Does your appearance reflect your own self-awareness? Do you understand your conscious and unconscious non-verbal cues through your choice of clothing and accessories?

Truthfully, there are many sides of you. There is the playful and casual side that is evident in the way you dress and behave when you are with your family and close friends. When at work, you may dress a bit more conservatively and more in keeping with the culture of the workplace. There is a romantic side when you are with the love of your life. Attitudes, beliefs, and values are often reflected in the type clothing we choose. It is appropriate to change appearances for different occasions and circumstances, but it is equally important to realize when to dress and groom in a particular manner.

Appearance is not just about the clothing, shoes, jewelry, and accessories that you choose, but also about grooming. Ask yourself the following questions:

- How does your clothing fit?
- Are your shoes polished?
- What colors do you choose?
- What styles appeal to you?
- What type hairstyle do you have?
- Are your clothes ironed or wrinkled?
- Does your clothing complement your accessories?
- Is your hair clean and styled?
- Are your fingernails manicured?

A few months ago, I had the pleasure of interviewing the Director of Talent Procurement for a Fortune 500 Company. During the interview, I asked if she looked for a particular type of clothing when she was scouting for new employees. She told me that she looks for candidates who are well-groomed and conservative and not for a particular clothing type. Different businesses reflect the culture of the business through the type clothing worn. She mentioned that for her organization, the most expensive suit was not always a bonus; however, she did want to see candidates wear clothing that was clean, ironed, and tailored to fit. As far as accessories, she said that haircuts, jewelry, and accessories often tell a great deal about the personality of the candidate. The most interesting thing she told me had to do with what the candidate was carrying! She shared that candidates who walked in with huge bags bulging with papers gave her the impression of an employee who was unorganized and messy. Instead, she preferred to see candidates walk in with a simple black folder or an iPad or tablet for note-taking. In today's technological world, anything that the employer may require can be sent with the touch of a key on the iPad or tablet. In other words, less is more!

As people prepare to make a speech presentation, they often wonder what they should wear. As a speech coach, I suggest that speakers dress according to the audience to which they will be speaking. Is it a casual or formal event? Are you speaking to people in your community or to the board of directors for your organization? In any speaking situation, it is always advisable to dress a bit more formally than the people who will be attending your presentation. Business casual or dressy business is always in good taste.

Using the SpeechShark app, you can write your speech and use the note cards available on your device. Consequently, you will not walk to the stage with a fistful of papers; instead, you can take your device and with a well-timed swipe of the screen, you can move to your next card to stay on target with your presentation. Again, less is more!

Physical appearance sends a positive or negative message about the speaker's credibility. For most speaking occasions, it is important to dress as if you are going to a job interview. Business casual dressing for a speech is always preferred. Occasionally, speakers may dress according to the topic they are presenting. For example, if you are giving a speech about cooking, you might wear a chef's hat and apron. But for the most part, your audience will appreciate the fact that you took time to dress professionally for the speech. Blue jeans and a t-shirt that says, "BITE ME," may not be the best choice if you want your audience to take you seriously. Overly bright outfits, unusual

styles or garments that do not fit properly can also be distracting. While it may be appropriate to show tattoos or piercings if your speech topic is about tattoos or piercings, it is a better idea to avoid clothing that flaunt these. Have you ever heard "You only get one chance to make a first impression"? What message are you trying to send? Dress the part, SpeechShark!

Posture sends a non-verbal cue about how you feel about yourself and your speech. Not only will good posture show self-confidence, but it has a positive effect on your breathing patterns and the way you project your message. Good posture also lends itself to effective movements and gesturing during the speech. Have you ever heard someone tell you to "Stand tall"? Hold your chin up, keep your eyes focused on your audience, and take your place among great speakers who know what it takes to deliver a strong message. As you are introduced to the stage, walk with a positive purpose to let your audience know that you are ready and prepared.

Poise is displayed with how you carry your body. Are you comfortable in your own skin? Shoulders should be up and eyes looking at your audience to display positive self-confidence. Speakers who walk to the stage looking at the floor and with shoulders drooping will send a negative non-verbal cue about themselves and their speech topic. When giving a speech, walk confidently to the lectern and pan the audience with your eyes, smiling at them and letting them know you are happy to be speaking to them. When you get on stage, avoid leaning on the lectern, shifting from one foot to the other, adjusting your clothing or hair, handling notes, or putting your hands in your pocket. All of these negative behaviors will send negative non-verbal cues to your audience and will be evidence of a poor self-image and lack of confidence in yourself and your topic. Yes, all eyes will be on you. Make sure you are showing them cues that will increase your credibility.

Gestures are the ways you use your hands, body, and facial expressions during the speech to communicate points. I've often had students ask me, "What should I do with my hands during the speech?" My advice is to get immersed in your topic and in your audience so that you do not think about your hands and body. When you do this, you will have more natural and meaningful gestures. Don't put your hands in your pockets, clench them in front of you, or hold them behind you. These movements send a negative non-verbal cue. Gestures should not seem rehearsed, but should enhance your delivery and make visual points about things you are describing. They should be natural movements. The important thing is to make sure your gestures mirror the message you are sending.

Facial expressions include eye contact, smiling, head nodding, and head tilting to send a non-verbal cue to the audience during communication. Positive facial cues send a message of your emotions and attitudes regarding the topic you are sharing.

Eye contact promotes goodwill and a connection with the audience. It also helps the speaker appear more credible and knowledgeable about the topic. As you enter the stage, establish strong eye contact and keep strong eye contact throughout the speech. I've heard people suggest looking at the back wall if you get nervous with all eyes on you; however, that will only help you to establish a connection with the back wall. Take a deep breath and establish direct eye contact to develop a connection with the audience. Believe it or not, but the smiles and head nods of audience members will give you the strength and self-confidence to complete your speech in a positive manner. You need them and they need you.

When you have a large audience, you may find it hard to establish eye contact with each member. In this case, start with looking toward one side of your audience and pan the entire side with your strong eye contact as you move your gaze to the other side of the audience. Looking at the entire audience will help them to feel valued and included in your speech. This is how you connect with them and have them invest in your topic. Avoid gazing at any one person or group of people for too long of a time. Share your eye contact and your attention with all audience members.

Smiling is a non-verbal cue that says, "I am happy to be here!" A genuine smile will send a positive message to your audience. As you smile, you will be pleased to notice that they will also smile at you. This reciprocal smile will help you not be as nervous as you might be without positive audience cues.

Head tilting and head nodding is a non-verbal cue which lets you know if your audience comprehends your point or if they still might have questions.

Proxemics is the study of space and how we use it. We send spatial cues to show whether we are comfortable or uncomfortable with the space placed between us and the person speaking. Have you ever noticed a person back up when you move in to speak to them? If they do this, you might be moving into their personal space. When speaking to a small audience, you will need to keep a distance between yourself and the first row of audience members.

There are four different designations for space that we use when discussing communication: public space, social space, personal space, and intimate space. Different cultures and different people will be more comfortable in the different types of spaces. Here are designations to help you understand this better.

Public space is the space designated for speakers and usually twelve to twenty-five feet away from audience members. It is appropriate to move closer to your audience when making a particular point, but advisable not to stay too close to any one audience member for too long of a period. If you do, you will notice that it will make the audience members nervous. If there is a table in front and you move closer to the table, the audience member may move their personal items closer to them and away from the speaker. If you see then, take the cue that you are too close and back away.

Social space allows you to get just a little closer. This is the space that others are most comfortable with when working with a co-worker or customer and is usually about four to twelve feet.

Personal space allows someone to get closer, but not closer than one to four feet. This area is usually reserved for meeting with friends or family members.

Intimate space is the closest and is usually one foot or less away and usually involves touching the person next to you. This area is reserved for very close family members and also a romantic partner. With intimate space, we usually allow someone there for a short period of time, but will expect that same person to move to the personal space area at a certain point. We often will allow someone in the intimate space for a quick hug or to bid farewell, but also expect them to move back to the personal or social space once the hug is over.

As we conclude this section about proxemics, remember these designated spaces are the standards we recognize most often in the United States; however, they can change due to diverse cultures and circumstances. In all cases, whether speaking to an audience or speaking one-on-one to another person, be sure to read carefully the non-verbal cues being sent. Space distances with one person or a group of people may be altered according to that person or group's comfort level.

Chronemics is the study of how we use time to communicate. If you arrive early or if you arrive late, you are sending a non-verbal cue about your time and the time of those who are expecting you.

I'm sure all of you have a friend who is constantly arriving late for all functions. In fact, you might even find yourself telling this friend the event begins thirty minutes to an hour prior to the time it actually begins, just so they will arrive in time. If your friend constantly arrives late, they are sending you a message that their time is more valuable to them than your time. This is true for personal events and for professional events. They are being rude to you. Don't forget it!

If someone always arrives a few minutes early or on time, this means that they honor your time and they value you and the event. This is a non-verbal form of communication that many people dismiss, but the way you handle this will determine how others consider you in the long run.

Why are time restraints important when presenting a speech?

When asked to present a speech, always ask the host about the time limit for your speech. Often other points of interest are included during the gathering and your speech will be just one portion of the event. Whether you are the key note speaker or a support speaker, timing is extremely important so that the event planner can keep the event moving according to a planned schedule. If your speech is longer than needed, the entire event may run overtime.

A good rule to follow is to meet the minimum time limit, but not go over the maximum time limit. A four- to six-minute speech should last five minutes. A twenty to thirty minute speech should last twenty-five minutes. It is always preferred to end your speech just short of the maximum time limit to keep your event host happy!

Your SpeechShark app has a built-in timer to help you stay on time! Just dial in the time that you have been asked to speak and the app will give you a visual reminder of the time left! The screenshot to the right will show what this looks like in your app. If a speech is designed to last eight to ten minutes we suggest you dial in nine minutes as your max time. This gives you a little cushion to make sure you do not go over time.

Haptics is the study of communicating through touch. This happens when we shake hands with a colleague, share a friendly pat on the back, or hug a family member. We send non-verbal communication through touch. Culture also plays an important part with touch and we should always be mindful of cues the recipient sends to us to let us know if the touch is welcomed or not.

SPEAK WITH CONFIDENCE: TAKING A "BITE" OUT OF THE FEAR OF PUBLIC SPEAKING

Just as a shark swims boldly forward to pursue his goal, you can also walk toward the stage with confidence and deliver your speech without hesitation! The first thing that you will want to do is to examine your own confidence level when speaking to an audience.

Here are some questions to consider:

Question	Answer Yes or No
Do you have a low level of anxiety about public speaking?	
Do you have moderate anxiety in most public speaking situations, but not so severe that you cannot cope and be a successful speaker?	
Do you have a moderately high level of anxiety and tend to avoid speaking in public when possible?	
Do you have a very high level of anxiety and will go to any length to avoid a public speaking situation?	

Unsure of whether your speaking anxiety level is low or high? Take this self-evaluation from **George L. Grice and John F. Skinner's** *Mastering Public Speaking.*

Directions: This instrument is composed of thirty-four statements concerning feelings about communicating with other people. Indicate the degree to which the statements apply to you by marking whether you **(1) strongly agree, (2) agree, (3) undecided, (4) disagree, or (5) strongly disagree** with each statement. Work quickly and record your first impression.

PERSONAL REPORT OF PUBLIC SPEAKING ANXIETY

1	2	3	4	5	Statements Concerning Feelings about Communicating with Other People
					1. While preparing for giving a speech, I feel tense and nervous.
					2. I feel tense when I see the words Speech and Public Speaking on a course outline when studying or on a job description.
					3. My thoughts become confused and jumbled when I am giving a speech.
					4. Right after giving a speech, I feel that I have had a pleasant experience.
					5. I get anxious when I think about a speech coming up.
					6. I have no fear of giving a speech.
					7. Although I am nervous just before starting a speech, I soon settle down after starting and feel calm and comfortable.
					8. I look forward to giving a speech.
					9. When the instructor announces a speaking assignment in class, I can feel myself getting tense.
					10. My hands tremble when I am giving a speech.
					11. I feel relaxed when I am giving a speech.
					12. I enjoy preparing for a speech.
					13. I am in constant fear of forgetting what I prepared to say.
					14. I get anxious if someone asks me something about my topic that I do not know.
					15. I face the prospect of giving a speech with confidence.
					16. I feel that I am in complete possession of myself while giving a speech.
					17. My mind is clear when giving a speech.
					18. I do not dread giving a speech.
					19. I perspire just before starting a speech.
					20. My heart beats very fast just as I start a speech.
					21. I experience considerable anxiety while sitting in the room just before my speech starts.
					22. Certain parts of my body feel very tense and rigid while giving a speech.
					23. Realizing that only a little time remains before a speech makes me very anxious.
					24. While giving a speech, I know I can control my feelings of tension and stress.
					25. I breathe faster just before starting a speech.

continued

1	2	3	4	5	Statements Concerning Feelings about Communicating with Other People
					26. I feel comfortable and relaxed in the hour or so just before giving a speech.
					27. I do poorer on speeches because I am anxious.
					28. I feel anxious when I hear an announcement of a speaking assignment.
					29. When I make a mistake while giving a speech, I find it hard to concentrate on the parts that follow.
					30. During an important speech, I experience a feeling of helplessness building up inside me.
					31. I have trouble falling asleep the night before a speech.
					32. My heart beats very fast while I present a speech.
					33. I feel anxious while waiting to give my speech.
					34. While giving a speech, I get so nervous I forget facts I really know.
					TOTAL Points

To determine Your Score on the PRPSA, Complete the Following Steps:

1. Add the scores for items in purple (1,2,3,5,9,10,13,14,19,20,21,22,23,25,27,28,28,30,31,32,33,34).
2. Add the scores for items in peach (4,6,7,8,11,12,15,16,17,18,24,26).
3. Complete the following formula: PRPSA = 132 – (total points from step #1) + (total points from step #2).
4. What is your score? _____

NOTE: Your score can range between 34 and 170. There is no right or wrong answer because this report just helps you to understand if you do have speaker anxiety and the level of speaker anxiety that you may have. Understanding Your Score:

- 34–84—Very low anxiety about public speaking
- 85–92—Moderately low level of anxiety about public speaking
- 93–110—Moderate anxiety in most public speaking situations, but not too severe that the individual cannot cope and be a successful speaker
- 111–119—Moderately high anxiety about public speaking. People with this score usually tend to avoid public speaking situations.
- 120–170—Very high anxiety about public speaking. People with these scores will go to considerable lengths to avoid all types of public speaking situations.

Whether your level is low or high, it is good to realize that we ALL get nervous when speaking in public; even sharks get nervous, especially when they are swimming in waters teaming with other sharks! So, that means you are normal! Yes, I said it—you are NORMAL!

Most of us are anxious because we think that the audience is staring at us and judging us. Dry mouth, shortness of breath, sweaty palms, increased heart rate—we experience all of these! We might even think that the audience members are sitting there silently wishing that we will run screaming from the stage.

In fact, the opposite is true. Audiences WANT speakers to succeed. Audiences WANT speakers to be amazing and to wow us with their presentations! Why? Because the audience is investing their time to hear your speech. They don't want to waste time, but want to hear a message that is relevant and riveting! You can be the SpeechShark that provides what the audience WANTS!

Using the SpeechShark app will help you to do just that! The app is designed to create a speech that is geared toward your audience and is designed to satisfy the purpose for which you have been asked to speak! SpeechShark provides you with prompts that will help you maneuver through murky waters so that you, too, can swim easily and confidently toward your goal and deliver a crowd-pleasing presentation without hesitation or FEAR!

Dealing with Speech Anxiety:

How do you cope with speech anxiety? What is stage fright? Stage fright is different for everyone and speakers compensate for stage fright by using techniques that work for them.

Some people like to use **breathing exercises** before the speech to help channel the adrenaline running through their bodies. Slowing down their heart beat will also slow down the flow of adrenaline and will help calm nerves. Learning to deal with stress associated with public speaking will be your key to speaking with confidence. We all get nervous, so the best thing to know right now is that you are normal! See, doesn't that make you feel better? As you speak, you will experience good stress and bad stress.

The feeling of stress is produced as adrenaline rushes through your body. **Adrenaline** is physiological and involves increased heart and respiration rate as a result of a situation perceived to be frightening or exciting. With this adrenaline rush, you may feel more energetic, excited, sometimes stronger and happier. This is good stress and will help you to rise to the challenge. Bad stress will cause you to feel fear and anxiety. Fear is a negative emotion which truly does not help the situation at all. With this in mind, I want to show you ways to focus on the good stress and alleviate the bad stress. Try all of these different strategies and you will soon discover the strategy that works best for you.

I've discovered that the people who have stage fright the most are the people who enter the stage unprepared. The best remedy for stage fright is again—**Plan, Prepare, and Persevere!** Know what you are going to say and most of the stage fright will disappear.

We've heard from lots of speakers who say that using the SpeechShark app (www.speechshark.com) helps them to be less anxious because it helps them to know what they should say during the speech. The app also provides note cards for presenting the speech.

PLAN

KNOW your audience, understand your purpose, and know what you need to say. If you can do that, you will have less stage fright and will be a more effective communicator! The **SECRET** is to do everything and anything that will help you be more confident. It is a confidence factor, not a personality or knowledge factor.

Here is what SpeechSharks do BEFORE the speech:

- **Walk around the room before the speech.**
- **Stand by the lectern and rehearse in the room where you will be giving the speech.**
- **Rehearse with people listening to you instead of rehearsing to an empty room.**
- **Rehearse by audio or video taping yourself.**
- **Rehearse in front of a mirror.**
- **Exercise positive self-talk.**

Rehearse, rehearse, rehearse—and rehearse some more. Change wording to make sure the words are coming to you comfortably. Believe in yourself! Feel comfortable with yourself, your location, and your content. As a result, you will be more confident and you will be happier with your presentation.

PREPARE

How do you cope with speech anxiety? The **SECRET** is to do everything and anything that will help you to be more confident. It is a confidence factor, not a personality or knowledge factor. Here is what SpeechSharks do BEFORE the speech:

- **Walk around the room before the speech**, instead of sitting in a chair and waiting to be called up front. It will help you to work off some of the nervous energy, and you can greet audience members as you move around the room waiting for the event to begin.
- **Stand by the lectern and rehearse in the room where you will be giving the speech.** This is difficult when the room is full, so arrive early and spend time rehearsing in the SAME PLACE where you will be giving the speech.
- **Rehearse with people listening to you** instead of rehearsing to an empty room. Having a rehearsal audience will give you a similar experience as having the presentation audience. That will help you to feel more confident because you can see how the audience will react to certain points that you make.
- **Rehearse by audio or video taping yourself.** Be AWARE of words that you tend to "chew" up. It may mean changing the wording so that your message will have a smoother delivery.
- **Rehearse in front of a mirror.** This is awkward, but it will help you see your gestures and facial expressions as you make the presentation. It will also give you a chance to check your appearance before you meet your audience.
- **Exercise positive self-talk.** Don't let anything negative come into your brain—tell yourself, "I am going to do a GREAT job!" "This will be my BEST speech!" "The audience is really going to LOVE my topic!" "Nobody in this room KNOWS this topic like I do!" "I am an EXPERT!"

PERSEVERE

Ultimately, the main thing you can do is rehearse, rehearse, rehearse—and rehearse some more. Don't quit. Move forward. Keep your goal in mind. Change wording to make sure the words are coming to you comfortably. Believe in yourself! Feel comfortable with yourself, your location, and your content. As a result, you will be more confident and happier with your presentation.

Look forward to your next speech!

Knock out stress using the **BAM** Approach:

B = Breathing exercises can help affect your state of mind, lower heart rate ,and bring stress under control. The trick to this is to use controlled breathing exercises. As you follow the breathing exercises, you will notice that your muscle tension will relax when providing your body with much needed oxygen. The result will have a positive effect on your thoughts and feelings. The Internet is packed with breathing exercises to use before your next speech!

A = Aromatherapy involves the sense of smell and uses scents to overcome stress and improve overall mental health. Certain scents may help you to feel more calm than others, so it is important to find the scent that helps you to feel "ahhhh!" Some popular scents used to calm stress are lavender, chamomile, lemongrass, and peppermint. Diffusers are readily available online and in department stores along with vials of essential oils. There are also mixtures of various essential oils designed to bring a sense of calmness to the user. Experiment to find the oil/scent which works best for you. Diffuse the oil as you sit in your home or desk prior to giving the speech. Dab a tiny bit of oil on the inside of your wrists before a speech. There are even diffusers available that plug in to your car so that you can experience the calming scents while driving to your speech location.

M = Meditation enhanced with music will calm stress. Use imagery and positive visualization to think your way to success! Positive self-talk and imagining a successful speech are achieved as you concentrate on feeling successful while communicating to others. First, imagine yourself walking confidently to the stage, delivering the best speech of your life, and then hearing the welcomed applause of audience members! Tell yourself, "I can do this! I know my topic. I am prepared for this speech. I have a message my audience needs to hear. I am the best person to share this topic to my audience. I will do a great job and my audience will be glad they heard this speech." Do not allow negative thoughts or feelings to enter this moment. Only

concentrate on positive thoughts and visualize your success. Using calm music or sounds of nature while meditating can intensify this effect and will help you feel composed and ready to meet the challenge.

There are several strategies available, but as with anything, it is important to do what works for you and understand your stress triggers and indicators. Be sure to review the chapter covering the Speech Day Checklist. Following a checklist will help you arrive feeling prepared and ready to take the stage!

What do you need to know about entering and exiting the stage area?

Whether you know it or not, your speech begins the moment you stand and enter the stage and does not end until you have been seated or exit the stage. Audience members watch you from the very first indication that you are going to be the speaker. It is for this reason that speakers need to enter the stage confidently, acknowledging the audience while approaching the lectern. If you are using notes, place them carefully on the lectern and then move away from the lectern toward the center of the stage. Avoid standing at the lectern and spending valuable time arranging and rearranging pages of notes. Notes should be in order before you enter the stage.

Once the speech is completed, take your notes from the lectern and again make eye contact and acknowledge your audience as you move back to your seat. BIG smiles and strong eye contact will convey the non-verbal cue that you are confident to give the speech and proud of the results once the speech is completed.

What do I need to know about movement during the speech?

Sharks are known for their uncanny way of maneuvering gracefully through murky waters. You can do this, too. The only difference is that you will be maneuvering gracefully across the stage—no murky waters for you!

Movement during a speech should happen naturally as you are making the presentation, but Speech-Sharks know ways to orchestrate movements that are effective and carefully placed during the speech. It is called movement with a purpose. Use the letter W in the alphabet to help you visualize movement during your speech. There are five points in a W. Here is a numbered diagram and movements to help you walk your way to success:

WALK YOUR WAY TO SUCCESS!

3	1	5
W		
2	4	

- Imagine a giant W in the middle of the stage area. Move from 1,2,3,2,1 and then from 1,4,5,4,1. This helps you move to the left side of your stage and to the right side of your stage equally.

- Begin your speech at area #1. While you are front and center of the stage area, this is where you should stand to deliver the attention step, establish relevance for the topic, establish credibility, and clearly state your thesis.

- Take two steps back and away from the middle front of the stage to area #2 as you transition to the first point.

- Then move to area #3 as you cover the first point. Use this area of the stage to cover point one.

- As you transition to the second point, take two steps back to area #2 of the diagram. Stay in this area during the transition. Move to area #1 as you cover the second point.

- After the second point has been covered and as you transition to the third point, move directly to area #4. As you lead into the third point, take two steps up to area #5. Stay in this area while you cover the third point.

- As you transition to the conclusion, move back to area #4.

- Following the transition move back to area #1 to complete the summary of three main points.

- Stay in area #1 to deliver the final Appeal to Action and end with a BANG while standing center of the stage area and close to your audience.

SpeechShark's Top Ten Tips for a Killer Presentation:

1. Start with a strong attention step.
2. Plan the speech for your audience.
3. Research the topic.
4. Add personal stories.
5. Show empathy for the audience.
6. Be conversational.
7. Move forward, even if you make a mistake.
8. Stay with your plan.
9. Use visual aids.
10. End with a BANG.

Presentation Skills

After reading this chapter, you will be able to answer the following questions:

1. What is the definition of verbal language? _____

    _____

    _____

2. What is the definition of non-verbal language? _____

    _____

    _____

3. What is the formula for Albert Mehrabian's communication theory? _____

    _____

    _____

4. What are the three primary areas of communication? _____

    _____

    _____

5. What are five areas of non-verbal communication? _____

    _____

    _____

6. What is the definition of paralanguage? _____

_____

_____

7. What is the definition of volume? _____

_____

_____

8. What is a larynx? _____

_____

_____

9. What is the definition of rate? _____

_____

_____

10. What is the definition of pitch? _____

_____

_____

11. What is the definition of pace? _____

_____

_____

12. What is the definition of color as used to describe a voice? _____

_____

_____

13. What type dialect do YOU have? _____

_____

_____

14. What are filler words? Do you use them? _____

_____

_____

15. What are kinesics? _____

_____

_____

16. What non-verbal cues do you send about yourself with your posture and pose? _____

_____

_____

17. What gestures send negative non-verbal cues? _____

_____

_____

18. What is a benefit of using strong eye contact throughout the speech? _____

_____

_____

19. What is the definition of proxemics? _____

_____

_____

20. Define the difference between public, social, personal, and intimate space? _____

_____

_____

21. What is the definition of chronemics? _____

_____

_____

22. Define the definition of haptics. _____

_____

_____

23. What is the definition of adrenaline? _____

_____

_____

24. What is the BAM Approach for speaking with confidence? _____

_____

_____

25. What strategy works best for you when you need to deal with speech anxiety? _____

_____

_____

26. Why do most of us experience speech anxiety in some form? _____

_____

_____

27. What symptoms are evident with speech anxiety? _____

_____

_____

28. Does the audience want you to succeed? _____

_____

_____

29. How do breathing exercises help with speech anxiety? _____

_____

_____

30. What can you do before the speech to calm your nerves? _____

_____

_____

Shark Bites

IMPROVING PRESENTATION SKILLS

Practice Eye Contact: Work in a group of four or five people. Put your chairs in a circle. Take turns speaking impromptu (Suggested Topic: Your favorite vacation). As you speak, make sure you are making direct eye contact with each person in your group. Spend two or three seconds looking directly at each person and then move your gaze to the next person. Continue doing this until your story is finished and you have held direct eye contact with each person in the group.

Practice Good Posture: Stand next to your chair. Place an object on your head (iPad or phone). Count to twenty slowly and keep your head balanced so that your device does not fall off your head.

Practice Good Gestures: Using your arms, hands, head, and face, practice gestures for the following: saying "no," saying "yes," showing how many numbers, showing how large or small something is, showing locations, showing you understand, and showing you do not understand.

Practice Using Note Cards: If you are using the SpeechShark app, note cards will be on your phone or tablet. Practice using them and swiping to move from one point to the next point.

Practice Using Different Verbal and Non-Verbal Cues: Make up hypothetical situations with a friend and respond using the following:

1. Angry response
2. Happy response
3. Confused response
4. Submissive response
5. Assertive response

Peer Evaluate each other to make sure verbal words and the responses aligned with non-verbal cues. Are there things you need to improve? What are they?

Shark Bites

TAKING A BITE OUT OF THE FEAR OF PUBLIC SPEAKING

List five things that cause you to have presentation anxiety:

1.

2.

3.

4.

5.

Rank these fears from 1–5. Assign 1 to the fear that causes the most anxiety.

Draw a line through the fear and add a positive thought beside each one.

Use BREATHING Exercises to help you feel calm:

Sit in a chair with both feet on the floor and your hands in your lap. Close your eyes. Breathe in and count 1, 2, 3, 4 and out 1, 2, 3, 4. Do this for one full minute (timing yourself with the timer on your phone).

Do this exercise again, but this time try to take only six to ten breaths per minute.

Take your hands out of your lap and let them hang loosely by your sides. Shake your hands as hard as you can for three seconds. Then drop your hands by your side and imagine all of your anxiety dripping out from your fingertips and landing on the floor. Stay in this position for ten seconds.

Return your hands to your lap. Again repeat breathing in and count 1, 2, 3, 4 and breath out 1, 2, 3, 4.

Think positive thoughts and tell yourself—I've got this! I'm a SpeechShark!

Chapter Fourteen

Rehearsing the Speech and Creating a Speech Day Checklist

In this chapter:

How do I rehearse my speech?

Why should I plan to rehearse using presentation aids?

What do I need to know about the timing of the speech?

What is a Speech Day Checklist?

You have heard it said that practice makes perfect. This is true, but only if you practice properly. You will do little to improve your speech delivery unless you practice the right things in the right ways. **Here is a five-step method that works well for presenters:**

1. Go through your outline to see what you have written.

   • Are the main points clear?
   • Do you have supporting materials?
   • Does your introduction and conclusion come across well?

2. Prepare your speaking notes. In doing so, be sure to follow the guidelines. Use the same framework as in the preparation outline. Make sure your speaking notes are easy to read. Give yourself cues on the note cards for delivering the speech.

3. Practice the speech aloud several times using only the speaking outline. Be sure to "talk through" all examples and to recite quotations and statistics. If your speech includes visual aids, utilize those as you practice. The first couple of times, you will probably forget something or make a mistake, but don't worry. Keep going and complete the speech as best as you can. Concentrate on gaining control of the ideas; don't try to learn the speech word for word. After a few tries you should be able to get through the speech extemporaneously with surprising ease.

4. Now begin to polish and refine your delivery. Practice the speech in front of a mirror to check for eye contact and distracting mannerisms. Record the speech to gauge volume, pitch, rate, pauses, and vocal variety. Most important, try it out on friends, roommates, family members—anyone who will listen and give you honest feedback. Because your speech is designed for an audience you need to find out ahead of time how it goes over with people.

5. Finally, give your speech a dress rehearsal under conditions as close as possible to those you will face in class. Some students like to try the speech a couple times in an empty classroom the day before they actually present the speech. No matter where you hold your last practice session, you should leave it feeling confident and looking forward to speaking in your class.

If this or any practice method is to work, you must start early. Don't wait until the night before your speech to begin working on delivery. A single practice session—no matter how long—is rarely enough. Allow yourself at least a couple of days, preferably more, to gain command of the speech and its presentation.

PRACTICE WITH YOUR VISUAL AIDS

We have mentioned several times the need to rehearse using your visual aids, but the point bears repeating. No matter what kind of visual aid you choose, be sure to employ it when you rehearse. Go through the speech multiple times, rehearsing how you will show your aids, the gestures you will make, and the timing of each move. In using visual aids, as in other aspects of speechmaking, there is no substitute for preparation.

If you are using presentation technology, don't just click through casually or rush quickly over your words when you practice. Make sure you know exactly when you want each slide to appear and disappear, and what you will say while each is on-screen. Mark your speaking notes with cues that will remind you when to display each slide and when to remove it.

Rehearse with the mouse, remote, keyboard, or iPad until you can use them without looking down for more than an instant when advancing your slides. Also concentrate on presenting the speech without looking back at the screen to see what is being projected. Rehearse with your tech team, if you need one!

Given all the things you have to work on when practicing a speech with any kind of presentation technology, you need to allow extra time for rehearsal. So, get an early start and give yourself plenty of time to ensure that your delivery is as impressive as your slides.

Practicing Visual Aids Checklist	Yes	No
• Have I checked the speech room to decide where I can display my visual aids most effectively?		
• Have I practiced presenting my visual aids so they will be clearly visible to everyone in the audience?		
• Have I practiced presenting my visual aids so they are perfectly timed with my words and actions?		
• Have I practiced keeping eye contact with my audience while presenting my visual aids?		
• Have I practiced explaining my visual aids clearly and concisely in terms my audience will understand?		
• If I am using handouts, have I planned to distribute them after the speech rather than during it?		
• Have I double-checked all equipment to make sure it works properly?		
• If I am using PowerPoint, do I have a backup of my slides that I can take to the speech with me?		

CHECK THE ROOM AND EQUIPMENT

For classroom speeches, you will already be familiar with the room and equipment. Even if you have used PowerPoint on previous occasions, you need to check the setup in the room where you will be presenting.

If you are using a computer that is installed in the room, bring your slides on a flash drive so you can see how they work with that computer. If your presentation includes audio or video, double-check them using the room's audiovisual system.

Sometimes, of course, it is not possible to visit the room before the day of your speech. Never assume that everything will be "just fine." Instead, assume that things will not be fine and that they need to be checked ahead of time.

Finally, always bring a backup of your slides on a flash drive. This may seem like a lot of fuss and bother, but anyone who has given speeches with PowerPoint—or any other kind of visual aid—will tell you that it is absolutely essential.

Have a Backup Plan

No matter how much time presenters invest in mastering the technology, they can still be undermined by technological glitches. This is why experts recommend that you always have a backup plan in case the technology fails. Because we have all encountered sabotage by technology at one time or another, audiences usually have sympathy for a presenter who encounters such problems. When in doubt, be prepared to present without technology.

Rehearsing the Presentation

After reading this chapter, you will be able to answer the following questions:

1. What are keys for preparing to rehearse your presentation?

   _____

   _____

2. What are the guidelines provided for a checklist for rehearsing with visual aids?

   _____

   _____

3. Why is it important to check the room and equipment prior to your presentation?

   _____

   _____

Shark Bites

List of Things to Do Before Speech Day:	Assigned to:

SPEECH DAY CHECK LIST

- Plan, Prepare, Persevere! The more planning and preparation you do before the speech, the more confident you will be.
- Think positively—YOU can do this!
- Understand what is expected of you for the speech.
- Pack all materials you need the day before your speech. Have a checklist planned to keep you on target.
- Take care of you!
    - Get a good night's sleep before the speech.
    - Eat a healthy high protein meal.
    - Stay away from milk products which can coat your throat.
    - Drink plenty of fluids before your speech, but avoid caffeine and sugar which can make you feel jittery.
- Rehearse with your tech team so they know what you need.
- Arrive early to become familiar with the speaking area.
- Rehearse using a microphone, if you need to use one.
- Rehearse using a remote for your PowerPoint, if you choose to use one.
- Visit with people as they arrive for the speech. It helps to create a bond with the audience prior to your presentation.

Consider these areas carefully and pre-pack for your presentation. Begin to pack a bag of things you will need to carry for the speech. If you need visual aids, you will also need to work with a tech team and have them rehearse with you to make sure they understand all that you will require them to do for your presentation. This means providing a script so they will know when to set up your table display for props or so they will know when to advance the slides of your PowerPoint presentation. Preparation also includes rehearsal.

First, rehearse *without* your tech team to smooth out the rough edges and to make decisions regarding the point in your speech when visual aids, sound, light changes, or PowerPoint slides should be introduced. Once you have worked through these details, then bring in the tech team.

CHECKLIST FOR A GREAT SPEECH

Before each presentation, follow this checklist to make sure every detail is in shipshape!

The Outline:
- ☐ Typed
  - ○ Correct outline format
  - ○ Header (name, company name/class name/date)
  - ○ Headings for each item is in bold letters
- ☐ Speech Category
- ☐ Title
- ☐ General Purpose
- ☐ Specific Purpose

Introduction:
- ☐ Full sentence format
- ☐ Attention Step
- ☐ Establish Need/Relevance
- ☐ Establish Speaker Credibility
- ☐ Thesis/Preview Statement (clearly states main points)

Body:
- ☐ Roman numerals (I., II., III.) Capitalized letters for sub-points (A., B., C.) and numbers for sub-sub-points (1., 2., 3.)
- ☐ Three main points (using key words or phrases)
- ☐ Transition sentences between the introduction step to the main points, between each main point, and between the last main point and the conclusion
- ☐ Each main point is covered equally

Conclusion:
- ☐ Full sentence format
- ☐ Signal to let your audience know you are concluding the speech
- ☐ Summary restates all main points clearly
- ☐ Final appeal keeps the audience thinking about the speech

Visual Aids:
- ☐ Visual aid explanation page is included with the outline
- ☐ PowerPoint/Prezi slides follow outline
- ☐ PowerPoint follows design requirements
- ☐ Handout is usable, designed by the speaker, and supplies one for each person
- ☐ Rehearse using visual aids with tech team

Research:

- ☐ Follow citation guidelines for the topic
- ☐ Include credible research sources
- ☐ Include the minimum number of sources required
- ☐ Vary types of research used
- ☐ Parenthetically cite research in the document
- ☐ Include a separate page for the Works Cited

Presentation:

- ☐ Rehearse using presentation notes
- ☐ Rehearse with the tech team
- ☐ Place a water bottle on the lectern
- ☐ Check EVERYTHING—lights, sound, computer, PowerPoint, notes folder

TECH TEAM CHECKLIST

Complete this form as you plan the use of visual aids so you are prepared for the speech. Speakers who use visual aids will need to make use of a tech team. It is the speaker's responsibility to meet with tech team members ahead of time, provide a script, and rehearse with the tech team to make sure they understand what is needed. Visual aids are an important part of the speech and a direct reflection of your credibility as a speaker.

Date: _____ **Time of Speech:** _____

Type of Speech: _____

Description of visual aids:

_____

_____

_____

_____

Note: In the area below, please list each tech team member's name and their assigned duties. Be sure to assign a member for the PowerPoint, sound, lights, setup, breakdown, and distribution of handouts. All duties may not be needed for all speeches.

Tech Team Member's Name: _____

Duties Assigned: _____

Tech Team Member's Name: _____

Duties Assigned: _____

Tech Team Member's Name: _____

Duties Assigned: _____

Tech Team Member's Name: _____

Duties Assigned: _____

_____

_____

COMMUNICATION TIPS FROM THE EXPERTS AT SPEECHSHARK

What is the worst thing that a person can do when trying to make a speech presentation?

If a speaker knows that a speaking engagement is approaching, the worst thing the speaker can do is to be so overly confident that he does not prepare for the event! Preparation includes knowing to whom you will be speaking and making sure you provide content that the audience needs. It also includes researching the topic to add support for your points and rehearsing the presentation several times.

How can you prevent that?

To prevent a failed presentation, the key is over-preparation. For example, if you are speaking to specific groups, learn the names of the directors and interject their names into the speech at an appropriate moment. Include projects or plans the group is making so they know you cared enough about the group to learn about them. Plan, prepare, and practice so your presentation will be perfect!

What are the characteristics of effective speakers?

- Effective speakers are great listeners. They listen to find out what is needed and then go the extra mile to research main points within the content and provide the audiences with credible information.
- Effective speakers are detail oriented and are planners. They LOVE using Speech Checklists! Once they have the content of the speech covered, they are effective in the delivery of the information.
- Effective speakers use energy to captivate their audiences so that enthusiasm and excitement for the topic is "caught" and not "bought"!
- Effective speakers learn to calm their nerves so they always appear confident and competent.

In a socially awkward situation like meeting someone for the first time, what is the best way to break the ice?

Let's face it, meeting someone for the first time can be very awkward. Understanding that there will be a short period of awkwardness before the relationship begins is a realistic way of approaching the situation. From a communicator's point of view, it is important to know your audience before speaking to them. What can you learn about this person before the meeting? What common ground might you have with this person? Do your homework before the meeting and the period of time between "Hello!" and "I'll look forward to seeing you again!" will be less awkward and more productive!

What sort of approach is best to avoid?

If you know your audience before the meeting, it will be easier to instigate conversation that is mutually satisfying. Stay away from topics and points that would cause a conflict. I am not saying that you should never speak about controversial matters, but that is a subject for another meeting once your relationship has progressed to the point where you can speak candidly about your thoughts.

"Do unto others as you would have them do unto you!" I know you have heard that a million times, but as you meet someone for the very first time, treat your new friend the way that you

would like to be treated. Be open to them and be a good listener. The awkwardness will soon pass and you will be the master of conversation before the meeting is over!

What can good communication skills do for someone?

Having good verbal and non-verbal communications skills are crucial to success in life! Effective communication skills will foster relationships, solve problems, promote teamwork, motivate and influence others, achieve goals, and the list goes on!

Non-verbal skills are just as important as verbal skills. Have you ever heard someone say, "What you do speaks so loudly that I can't hear what you are saying"? The truth is that people believe what they see before they believe what they hear. If you are going for a job interview, ask yourself the following questions:

- What will my potential employer see when I walk through the door?
- How are you dressed?
- What are you carrying with you?
- How is your poise and confidence?
- How is your handshake?
- Are you wearing a big smile?
- Are you demonstrating enthusiasm in your walk and the way that you carry yourself?

If all of these are positive, then you could very well get the job as long as your resume is as impressive as you are! If they are negative, then you will need to keep job searching, but please work on non-verbal skills before going to another interview.

I was speaking to a businessman the other day who shared with me that he likes to hire people who belong to Toastmasters International Clubs. He said that people who actively work on their images by improving their communication skills are also going to be conscious of improving the image of the business they represent. None of us are perfect communicators. Learning effective communication skills is not a destination, but a journey and something that we continue to improve as we move toward success!

Why do you think so many people fear public speaking?

It is no secret that most people fear public speaking more than they fear death. The truth is, everyone gets nervous when they need to speak in public. The good news is, no one has ever died from public speaking! Now, I know that the fear of public speaking is no laughing matter; however, if we realize we are perfectly normal and that everyone gets nervous, then we do not enter the stage feeling like we are the only nervous speaker in the world! We simply need to learn how to handle our own fears so that we can be effective speakers.

Usually people fear public speaking because they think everyone in the audience will be judging them—judging their appearance, voice, accent, body movements, content of speech, and the list goes on and on. Truthfully, people do not judge negatively and "take the speaker apart piece by piece." Instead, they want the speaker to be successful. After all, they are investing their time to hear this person speak and they don't want to waste their time. So, the audience is hoping for a knock-you-out-of-your-chair speech.

The question is not so much, "Why do so many people fear public speaking," but "How do I overcome my own fear of public speaking?" The answer to that is:

- Conduct an audience analysis prior to giving a speech.
- Choose a topic that is relevant for the audience.
- Conduct research to make sure you are covering points the audience wants to hear.

- Plan visual aids that support points.

- Craft a speech outline that includes an introduction, body, and conclusion. Let the first words you say grab your audience's attention. Establish why the audience needs to hear your speech. Establish why you are the person credible to speak to them. Clearly state the three points you will cover. Plan effective transitions between each main point. In the conclusion, clearly restate the three main points you covered. Finally, end with a BANG! Make sure your last words are something that will keep your audience thinking about your topic and about your speech.

- Rehearse, rehearse, rehearse! I say this three times because a speaker should rehearse speeches a minimum of three times before making the presentation.

- Positive self-talk will take you from "I can't do this" to "I can do this and I will do a great job!"

- Breathe! That's right, breathing exercises prior to the presentation can help you calm your heart rate and slow the flow of adrenaline in your body.

- Walk confidently to the stage realizing that you have earned the right to be the speaker of this particular event. Establish strong eye contact with your audience as you move toward the lectern, smile at them, and send non-verbal cues that send the message of your confidence and competence to speak!

- Do your best, but understand that you will never give a perfect speech. There will always be that one thing you forgot to say or there may be a time when you trip over your own words. Remind yourself that you are human—just like everyone in your audience—and do not beat yourself up over mistakes. Instead, dwell on all of the great things that you do!

- Be proud of yourself! Pat yourself on the back! Get ready for the next speech.

I am a SpeechShark! What is your super power?

Speech Day Check List

After reading this chapter, you will be able to answer the following questions:

1. What will help you to be more confident the day of your speech? _____

    _____

    _____

2. When should you pack your speech materials? _____

    _____

    _____

3. What should you do before the speech to take care of YOU? _____

    _____

    _____

4. When should you arrive for your presentation? _____

    _____

    _____

5. What should your outline include? _____

    _____

    _____

6. What are research requirements to include? _____

_____

_____

7. What should you check prior to the presentation? _____

_____

_____

8. How many Tech Team members will you need? _____

_____

_____

9. What is the worst thing you can do when preparing for a speech? _____

_____

_____

10. What are the characteristics of effective speakers? _____

_____

_____

11. Why does the audience want YOU to succeed? _____

_____

_____

12. What are the benefits of good communication skills? _____

_____

_____

13. Why do people fear public speaking? _____

_____

_____

14. What strategies do you use to overcome the fear of public speaking? _____

_____

_____

15. Are you ready for your next speech? If not, what do you need to do in order to be prepared? _____

_____

_____

Shark Bites

GETTING READY FOR THE BIG DAY!

Complete the following Outline Checklist:

The Task (Outline)	Completed	Needs More Work
☐ Typed ☐ Uses Standard Outline ☐ Header (name/company/date) ☐ Headings for each item ☐ Speech Category ☐ Title ☐ General Purpose ☐ Specific Purpose		
Introduction Step: ☐ Full Sentence Format ☐ Attention Step ☐ Establish Need/Relevance ☐ Establish Credibility ☐ Thesis/Preview Statement		
Body: ☐ Roman Numerals I., II., III. ☐ ABCs for Sub-Points ☐ Three Main Points ☐ Transition Sentences		
Conclusion: ☐ Full Sentence Format ☐ Signal to Conclude Speech ☐ Summarize Main Points ☐ Appeal/Closing Statement		

Shark Bites

CHECKLIST FOR THE VISUAL AIDS AND RESEARCH!

Complete the following Task Checklist:

The Task	Completed	Needs More Work
Visual Aid ☐ Include a Visual Aid Explanation Page with Outline ☐ PowerPoint/Prezi follows Outline ☐ Handout is Usable ☐ Handout is Designed by Speaker ☐ One Handout for Each Audience Member ☐ Rehearse Visual Aids with Tech Team		
Research ☐ Follow Citation Guidelines for the Subject ☐ Use Credible Sources ☐ Include Minimum Required ☐ Vary Types of Research ☐ Parenthetically Cite Sources in the Outline ☐ Include a Works Cited or Bibliography Page with the Full Citation		
Presentation ☐ Rehearse, Rehearse, Rehearse ☐ Rehearse Using Presentation Notes ☐ Rehearse with Tech Team ☐ Double-Check EVERYTHING—lights, sound, computer, PPT, notes, water		

Chapter Fifteen
Evaluating the Speech

In this chapter:

What do I need to know about self-evaluations?

How do I conduct peer evaluations?

How will I be evaluated during my speech?

How will my outline be evaluated?

SPEECHSHARKS HAVE THICK SKIN

It's no secret, SpeechSharks have thick skin. Most people who are working hard to improve their speech presentations often ask others to evaluate or critique their speeches. As speakers work to improve stage presence, they will often video and audio record presentations then play the recordings over and over again searching for ways to improve. You need thick skin for this!

Speakers welcome evaluations and critiques that recognize their strengths, but also evaluations that offer suggestions and tips for overcoming weaknesses. The purpose of an evaluation is to coach, help, build, mold, and encourage. ALL of us can improve. Not only do SpeechSharks understand this concept, but they have the thick skin needed to welcome feedback in all types of forms. Here is a strategy to help you evaluate other speakers:

I lovingly call this "The Sandwich Approach." This strategy involves building an evaluation the way that you would build a sandwich. The best part of any sandwich is the bread, but without the meat and cheese, it's just a piece of bread —a snack, but not a meal. The same is true with an evaluation. Consider the two slices of bread as the (1) Introduction Step and the (2) Conclusion Step. Consider the meat and cheese as the Body of the speech.

Start the evaluation with the first piece of bread, the Introduction Step. Do this by showing how the speaker got the audience's attention, established need for the topic, established why the speaker was credible to speak about the topic, and clearly detailed the three main points in the thesis. Also, add the strengths you noticed during the first part of the evaluation. Was the speaker prepared, did she use research effectively, was she dressed professionally, and how were her vocal skills?

Now, it is time to evaluate the message delivered. This is the meat and cheese of the sandwich and includes the content and purpose of the speech. Are the points clear, do they make sense, did the speaker use research or personal experience to clarify the points? This is also a good time to share any issues you noticed that the speaker should strengthen.

Finally, it's time for the last slice of bread. This one will cover the conclusion. How was her summary and appeal to action, did she end strong, and did her final words keep you thinking about the message she delivered. Before you finish the evaluation, be sure to add one more thing that you noticed the speaker do that was really over the top! Leave the speaker with a last word that leaves the speaker motivated to continue working on her communication skills.

It takes skill to build an evaluation that motivates, encourages, and also highlights areas to improve without making the new speaker feel defeated. Sure, SpeechSharks have thick skin. Evaluators also need thick skin, but with time and experience, evaluations can be delivered as a tender morsel to be savored, enjoyed, and appreciated!

Evaluations of presentations allow you to recognize and be prepared to capitalize on your strengths as a speaker and identify areas for improvement. Generally, a one- to two-page document is sufficient to evaluate your overall speaking strengths and areas in need of improvement.

In a learning environment, speakers may also be asked to offer written or oral speech evaluations of their peers. Written evaluations are conducted during the presentation in the form of a rubric or guideline as found below. Oral evaluations are usually presented immediately following the speech and may be delivered by a member of the audience or by the speech coach. In any case, evaluations are an excellent tool to help us become better speakers.

Consider asking a friend or colleague to video record your speech. Plan to watch the video twice before completing a self-evaluation.

The first time, watch the video without sound so that you pay careful attention to non-verbal cues that you may send. These will include the way you are dressed, movements, gestures, and facial expressions.

The second time, watch the video with sound and pay careful attention to your vocal skills and to the content delivered.

SUGGESTED GUIDELINES FOR SELF-EVALUATION

Evaluate your last classroom presentation by responding to the questions listed below. As you analyze your performance, consider your own reactions, your personal opinion of your performance, and audience reaction during your presentation. Respond to all questions:

SELF-EVALUATION

Areas to Consider	Questions to Ask
Self	Did the audience see you as a credible speaker? If yes, why? If no, why not?
Others	How well did you analyze and adapt to your audience?
Purpose	How successful was your presentation? How well did you achieve your purpose?
Context	How did you handle the logistics of your visual aids, time frame, etc.?
Content	How well did you include appropriate content substantiated with strong and valid supporting material?
Structure	What made your introduction and conclusion effective or ineffective? How well did you organize the overall presentation?
Expression	What are your delivery strengths? How will you endeavor to improve your delivery in future presentations?

Just as it is imperative to evaluate your own performance, it is critical that you have the ability to critique and evaluate your peers' presentations. Please use the Peer Evaluation Template when asked to evaluate your peers. It is not necessary to post a score, but showing a rating scale of 3–1 will help the speaker to know his/her own strengths and weaknesses. Please use the "Notes" area to acknowledge great work or to add suggestions to help the speaker.

Suggested Guidelines for Peer Evaluations

Please rate the speaker's use of each element on a scale of 3–1 as defined below:

3 = Element was evident and very effective

2 = Element was present, but could be revised for greater impact

1 = Element was NOT evident or effective

Introduction:

When starting the speech, did the speaker—

_____ 1. Gain attention through an interesting question, story, statistic, example, etc.?

_____ 2. Clearly state thesis/purpose statement and preview the main points?

_____ 3. Establish credibility by citation of sources and establishing speaker's own experience with the topic?

Notes:

Body:

In developing the body of the speech, did the speaker—

_____ 1. Identify and organize main points in a manner that was easy to follow?

_____ 2. Use well chosen examples and/or personal experience?

_____ 3. Effectively use support materials such as statistics and quotations?

_____ 4. Properly cite sources (verbal citations)?

Notes:

Conclusion:

When moving to finish the speech, did the speaker—

_____ 1. Clearly indicate the speech was concluding by providing a signal word?

_____ 2. Review main points?

_____ 3. End the speech with a memorable statement?

Notes:

Presentation and Visual Aids:

_____ 1. Incorporate relevant and well-designed visual aids?

_____ 2. Effectively handle presentation aids, avoiding any distraction?

Notes:

Delivery:

During the speech, did the speaker—

_____ 1. Utilize voice appropriately by varying inflection, tone, and volume?

_____ 2. Speak words clearly with proper grammar and pronunciation?

_____ 3. Physically move and gesture with purpose, avoiding distracting mannerisms?

_____ 4. Establish and maintain eye contact, while balancing use of note cards?

_____ 5. Appear confident, poised, and in control of the presentation?

Notes:

Overall Evaluation:

Considering the speech as a whole, did the speaker—

_____ 1. Choose an appropriate topic and purpose statement?

_____ 2. Meet the assignment requirements, including time limits?

Additional Comments:

Whether you are completing the speech for a grade in a class or working toward a personal goal, you may want to know how you will be evaluated and what your audience expects. Here are two more evaluation rubrics. These can be adapted to any type of speech. When Research and Visual Aids are not required, add the extra points to the Introduction and Conclusion steps.

SPEECH EVALUATION RUBRIC

Speech Performance 100 possible points	Excellent 5 points	Good 4 points	Average 3 points	Fair 2 points	Poor 1 point	N/A 0 points
Introduction Step: Attention Step: Establish Need/Relevance: Establish Credibility: Thesis:						
Body: Point #1						
Body: Point #2						
Body: Point #3						
Transitions (4) To first point To second point To third point To conclusion						
Conclusion Step: Summary: Appeal to Action:						
Use of Research Verbal Citations: Number Sources Used: Research Supported Topic:						
Visual Aids Types: _____ _____ Setting up Handling of Aids (Use) Design Visibility						

Speech Performance 100 possible points	Excellent 5 points	Good 4 points	Average 3 points	Fair 2 points	Poor 1 point	N/A 0 points
Language Skills Vocabulary Sentence Structure Grammar Usage						
Vocal Delivery Skills Voice Volume Rate Vocal Variance						
Enthusiasm for Topic Energy/Passion						
Gestures						
Eye Contact						
Poise and Confidence						
Appearance						
Movement: Entrance to Stage Exit from Stage Stage Movement						
Time of Speech						
Management of Tech Team						
Professionalism						

Additional Comments for the Speaker:

OUTLINE RUBRIC

Outline	Possible Points = 100	Points Earned
Standard Outline Format	20 points	
Typed	5	
Roman Numerals I, II, III	5	
ABC	5	
123	5	
Introduction Step:	20 points	
Attention Step:	5	
Establish Need/Reliance:	5	
Establish Credibility:	5	
Thesis:	5	
Main Points	15 points	
#1	5	
#2	5	
#3	5	
Transitions (4)	10 points	
#1	2.5	
#2	2.5	
#3	2.5	
#4	2.5	
Conclusion:	10 points	
Summary:	5	
Appeal to Action:	5	
Research	25 points	
Required Sources Used	5	
Parenthetical Citations	5	
Works Cited Page	5	
Follows Citation Guidelines	5	
Copy of Research Included	5	

Evaluating Presentations

After reading this chapter, you will be able to answer the following questions:

1. Why is it important to evaluate your own presentation?

   _____

   _____

2. How many elements are generally assessed when conducting a self-evaluation?

   _____

   _____

3. What are some suggested guidelines to follow when assessing a peer's presentation?

   _____

   _____

Chapter Sixteen
Specialty Speeches

In this chapter:

What are TED Talks?

What are PechaKucha Presentations?

What do I need to know about Competitive Speaking?

How do I present a Humorous Speech?

Specialty Speeches are in a league of their own and involve situations that may require unique preparation strategies and varied delivery skills. This chapter will highlight several types of speaking opportunities that do not fit the descriptions of other speech types traditionally covered; however, these are presentations commonly found and enjoyed. There are as many different types of specialty speeches as there are different types of sharks in the ocean, but we will attempt to highlight just a few that many of you enjoy on a regular basis. The purpose of most specialty speeches is to provide the audience with something they may not be expecting, yet will produce the end result of reaching your speaking goals.

TED Talks

You've all heard about TED Talks. You watch them on your phone while waiting for an appointment to begin. You share them with your friends when you see a topic you think they will find interesting. You dream that one day YOU will give your very own TED Talk. But, what do you really know about it? It is my belief that Speech-Sharks should know everything there is to know about speaking and speaking opportunities, so I would be remiss if I didn't include a segment here about TED Talks.

TED is an acronym that stands for **T**echnology, **E**ntertainment, and **D**esign. This organization first began as a method for delivering brief speeches (talks) about great ideas in a conference setting. Since that time, it has grown so that annual conferences are now held throughout the world. These days the topics are unlimited and include a way to share research, ideas, and stories to bring home a point. Speakers may include names that you would recognize along with Nobel Prize winners and speakers that you may never have heard of before the moment that you watch their TED Talk. Thousands of TED Talks are available to view online and many have been watched hundreds or thousands of times by viewers all over the world. Each TED Talk can last up to eighteen minutes and the speakers are challenged to share their ideas in the most engaging way possible. Many choose to use storytelling as their method.

TEDx conferences are like TED Talk conferences, but they can be organized by folks who obtain a free license from TED and agree to follow the TED basic principles. Since both groups are non-profit, they rely upon admission fees or conference fees to cover the costs of renting the venues, staging, lights, sound, tech crews, and all of the other expenses that go into operating a conference. There is also a division called TED-MED which focuses on the medical field, but it doesn't stop there. We can purchase TED Books, join TEDEd Clubs, attend conferences for TEDWomen, and participate in smaller events called TED Salon or listen to podcasts from the TED Radio Hour. If that isn't enough, you can also listen to TED Talks for Kids! To look through the different talks that have happened recently and in the past, please check out their Web site at https://www.ted.com/talks.

Yesterday I watched Richard J. Berry's "A practical way to help the homeless find work and safety" at: https://www.ted.com/talk/richard_j_berry_a_practical_way_to_help_the_homeless_find_work_and_safety/ up-next. This is a short talk that could very well change your community! Think for a moment about this. If Mr. Berry gave this speech for his senior citizens monthly meeting in Albuquerque, New Mexico, only fifty people might have heard his message. But since he gave this speech as a TED Talk, thousands and thousands have heard this story about his idea to help the homeless and there is no telling how many lives his story might have changed. We already know that several other states are implementing the same experiment that Mr. Berry tried in his town.

Mr. Berry asks at the end of his speech, "Who is next?" (Berry). He is talking, of course, about his idea of helping the homeless, but I am going to ask YOU, "Who is next?" Could YOU be the next person to share your own ideas or thoughts through a TED Talk?

If that isn't enough, try watching Becky Blanton's "The year I was homeless," TED talk has had over a million views at: https://www.ted.com/talks/becky_blanton_the_year_i_was_homeless/up-next.

Ms. Blanton is simply telling her story, but as she tells her story to millions of people during a TED Talk on the Internet, Ms. Blanton is able to deliver the moral of her story—her message—"People are not where they live. People are not where they sleep. People are not where their life situation is at any time . . . Hope always finds a way!" (Blanton).

As a speech instructor and speech coach, I've watched many, many TED Talks throughout the years and I've enjoyed them all. I may not have always agreed with the speaker's point of view, but I always learned something from each one. Often, I will refer various TED Talks to my students or co-workers. I'm sure you have done the same thing. If you've never watched a TED Talk and never heard about this amazing platform for sharing ideas, I would like to invite you to watch just one. Choose the one you would like to watch.

PechaKucha Presentations

OK, SpeechSharks, get ready for a little fun as we dive into the world of PechaKucha. Here are things you need to know about this type of presentation that has become quite popular in and out of the speech classroom!

According to the PechaKucha Web site at www.pechakucha.org, "The presentation format was devised by Astrid Klein and Mark Dytham of Klein Dytham Architects . . . PechaKucha Nights are informal and fun gatherings where creative people get together and share ideas, works, thought, holiday snaps—just about anything, really—in the PechaKucha 20×20 format"("Frequently Asked Questions"). The architects who developed this were inspired because they were tired of presentations that went on and on forever. It was also developed as an anecdote to the dreaded "Death by PowerPoint" where a speaker reads PowerPoint slides to his audience. You've all been there, right? I'm sure you also would prefer a system to get the information in a more interesting format.

PechaKucha is synonymous with 20×20. If you've never heard of this type of presentation, then you are in for a wonderful "Shark-o-licious" treat. My first PechaKucha experience was at a National Communication Association Conference for communication and speech professionals. The speaker took the stage and began to describe this strategy which involved showing twenty slides that were timed for twenty seconds per slide. Each slide would advance automatically at the twenty-second mark while the speaker talked using images that were designed to define, demonstrate, and inform us about PechaKucha Presentations.

One of the slides included the interesting ways in which people pronounced the term. We were all laughing before that twenty-second segment was over. SpeechSharks, do you want to know the correct way to pronounce PechaKucha?

- It should be pronounced as it is spelled, Pe-cha-ku-cha with equal time spent on each of the four syllables.
- It should NOT be pronounced as Pet-cha Koot-cha.
- Nor should you pronounce it as Pek-chak-u-cha.

Are you trying it out as you read this? Are you laughing? For some reason, it can be quite funny to sit around with your friends planning the next PechaKucha night and try to see the many different ways people pronounce this. It really doesn't matter how you pronounce it, the event is fun and can be a great way to share your sharky ideas or creative projects.

PechaKucha Nights are events held in public places that are equipped for showing PowerPoint, Prezi, or Haiku Deck slides. The events can center around a particular theme or various topics and include just a few speakers or many speakers. The purpose is to inform the audience about a topic in a fast-paced environment. I can already see your mental calculators working as you are trying to figure exactly how long this type of speech should last. The answer is that in four hundred seconds or six minutes and forty seconds, the speaker will cover a topic.

Would you like to see a PechaKucha Presentation? Just go to YouTube in your Internet search and type in PechaKucha Presentations. There are hundreds to see and some are better than others, but they are all quite entertaining. You can also visit the PechaKucha Web site at www.pechakucha.org/watch and choose presentations posted there.

Here are tips to help you plan a PechaKucha Presentation:

- Watch a PechaKucha Presentation before you plan to present one.
- Each presentation needs to cover one really big idea.
- Organize your ideas so that they are interesting, but use the slides so they offer details which support the big idea.
- Plan your speech first before you create the slides.
- Use an outline and not a manuscript.
- As you plan slides, realize that twenty seconds may not be long enough to cover some points and may be too long to cover other points. Be open to adjusting the content so that it stays within the twenty-second goal.
- Use conversational language instead of a memorized script.
- Since a PechaKucha Presentation uses lots of images, make sure the images are clear and make sense to the presentation.
- Set the timing in PowerPoint to have twenty seconds for each slide.
- Rehearse with a stopwatch to make sure you are keeping to the twenty seconds for each slide. Speakers should only speak about the slide/image that is being shown. Timing for this speech is crucial to the success of the speech.
- Avoid looking at the slides while you make the presentation. Establish good eye contact with the members of your audience.
- Use gestures and connect with your audience.
- Appoint a Tech Team person to start the slide show as you begin talking and will take it down after the speech concludes. You will not use a remote or Tech Team member to progress the slides because each slide will be timed within the PowerPoint presentation.

Does this sound like fun to you? If so, give it a try!

Competitive Speaking

Competitive Speaking is a lot of fun and getting involved in this arena will help you to hone your communication skills to a level beyond basic public speaking. In this section we will be sharing details about debates, storytelling, oral interpretation, and improvisational speaking.

When speaking of **debates**, most of us automatically conjure up the image of high school or collegiate debate leagues while others immediately move toward political debates. While the two can be quite different, they also have similarities and share basic features and formats. Debates are more competitive than other types of specialty speeches because they usually involve a judge that will determine a winner between two debaters or two teams. The very term—debate—brings to mind definitions of formal discussions which often become quite heated. They may sound like organized arguing or quarreling in order to voice a view regarding a controversial topic.

Although the first recorded political debate for the United States was in the 1800s, political debates are now commonplace to allow candidates a platform for speaking to voters about their positions on various issues. During the last presidential election, we were all glued to the television watching the initial lineup of candidates as they squared off to face each other in an organized game of "he said, she said." The result noted a winner, but most of us noted frustrations realizing it was time spent that truly did not yield more information than we already knew. In other words, we enjoy debates that cover the issues.

Debates involve appealing to the audience's logic using credible research to document facts interlaced with an emotional appeal to sway the audience's opinion of the topic. It takes a competent speaker to be able to mix so many different elements and effectively deliver a message which demands a resolution.

Debates can be formal or informal and involve two sides: the affirmative side which supports the status quo, or current view, and the negative side which supports an opposing view. Each side will be given the same amount of time to define, support, and defend their view of the topic which will be divided into two sections. During the first section, the speaker or team will lay the foundation for the debate in what is often called the constructive phase. The last section is called the rebuttal and is an opportunity for the affirmative and the negative sides to offer rebuttals for points brought up by the opposing team. Both sides alternate turns delivering their portion of the debate and end the debate by stating a resolution. It then becomes the task of the judge to decide which debater or team has achieved the purpose of refuting all points made by the opposition. Miss one point and the debate will be lost.

High schools and colleges are supporters of debates because this type of presentation involves the development of critical thinking and problem-solving skills as debaters or teams share different viewpoints of the same topic. Preparation for a debate requires that teams work together to research both sides of the topic. The affirmative team should know every point of reference that may be made by the negative team so they can establish a platform and be ready on-the-spot with points and research to refute points made. The same is true for the negative team. In high school and college debates, the team often does not know whether they will be debating the affirmative or negative side of the topic until they arrive at the debate and receive their orders. This further solidifies the importance of researching and understanding both sides of the topic.

As social networking and online access has evolved through the years, so has the online debating formats. This allows debaters to contribute in short "mini" debates using instant messaging, Twitter, or video conferencing. This method of debating is becoming quite popular and is a great way to hone communication skills, especially when you have to figure out how to deliver a message and achieve a purpose with a limited number of characters! As technology improves, we may see more online debating opportunities surface.

Different types of team debates include the following and are listed alphabetically:

- American Parliamentary Debates
- Australasia Debates
- British Parliamentary Debates
- Canadian Parliamentary Debates
- Cross Examination Debates
- European Square Debates
- International Public Debates
- Karl-Popper Debates
- Legislative Debates
- Lincoln-Douglas Debates
- Mace Debates
- Mock Trial Debates
- National Debate Tournaments
- Oxford-Style Debates
- Policy Debates
- Public Forum Debates
- Team Policy Debates
- World Universities Debate Championships

Have you ever tried to use **storytelling** to get your message across to an audience? Whether you are telling your story or someone else's story, a good storyteller will always include the moral of the story and will weave a tapestry of events together in order to bring the story to life. Storytelling is the process of sharing stories to educate, inform, and entertain. We all love a good story, especially when the story is used to illustrate something more. Good stories have the power to engage audiences and instill lessons that connect the past with the future. Storytelling can also be used as a way to share values and teach ethics in an environment that is warm and inviting.

I grew up sitting captivated at the feet of my parents and grandparents hanging on to each detail of stories they would tell. Whether the stories were told around a campfire in the dark as we huddled beneath warm blankets or at church in a Sunday School classroom, my happiest memories as a child involved listening to stories being told by my elders. As a grandparent, I find myself telling tall tales to my own grandchildren and hoping that the moral of the story is clear and will strike a chord with these little ones. We've all heard stories told in the form of fables, legends, folklore, and fairy-tales. Often stories reveal the same plot but with different characters and different strategies for sharing the story.

As a speaker, it is a great idea to incorporate stories in order to support points that you wish to make. Personal stories sharing real events that you have experienced will often make a stronger impact than supporting points with mounds of research, data, and statistics.

Here are tips to remember about storytelling:

- All stories do not have to begin with . . . "Once upon a time, a long, long time ago, there was a . . ."
- Good stories are designed with three parts as the foundational structure. The story begins, an event (confrontation, problem, or misunderstanding) occurs, and the story ends with a resolution.
- First, the speaker needs to set up the story. This part of the story will help to bring the listener up to speed by giving a bit of the history behind the story and a brief preview of what is to come. Describe the characters in your story so that your listener will recognize them as they make their appearance.
- Secondly, the speaker will need to detail the confrontation or the problem. After all, there should always be a little action or intrigue and a bit of excitement for each story you tell.
- Finally, the speaker will need to artfully move the confrontation to a desired resolution. Yes, we all still enjoy happy endings, but the main idea of the resolution is to make the moral of the story absolutely clear.
- Tell stories so they can be re-told. You'll soon find that people will remember the stories you tell before they remember the points in a speech. Weeks after your speech, it will be the stories they remember!
- Involve your listeners in the story by painting vivid pictures with your words, using their senses to hear sounds described, see images unfold, and feel movements or passions involved.

We hear this termed as the "Art of Storytelling" and indeed it is an art, one that is developed through years of practice and rehearsals. Good storytellers often tell the story a bit differently with each audience and they do this to make the stories fit to various occasions. Young and old alike enjoy a good story and are eager to hear them.

Did you know there is actually a World Storytelling Day? It happens every year in March and is a celebration of the art of storytelling. Another interesting fact about this event is that it follows a different theme for each year. Do a little research and you will soon find out the date for this year's World Storytelling Day. Perhaps you can volunteer at your local library or school to share your story!

Oral Interpretation involves making careful material selections and using interpretive or dramatic readings of prose, poetry, drama, plays, or oratorical speeches. Oral Interpretations may be presented as a Solo or as a Duo Interpretation and may involve a competition element also found in debates.

While reading the selection, the speaker will express meaning through vocal variety, gestures, and carefully planned movements. Oral interpretation is a basic part of all performance art as the speaker/dancer works to interpret the author's meaning using their vocal skills and movement. This is another form of storytelling because it is the speaker's job to bring stories to life; however, the speaker is interpreting the author's words and meanings instead of sharing his own words.

When presenting an oral interpretation, the speaker is charged with honoring the true meaning or integrity of the written word and delivering the message as the author intended. While this may be a hard task to do, it is often made clearer once the speaker researches the work being interpreted, the author's intention for the work, and also his viewpoint regarding the work at the time it was written. This will involve analyzing the various dimensions of the characters used in the texts. The reader should understand their emotional, social, and physical descriptions in order to adequately portray the character intended by the author and to give the illusion that the speaker is reading from the script.

Care must be taken to understand the pronunciations and meanings of each word and know the setting for the selection. Gestures and movement are a big part of oral interpretation by using shifts in posture, head nods, and hand gestures to correlate with the script being read. Vocal variance in the form of varying pitch, volume, rate, and effective pauses will help the speaker to bring the document to life.

Here are tips for presenting an oral interpretation:

- To present an oral interpretation of selected materials, be sure to start with a short preview from the materials that will get the audience's attention.
- Mention something of value about the material and the author.
- Establish a need/relevance for the audience to hear the interpretive reading and relate it back to an experience they may have had.
- Set the scene so that the audience will know the background of the scene and will be ready to hear a brief description of the characters included and the theme of the selection.
- Clearly state the title of the document and also state the name of the author before beginning.
- Rehearse, Rehearse, Rehearse.
- To conclude, restate the author's message with the document and thank your audience for their attention as you worked to entertain, educate, or enlighten your audience.
- Oral Interpretations are another type of specialty speech that speakers will enjoy using at different times and for different purposes.

For material selection, remember there is a difference between prose and poetry. Prose expresses thought through language presented in sentences and paragraphs, whereas poetry expresses thought through a creative writing of words according to their sound, rhythm, and meaning.

If making the presentation as a team, please make sure you rehearse as a team and use enough team members to cover all characters involved within the document. Don't be afraid to channel your inner drama queen when working to present an oral interpretation. The most important thing is to have fun!

Team up with other SpeechSharks to give this type of competition speaking a try and you will find that **Improvisational Speaking** combines several elements which include movement, technology, imagination, and discussion on a stage or in a classroom setting. This type of speaking will allow speakers the opportunity to think on their feet with no prior preparation and will help develop problem-solving and critical thinking skills. A keen awareness of self and location is important for Improvisational Speaking.

Are you ready to give it a try? This usually begins with an instructor or a group leader giving the group a challenge. The group can be as few as six people or as many as twenty people. The challenge can be designed according to who is in the group and the nature of the gathering. For example, if you choose to do this in a business setting, the challenge may deal with something going on within the department or a project that the group may be working on together as a unit.

Whatever the setting, once the challenge has been offered, each person in the group will pair up with one or two others and then quickly share their response to the challenge. Once they agree on a response to the challenge, they move over to join another group to see if their idea is better or if the other group's idea is better. They settle on one idea and then move to combine with yet another group. In the beginning stages, it will feel like a brainstorming session, but with movement. Everyone should have an opportunity to speak and in doing so, it helps the group members to move a bit outside of their comfort zone, but to become more comfortable with those within their group. Quickly it will become obvious which group members are more vocal than others and they may be tempted to run with the challenge and ignore the quieter ones; however, care should be taken to include ALL group members.

The goal or purpose of this type of speaking is to use each member's natural impromptu speaking skills and as they move from one group to join with another, they should become more comfortable presenting their joint ideas with confidence. The goal is also to help the quieter ones in the group to have opportunities to improve their speaking performance through normal interactions with others in their group.

If you choose to give this specialty speech a try, you may find that in the beginning many of the group members will tend to stand back and not join in 100%. They are doing this to see how the other members are reacting. This will be a bit awkward sometimes, but keep the challenge moving forward. Watch how the quieter ones will begin to become more vocal and to play a bigger part in the resolution of the challenge.

If you ever attended a meeting and wanted to stand up to share your thoughts or feelings about a subject, but didn't have the confidence to speak up, **Improvisational Speaking** may give you the practice you need to improve your speaking confidence.

Have you ever watched the television show, *Whose Line Is It Anyway?* The actors on the show are placed in a particular scene and sometimes assigned to play a certain character and they would have to act out the scene or play that character with no prior warning or rehearsal. Their performance would be hilarious and the entire cast along with people watching the television show would burst into uncontrolled laughter. This is one of those situations where we learn by playing, but you have to be open and vulnerable enough to play without thinking of the final outcome so that you can truly be creative. Too much thought about what you may say, how you may move, and what your actions may look like, will cause you not to be creative and to hold back.

You are SpeechSharks, so I already know you are brave! Would you like to give it a try? Check out the examples for Improvisational Speaking in the "Shark Bites" section of this chapter and think of one type that you might like to try at your next gathering with friends or family. Try these at your upcoming Toastmasters International meeting. Just choose one, take a deep breath, and jump in! The results will be unforgettable and you may discover this is your favorite specialty speech of all times!

Humorous Speeches

The purpose of a **humorous speech** is to warm up the audience, make them laugh, and keep them laughing! We saved this specialty speech for last because it is so entertaining. After you have given it a try, it may be one of your favorites, too!

Now, I can already hear you saying, "I am not funny! When I try to be funny, it falls flat before I can get to the punch line." That may be true, but with careful planning and a little practice you will be able to create a humorous speech and will have your audiences laughing in no time at all!

Before you can plan your first humorous speech, consider the idea you would like to use for the subject. Remember that the subject doesn't have to be funny.

It is what you say and how you say it that can get the laughs from your audience. Did I say, audience? Yes, I did and that means that as with all speeches, we need to consider who is in the audience before we decide the subject or topic of the speech. Here are questions to ask before you plan the speech:

- What is a common denominator with the audience members?
- Is there a particular type of subject to which they can relate?
- What type of humor will tickle their funny bones (make the audience laugh)?
- Do you want the topic to be informative or just funny?
- Is your primary purpose to make them laugh?
- Is there a topic that might lend itself to your personal sense of humor?
- What topics will be funny to your audience?

As we began the chapter, we mentioned that some of the specialty speeches do not follow the organizational plans that we follow for other types of speeches. Normally, you are accustomed to planning introduction steps for all of your speeches. The introduction step includes an attention getter, establishes need for the topic, your credibility for speaking about the topic, and a clear thesis to detail the three main points. We have to throw all of that out of the window as we plan a humorous speech. The most effective way to start a story is to go directly into the story. Begin with the "hook" that will get your audience laughing and will keep them interested. You can do this by including a personal story, providing "WOW" examples that will surprise or entertain your audience. You can even ask direct questions to give the audience a chance to laugh at themselves.

After you start the story, disclose the main points you are covering during the speech. Outlines are the way to go when planning a speech. Write first your three main ideas about the main point. Then go back and add sub-points to each of the three main ideas. The important tip here is to write simply and clearly. Write down the main points and sub-points, but avoid writing long, complicated sentences. Plan your speech by using vivid adjectives to paint a clear picture for your audience.

Repetition is a good strategy for this type of speech. As you repeat a sentence two or three times in succession, your repetition helps to escalate your audience to the punch line that you choose to use.

Self-deprecating in a humorous speech can be effective, but don't go too far into the other direction or you will turn into a "Rodney Dangerfield." If you are not old enough to remember this comedian, Google him to see a video of his self-deprecating humor. He was constantly saying things like, "I get no respect! When I was a kid, nobody would play with me. My mom would tie a bone around my neck just to get the family dog to play with me and the dog would still rather play with the cat. Yea (long pause), I get no respect!" Some people enjoy this type of humor, but it really has to be crafted just right in order to be effective and appreciated.

Don't lose sight of the main purpose of your speech—to speak about the topic you choose. Work humor into the text after you have completed the foundation for your speech. Read the points you have established and brainstorm ways to relate this information with specific things that will make your audience laugh. If it makes YOU laugh, it will probably make your audience laugh, too. Avoid jokes or humor that are not culturally sensitive and keep the humor you do use relevant for the topic.

Now that the speech is written, rehearse and make note of areas where you will need to edit the outline and revise the speech. As you rehearse, check to make sure your punch line punches hard. This may mean that you will need to practice in front of family or classmates to have them offer an evaluation of your humor!

Specialty Speeches, as you can see, are not a one-size-fits-all presentation. Be creative, follow our tips, and enjoy diving into clear waters to once again move toward your goal!

Specialty Speeches

After reading this chapter, you will be able to answer the following questions:

1. List the types of Specialty Speeches described in this chapter:

   _____

   _____

2. What is the acronym used to named TED Talks?

   _____

   _____

3. How many slides are used in PechaKucha Presentations?

   _____

   _____

4. How many seconds does each slide show last in a PechaKucha Presentation?

   _____

   _____

5. Of the Competition Speeches described in this chapter, which one do you think would be the hardest to present? Why?

   _____

   _____

_____

_____

6. What are the two sides that are represented in a debate?

_____

_____

7. Describe the process of Storytelling:

_____

_____

8. Fill in the blanks: Oral Interpretation involves making careful _____ selections

and using _____ or _____ readings of _____ ,

_____ , _____ , _____ , or _____

_____ . Oral Interpretations may be presented as a _____ or as a

_____ Interpretation and may involve a _____ element.

9. Improvisational Speaking combines several elements which include _____ ,

_____ , _____ , and _____ on a stage or in a class-

room setting.

10. What is the purpose of a Humorous Speech?

_____

_____

Shark Bites

GETTING TO KNOW TED

Go to https://www.ted.com/talks to look at the different topics posted in TED Talks. Choose one topic that interests you and complete the questions below:

1. Which TED Talk did you choose?

2. What is the URL address for the TED Talk you chose?

3. What is the title of the TED Talk?

4. Who delivered the TED Talk?

5. Did you enjoy hearing about the topic? If so, what did you learn? If not, what was the problem?

Shark Bites

CHECKING OUT PECHAKUCHA

Go to www.pechakucha.org/watch to look at the different PechaKucha Presentations. Choose one topic that interests you and complete the questions:

1. Which PechaKucha did you choose?

2. What is the URL address for the PechaKucha you chose?

3. What is the title of the PechaKucha?

4. Compare this PechaKucha Presentation to the TED Talk that you watched.

5. What did you think about the images shown by the speaker?

Shark Bites

Try one of the following options for completing an Improvisational Presentation:

1. **Imaginary Object:** Pick up an imaginary object from the table and begin to interact with it. Pass it on to the person next to you. They will also interact with it, and continue to pass it around to others. For this to work well, the first person will need to make it very clear the subject of the object so that others will know how to interact.

   - Example: Pick up an imaginary apple, hold it up, and brush it against your sleeve to wipe away dirt or germs before taking a nice large imaginary bite. Pass the imaginary apple to the next person and watch how they also interact.

2. **Narration Station:** Two or more people will play this game. One or more of the people will be an actor who will act out the story and the other person is the narrator. If using more than one actor, be sure to identify the character for each actor. As the narrator tells the story, the actor acts out the story and the narrator responds by describing what the actor is doing.

   - Example: Poem—"The Old Woman Who Lived in a Shoe." One person will be the old woman. Other actors will be the children. As the narrator recites the poem, the actors will act out the story.

3. **Q&A:** This will involve two people. One person asks a question. Instead of an answer, the other person will ask a question that expands on the other person's question. No answers are ever given, just more questions.

   - Here is what this might look like:
     - Person #1: Do you like sweets?
     - Person #2: What type of sweets?
     - Person #1: What about cakes?
     - Person #2: Chocolate or vanilla?
     - Person #1: What about caramel?
     - Person #2: Does caramel interest you?
     - Person #1: Do you have pecans that can go on the cake?
     - Person #2: Do you want the pecans toasted or not?
     - Person #1: Could you also add birthday candles?
     - Person #2: Is it your birthday today?
     - And the story goes on and on until they run out of questions.

Glossary

Active Listening: listening to understand

Adrenaline: is physiological and involves increased heart and respiration rate as a result of a situation perceived to be frightening or exciting

APA: the American Psychological Association style of citing research

Appreciative Listening: showing enjoyment of a speaker and the content exhibits appreciative listening

Aromatherapy: a strategy by which the user engages scents/smells to bring about a feeling of calmness

Attention Step: a step in the Introduction of the speech which gets the attention of the audience

Attitudes: to look at a topic with a favorable or unfavorable manner

Bar Graph: a diagram used to show comparisons among two or more items

Behaviors: a combination of personal values, beliefs, and attitudes, which causes us to behave a certain way when reacting to these three different areas

Beliefs: involves a perception of something to be true or false

Bibliography: itemized list of sources used for presentations that follow APA guidelines

Blogs: a written view of a person or organization, but not necessarily a credible source

Body Language Cues: communication signals that we send non-verbally

Breathing: a strategy whereby the speaker can breathe in managed, steady breaths in order to bring about a calming effect and to relieve speech anxiety

Causal Order: an ordering strategy in which the writer arranges information according to cause and effect

Category: a step for narrowing a topic

Central Idea Speech: a speech that begins with one general informative topic, but is narrowed down to one key/central idea

Ceremonial Speeches: include installation, presenting an award, accepting an award, dedication, eulogy, commemorative, and commencement speeches

Chart: a visual aid effective for summarizing large blocks of information

Chronemics: is the study of how we use time to communicate

Chronological Order: an ordering strategy in which the writer arranges information according to time

Citation: the written or verbal posting of credentials to give credit for an author's thoughts or ideas

Closed Questions: limit the amount of information that can be gathered about a topic. Closed questions are usually answered with a simple "yes" or "no"

CMS: the Chicago Manual of Style for research citations

Color: a way to describe a voice that shows passion, energy, and enthusiasm

Communication: a process in which ideas or information are transmitted, shared, and exchanged

Connective: a term used to indicate a transition or link within an outline and used to help tie a speech together

Connectors: another term used for transitions/links

Conversational tone: a preferred tone for speakers to use because it causes the audience to feel like the speaker is engaged in a direct conversation with them and helps the speaker to connect with the audience in a more intimate manner

Conversational Quality: maintaining a prepared, yet spontaneous element to a presentation

Credibility: implies how the audience perceives a speaker's ability to present information about a particular topic

Critical Listening: resisting outside noises and distractions

CSE: the Council of Science Editors guidelines for research citations

Decoding: a process by which we translate or interpret the content into meaning

Debate: a presentation in which two sides, affirmative and negative, are argued and resolved

Delivery Cues: items to consider when presenting the speech

Demonstration Speech: an opportunity to demonstrate a process or procedure needed to complete a task

Dialects: a form of language used by people living in a particular region. Dialects are often referred to as local speech, regional speech patterns, languages, linguistics, vernacular or accents

Empathetic listening: trying to see the speaker's point of view, even if you do not share the speaker's views

Empathy: is the act of seeing another person's point of view

Encoding: a process by which a person derives meaning and understanding

Entertaining Speech: speeches with a purpose to invoke laughter, humor, and happiness

Establish Credibility: this is a step within the Introduction of a speech in which the speaker shares his own experience with the topic and establishes himself as a credible speaker

Establish Relevance: this is a step within the introduction of a speech in which the speaker shares the relevance of the topic with the audience

Ethos: an appeal to ethics

Extemporaneous Speech: a presentation carefully planned, rehearsed in advanced, usually containing visual aids, research to support points, and includes brief notes

Eye contact: promotes goodwill and a connection with the audience and helps the speaker to appear more credible and knowledgeable about the topic

Facial Expressions: include eye contact, smiling, head nodding, and head tilting to send a non-verbal cue to the audience during communication

Feedback: helps the speaker to know if the content delivered has been effectively decoded and received

Filler Words: types of phrases, sounds, or words that speakers use to fill in silence when trying to communicate a thought or make a speech presentation

Font: imagery to ensure your presentation technology can be seen

GALILEO: Georgia Library Learning Online—an Internet-based virtual library

General Purpose: the purpose of the speech is to inform, entertain, or motivate

Gestures: ways we use our hands, body, and facial expressions during the speech to communicate points

Goodwill: measures a speaker's intent

Graph: a visual aid diagram used to illustrate complex series of numbers

Group Presentations: presentations made with three or more people

Haptics: a non-verbal cue that involves touch

Head Tilting and Head Nodding: a non-verbal cue from your audience to indicate comprehension of message delivered

Humorous speech: a presentation designed to warm up the audience, make them laugh, and then keep them laughing!

Imagery: this is the act of painting a visual picture for audience members during a speech

Impromptu: presentation delivered with little preparation and no rehearsal

Improvisational Speaking: a method which combines several elements to include movement, technology, imagination, and discussion on a stage or in a classroom setting

Information gathering interviews: conducted with many people responding to a question asked

Informative Listening: taking notes during a speech will incorporate informative listening skills

Informative Speech: an opportunity to share something of value with your audience

Internal Summary: an opportunity to clarify and reinforce main points to be covered in a speech

Interview: the asking of specific questions with the intent to gather information from the person being interviewed

Intimate Space: is the closest and is usually one foot or less away and usually involves touching the person next to you

Job interviews: structured conversations with a goal to discover if a person is suitable for an open position within a company

Key Idea/Central Idea Speech: a speech that begins with one general informative topic, but is narrowed down to one key/central idea

Key Words: words used for the purpose of gathering information

Kinesics: physical cues that we see as we evaluate physical appearance, posture, poise, gestures, facial expressions, eye contact, smiling, and body movements

Larynx: voice box which produces sound

Logos: an appeal to logic

Main Points: identifies key points to be covered in a speech

Manuscript Speech: presenting a crafted speech reading a script word-for-word

Meditation: a strategy used to relieve speech anxiety in which the participant finds a quiet place to intently focus on a calming place or thought to bring a feeling of peace and tranquility

Mehrabian, Albert: a scholar who conducted non-verbal research and reported his findings in a book entitled *Silent Messages*

Memorized Speech: committing a presentation to memory

MLA: the Modern Language Association style of citing research

Moderator: the lead speaker of a group presentation

Monotone: a constant pitch results in a monotone voice

Motivational Speech: a speech delivered with the purpose to motivate the audience to action

Movement: calculated movement from one place to another while onstage presenting a speech

Narrow: a step to break down a large topic into a more manageable topic

Noise: distractions in the speaking environment including preconceived notions, opinions, and ideas

Non-Verbal Communication: the act of communicating without words

Open Question: broad questions that cannot be answered with a simple "yes" or "no" answer

Oral Interpretation: involves making careful material selections and using interpretive or dramatic readings of prose, poetry, drama, plays, or oratorical speeches

Pace: is the rate at which you say syllables in a word

Paralanguage: is the vocal part of speech and involves volume, rate, pitch, pace, and color

Paraphrasing: the sharing of research without offering a direct quote; in this case, the author's name, title of the publication, publisher, and published date are also provided either in written format or verbally

Pathos: an appeal to emotion

PechaKucha: a presentation that uses twenty slides shown for twenty seconds each

Performance reviews: considered interviews and are initiated by management authorities in a company to review the performance of employees

Personal Space: one- to four-foot area usually reserved for meeting with friends or family members

Persuasion Speech: a type of speech in which the speaker provides useful information and supporting research that will motivate the listener to action

Pie Graph: a visual aid diagram used to show the parts of a whole

Pitch: is determined by sounds produced by vocal cord vibrations

Physical Appearance: sends a positive or negative message about the speaker's credibility

Plagiarism: the act of using someone else's ideas or work as if they are your own

Poise: a term used to describe a speaker who has good posture and exhibits self-confidence while speaking

Posture: sends a non-verbal cue about your self-confidence

Preparation Outline: an outline created to assist with organizing the speech

Presentation: a speech, whether impromptu or extemporaneous, with the intent of informing, entertaining, or motivating

Preview Points: presentation of points to be covered in the body. This is also called a thesis.

Problem-Solution Order: a strategy for arranging information addressing the problem and following it up with a solution

Problem-Solving Interviews: designed to bring peace or solve grievances between two parties. A mediator is usually present in the event of a problem-solving interview

Probing Questions: encourage the interviewee to elaborate about the topic

Proxemics: is the study of space and how we use it

Public Domain: property not protected by copyrights laws and available for the general public to use

Public Space is the space designated for speakers and are usually twelve to twenty-five feet away from their audience members

Public Speaking: a communication process in which speakers and listeners participate together

Question and Answer Session: also known as a Q&A Session is a point in a group presentation in which the audience members can ask questions of the group and receive answers not covered in the group presentation

Questions of Fact: point delivered during a persuasion speech that covers fact by using credible research to support points

Questions of Policy: point delivered during a persuasion speech that offers solutions which involve changing laws, enforcing existing laws, or revising procedures

Questions of Value: point delivered during a persuasion speech that covers questions of value—whether something is moral or immoral, just or unjust, good or bad

Rate: the method we use to determine how fast or slow someone is speaking

Rehearse: an opportunity to practice a speech prior to making the presentation

Research: the process for finding support materials, data, and credible information

Rhetorical Question: a question posed without a verbal response

Sales Presentation: a type of speech in which the speaker's purpose is to sell a product or service to the listener

Scripts: copy of speech outlines highlighted to show tech team member responsibilities

Shark-o-licious Treat: a way to describe a great speech to a group of soon to be SpeechSharks

Signpost: signals offered by the speaker to indicate points covered and points yet to cover

Smiling: a non-verbal cue that says "I am happy to be here!"

Social Space: the space that others are most comfortable with when working with a co-worker or customer and is usually about four to twelve feet

Spatial Order: a strategy for arranging information according to geographical location

Speaking Outline: an outline created with brief notes to jog memory during a speech presentation. This can also be called a presentation outline.

Special Occasion Speeches: speeches given during events that are work-related, social, or ceremonial

Specialty Speeches: presentations which involve situations that may require unique preparation strategies and varying delivery skills

Specific Purpose: a purpose statement made that details the topic and the speaker's purpose for presenting the topic

Speech Anxiety: a feeling of stress felt by some speakers when faced with the duty of making a presentation in public

Startling Statement: a strategy used to get the audience's attention in the beginning of the speech

Storytelling: the process of sharing stories to educate, inform, and entertain

Strategic Organization: an organizational skill critical to outlining speech content

Supporting Materials: items used to enhance content of the speech

SWOT Analysis: a strategy in which the user determines strengths, weaknesses, opportunities, and threats and makes a plan based upon these four areas

Tech Team: a group of people qualified to help you complete your speech presentation by setting up or breaking down, managing the PowerPoint/Prezi slides, managing lighting and/or sound requirements, and distributing handouts

TED Talks: began as a method for delivering brief speeches (talks) about great ideas. The name, TED, is an acronym taken from the words **T**echnology, **E**ntertainment, and **D**esign

Thesis: the point in the introduction step of a speech in which the speaker details the three main points that will be covered

Topical Order: a strategy used to arrange information according to topic

Transitions: sentences used as a bridge/connector/link between one main point and another main point in a speech

Verbal Communication: a form of communication using words

Vocal variance: incorporates varying degrees of volume, rate, pitch, pace, and color

Volume: is the level at which a sound is heard

Wikis: an Internet source of research not always deemed credible

Works Cited: itemized list of sources used for presentations that follow MLA guidelines

Shark Bites

UNDERSTANDING SPEECH TERMS

Do you know the terms to the words found in your glossary? Find a partner and make a game of asking the term and responding with the correct definition.

Works Cited Page

Adichie, Chimamanda Ngozi. "The Danger of a Single Story." *Chimamanda Ngozi Adichie: The Danger of a Single Story.* TED Talks. Accessed 28 May 2017.

<https://www.ted.com/talks/chimamanda_adichie_the_danger_of_a_single_story>.

"APA Central." American Psychological Association. 2017. Accessed 8 Feb. 2017. www.apastyle.org/.

"Benjamin Franklin Quotes." Your Dictionary. 2017. Accessed 12 March 2017. Lovetoknow.com

Berry, Richard J. "A practical way to help the homeless find work and safety". TED Talks. 2017. Accessed 15 Sept. 2017. www.ted.com/talk/richard_j_berry_a_practical_way_to_help_the_homeless_find_work_ and_safety/up-next.

Blanton, Becky. "The year I was homeless." TED Talk. 2017. Accessed 15 Sept. 2017. www.ted.com/talks/ becky_blanton_the_year_i_was_homeless/up-next.

Chicago-Style Citation Quick Guide. The Chicago Manual of Style. 2017. Accessed 15 March 2017.

http://www.chicagomanualofstyle.org/tools_citationguide.html.

Frequently Asked Questions. PechaKucha 20X20. Klein Dytham Architecture. 2017. Accessed 15 Sept. 2017.

www.pechakucha.org.

Frymier, Ann Bainbridge, and Gary M. Shulman. "What's in it for me?" *Communication Education Journal,* vol. 44, no. 1, May 22, 2009.

Grice, George L., and John F. Skinner. "Personal Report of Public Speaking Anxiety (PRPSA)." *Mastering Public Speaking.* 6th ed., Allyn & Bacon, 2007.

Mehrabian, Albert. *Silent Messages: Implicit Communication of Emotions and Attitudes.* 2nd ed.,

Wadsworth Publishing Company, 1980.

"MLA Style Manual." Modern Language Association. 2017. Accessed 4 March, 2017. https://www.mla.org/.

Mortensen, C. David, Ed. *Communication Theory.* 2nd ed., Transaction Publishers, 2008.

Pollan, Michael. *Cooked.* The Penguin Press, 2013.

"Public Domain." Merriam-Webster. 2017. Accessed 6 April 2017.

Quast, Lisa. "8 Tips to Dress for Interview Success." *Forbes.* 2014. Accessed 12 March 2017.

"Scientific Style and Format." Council of Science Editors. 2017. Accessed 4 March, 2017.

www.councilscienceeditors.org/ publications/scientific-style-and-format/.

Smith, Chris. "Dress to Impress: what to wear for a job interview." *The Guardian.* Guardian Careers. 2017.

Accessed 12 March 2017.

"Zig Ziglar Quotes." 2016. Accessed 12 March 2017. AZQuotes.com.

Shark Bites

FEATURES FOUND IN SPEECHSHARK, THE BOOK:

SpeechShark is a guide book to public speaking and offers sixteen chapters of content to help as you begin your public speaking journey. Within each chapter, you will find instructional materials, tips, and tools for speaking.

Following each chapter, you will find **Shark Attack**. This is a list of questions so that you can test your understanding of the subject matter. In a college or university course, speech instructors may use this list as an assignment to be graded following each of the chapter readings.

The last section of each chapter has a helpful section that we named **Shark Bites**. This section will help you to sharpen your skills and practice your newfound speech strategies by actively completing the exercises and suggestions found in Shark Bites.

This public speaking guide book is unique from other speech texts because it was written as a companion book for the SpeechShark app, available for Android and iOS phones and electronic devices. Visit your

GooglePlay or Apple Store through your phone or electronic device and search SpeechShark  to download the app. Let us know how you enjoy using it!

Visit our Web site at www.SpeechShark.com and download the SpeechShark app for iOS and Android phones and devices!

Index

Photo Credits